D1593251

SAVE

OR

SLAVE

HOW TO SAVE MONEY LIKE YOUR FREEDOM DEPENDS ON IT

SAVE

OR

SLAVE

CHRISTOPHER POLLARD

Library of Congress Control Number: 2020923142

Paperback ISBN: 978-1-7359829-0-8
eBook ISBN: 978-1-7359829-1-5

Cover images © Shutterstock.com

"It is well enough that people of the nation do not understand our banking and monetary system, for if they did, I believe there would be a revolution before tomorrow morning."

—Henry Ford

Contents

INTRODUCTION

Modern slavery has nothing to do with color—it has to do with finances. You either save money, or you will end up spending your life SLAVING away for others who *did* save money.

Until you build up a war chest of savings with which to invest, you will forever be forced to work for money, never getting to experience the wonder of having money work for you. Fortunately, you have made what will prove to be one of the best purchases in your life – this very book you are holding in your hand right now.

You! Yes, you reading this right now. I'm sending this message to YOU. Everything that has been holding you back from financial success and freedom is over. Every test you've been put through, you have survived. You might not be exactly where you planned, but **today** marks the start of your new life.

Your mindset has shifted to such a high level that it was on a frequency that brought you to this book right here. Now, you're on the right track. You're blessed and a new chapter of your life has just started!

No more self-sabotage, no more weighing yourself down with bad debts. No more being a victim to scams and living paycheck to paycheck. No more nights spent worrying how you're going to make ends meet.

I'm truly excited for what's about to happen to you as you read this book, implementing the hacks and strategies contained within, setting yourself up to achieve the life of your dreams. By reading this book, you WILL learn the lost art of saving and how to emancipate yourself from indebtedness; you will almost guarantee yourself a life of freedom, being able to do what you want when you want.

This book isn't going to be another "save a thousand dollars a year, invest, and by the time you're 80, you'll have $200,000" nonsense. That's a textbook plan for financial mediocrity. This book is going to equip you to not just save a few hundred or a few thousand dollars a year; we want you saving and investing tens of thousands of dollars a year and more as you level up in the personal finance game.

The economic events of 2020 should make clear how badly most people have underestimated the importance of savings and the security it gives you to weather hard times and unexpected disasters. The strategies you will learn in this book for increasing your savings and eliminating your debts **will work in any economy**, whether we're in a roaring boom or a depressionary bust, this book has your back.

Treat this book as your own personal finance toolbox. You may find it most helpful to skip to chapters on topics you think are most relevant to your situation. Or, if you read it front to back, it's advised to read no more than one chapter per day, as you may want to give yourself time to ponder some of the strategies and hacks covered in each chapter, so as to come up with ways for incorporating them into your daily life.

The point of this book isn't just to become more educated in the field of personal finance, it's to **take massive action!** Only through massive action will you see meaningful results in your savings and financial freedom.

What this book will **not** do is teach you how to be a real estate investor or how to trade Eurodollar interest futures. Those books already exist. That said, you **need** savings to invest. Notwithstanding, in the final chapter we will cover some basic principles of investing to help get you started (tailored for the new economic landscape of the 2020s).

WE'RE NOT IN THE 1990S ANYMORE

This book will empower you to cease accumulating debt, avoid falling into common financial traps, extinguish your existing debts, build up a sizeable savings, and wisely invest and grow those savings. You will avoid the mistakes most people make by using outdated strategies they or their friends and family heard from mainstream news blurbs, personal finance books, and gurus regurgitating strategies that worked in the 1980s and 1990s.

These outdated strategies no longer apply to the modern economy due to changes in: technology, demographics, consumer and investor behaviors, geopolitics and trade, the evolution of fiscal and monetary policies, the explosion of public and private debt, tax policy, and our positioning in the later phase of the credit cycle.

Following advice from the 1980s and 1990s that is no longer applicable will seriously hold you back. Just a few examples of the outdated principles still being propagated today:

- The **10% rule** of saving money. Today, saving only 10% of your gross income will not get you anywhere and will almost guarantee you will lose in the game of savings and building wealth.

- The **Snowball Method** of paying off your debts. This method is clearly less efficient and will add additional years to your indebtedness than another method, which will be revealed in Chapter 8.

- The **"you need to go to college in order to be successful"** platitude. You should "just get that degree" at all costs, no matter what the degree is in, what skills you learned, what your opportunity cost is, and how much debt you have to take on to do it.

- The **"get your car at a dealership"** scam. Wait until you see how hard the entire auto industry has been milking the lower and middle classes in Chapter 9. We're going to give you some powerful hacks when it comes to vehicles that will create a huge difference in your finances.

- The **"your home is an investment"** lie. This is completely not true today; you cannot just assume home values will rise or that your home is nearly as liquid as in previous years given today's deflationary forces on the housing markets. And even if your home's value does rise significantly, you're still not going to make the profits you think you would. This myth is largely responsible for people buying WAY more house than they can really afford, leaving no income left over to save and invest.

- The **60/40 rule** of structuring investment portfolios to 60% equities and 40% bonds. This rule is preached religiously in personal finance, and frankly is a complete joke today. Bonds are negative **real yielding** (i.e., nominal yield less inflation) as of 2020… long-term investors that aren't active bond traders are guaranteed to lose wealth when 40% of their portfolios are comprised of bonds under this outdated strategy.

CONSEQUENCES OF NOT SAVING?

If you don't have a consistent savings and investing habit, your life will not be as epic as it should be, and could be plagued by mediocrity or even poverty, with brief periods of joy quickly followed by long periods of hardship. Some of the hardships that often follow poor personal finance skills include:

- Having debt follow you around like a ball and chain, stealing any spare income you have left over after living expenses;

- Not being able to give as much as you otherwise could to your church or charitable causes you believe in;

- Not having the freedom to take vacations or travel when you want;

- Not being able to build or keep quality interpersonal relationships due to the stress and distraction that comes with financial woes (one of the leading causes of divorce);

- Being trapped in a job you no longer enjoy;

- Feeling like you never get ahead, like all your work simply gets you to the next month, still saddled with bills and loans;

- Having to choose cheap junk food that wreaks havoc on your health and your lifespan over the more expensive healthy nutritious food;

- Losing most of your savings in a stock market or real estate crash.

If you have a family or a strong desire to have a family one day, the perils of financial hardship become magnified.

GOOD NEWS!

With this book as your shield, you're going to keep financial hardships out of your life and out of your loved ones' lives. You will be amazed by how much money you can save using the hacks, tools, and mindsets contained in this book, all the while increasing your quality of life.

Employing the knowledge in *Save or Slave* will enable you to retire early if you'd like, or pursue other avenues that you may have always had an interest in but haven't been able to fully pursue because of financial constraints.

It enabled me to have enough savings at 31 years old to live comfortably for the rest of my life. That said, I have no intention of retiring. I've used my freedom from the corporate hamster wheel to write this book and try to help as many people as I can.

My goal is to help free you of any chains of debt you currently have or would otherwise have in the future, and illuminate the truths which the beneficiaries of our present monetary system do not want people to know.

These beneficiaries would prefer you not read this book; they want us to remain unaware of the hidden theft of our labor through **inflation** (*an increase in prices and a fall in the purchasing power of the currency we hold*) and ignorant about the personal consequences of living a life on credit.

BECOME A *RATIONAL SAVER*

Increasing your savings and financial prosperity doesn't just come from doing X, Y, and Z. It flows from who you become as a person.

The hope is that after reading this book, you will become a *Rational Saver*, which we'll define as one who:

- **has ZERO consumer debt** (credit card debt, car payments, home mortgages, student loans, and so forth);

- **has sizeable savings that gets bigger every month** by employing (or working towards) the **50% Rule of Savings;** and

- **is consistently investing** to accelerate the growth of their net worth.

YOUR RETURN ON THIS BOOK

You'll be surprised at some of the tips you find in this book. I know that after reading and employing even only a few of the tools provided, this book will save you tens of thousands, possibly hundreds of thousands or even millions of dollars over your lifetime. Heck, even if you only use a few of the tips in this book and save $1,000 a year over a 10-year period and end up saving $10,000, if the book costs $22.50, your yield or IRR (an important tool for your freedom, see Chapter 16) on that $22.50 investment would be over 4,400%...Try getting that kind of return elsewhere!

IT DOESN'T MATTER WHERE YOU START; WHAT MATTERS IS WHERE YOU GO

Boosting your financial IQ and savings will help your life tremendously, even if you currently have $0 to your name and make $10 an hour waiting tables. **Do not** put off learning how to save money because you think "I'm in no position to be looking at savings; I can barely make rent as it is."

You will be shocked at ways you don't even realize you're leaking money and things you can do to improve your situation dramatically. Even small things that you may never have thought of will make a **big difference**. All of that is contained in this book, and will noticeably alleviate the "barely making ends meet" problem.

ONLY YOUR HEALTH AND HAPPINESS IS AT STAKE

You have the power to curtail wasteful purchases and start saving and investing your income! Having a strong knowledge of how to save and grow your money is *absolutely crucial for your health and happiness*. It's hard to be happy when you're always in fight or flight survival mode – worrying whether you'll have enough money to pay your rent/mortgage(s), car payments, credit card debt, food, tuition, the list goes on.

While those first-world concerns may seem trivial to the challenges many people are facing around the planet—such as starvation, war, and disease—our bodies and minds are evolutionarily wired to still perceive these lesser threats similar to the way we'd perceive having a knife to our throat.

Regarding the health effects, statistics show a significant increase in life expectancy for the wealthy over the poor. A study co-authored by two MIT researchers shows that in the United States, the wealthiest 1% of men live 14.6 years longer on average than the poorest 1%, and among females, the difference is 10.1 years.[1] Wouldn't you like to live 10-15 years

1 Peter Dizikes, "New study shows rich, poor have huge mortality gap in U.S." *MIT News* (Apr 11, 2016), news.mit.edu/2016/study-rich-poor-huge-mortality-gap-us-0411

longer? To have 10-15 more years to spend with your friends, family, and loved ones?

A large percentage of adults today are stuck in a metaphorical hamster wheel—a state of perpetual hopelessness, feeling like they're continually trading away the precious weeks, months, and years of their lives only to get by, not get ahead. They feel like they'll have to do this for the rest of their lives, losing the best years of their life only to regret those decisions in their old age.

This is why alcohol and drug abuse and overindulgence of movies, TV, and video games are so prevalent—they're an escape from the realities of most people's lives. The reality is that most people are in a never-ending work cycle in which they don't get ahead, a state of perpetual limbo (even when they progress up the ladder in their respective industry, most are still strapped for cash due to poor financial IQ).

There are many people that will acknowledge that they should save, yet don't actually do it, or if they do, they think they're saving a lot when in reality they are only saving a fraction of what they're capable of, simply because they don't have the right tools or strategies to lower their living expenses, make better decisions, and accelerate their savings.

Just opting for your company's 401(k) plan doesn't cut it today. That's a beginner technique with high fees, limited liquidity due to all sorts of limitations on withdrawing *your* money, and is tied to the stock market bubble (see Chapter 15).[2]

School does *not* teach people about wealth creation. This is evidenced by the fact that you often hear people of all ages parrot things like "you should use a credit card so you can build up your credit score." This is utter financial nonsense. When you understand money, you understand that your credit score

---

2 Robert Kiyosaki, "The 401(k): Robbing Americans for 40 Years Now" *RichDad.com* (Nov 6, 2018), richdad.com/401k-robbing-americans

shouldn't even be a factor in any of your thinking when making financial decisions (see Chapter 7).

Government education bureaucrats have deemed subjects like chemistry more useful than sound financial intelligence. I believe this critical defect in the modern education system is intentional and not an oversight.

This book is the antidote to our educational failure that has caused millions of people to struggle financially and live lives that are not nearly as happy as they could have been if they'd been taught even some of the principles in this book. Humans are most happy when they feel they are thriving—getting ahead, improving their lot in life, making progress. By reading and employing the rules and strategies contained herein, you will thrive and get ahead. ***This book is your ticket to freedom***.

Imagine how you'd feel if you had an extra $100,000.... $500,000 or $1,000,000 (in liquid assets, not home equity). Imagine if you didn't have to make any car payments, rent payments, mortgage payments, student loan payments, credit card payments...

Would you breathe easier? Would you enjoy the sounds of birds chirping a bit more, would you take more vacations and travel more? Would you focus more on your romantic relationships, or spending time with friends and family? Would you spend more time pursuing hobbies that bring you joy? Would you feel less vulnerable in periods of economic turmoil?

GIVE YOURSELF AN INSURANCE POLICY WITH NO EXCLUSIONS!

For anyone who has met Mr. Murphy and had to deal with making a claim on an insurance policy, you'll probably remember having to fight tooth and nail with the insurance company, or being outright denied, due to one or a multitude of policy "exclusions." These are policy provisions that eliminate coverage. It's not a stretch to say that most insurance policies today are *filled* to the brim with exclusions, almost to the point that you wonder what insurance is for in the first place, and how that business can be legal.

But when you've built sizeable savings, you've essentially given yourself an insurance policy with NO exclusions. It's an insurance policy for medical emergencies, for loss of employment, for separation from your partner, legal troubles, for your car or home HVAC breaking down and needing repairs or replacement, and most of all, it's an insurance policy that you will have a better quality of life with significantly less stress.

GIVE YOURSELF A RAISE!

One of the benefits of having a strong financial IQ is it is like giving yourself a substantial raise. Let's say you were making $60,000 per year prior to picking up this book, and you read and diligently employ the rules and strategies contained herein and double your savings rate, the effect on your net worth would be the same as if your salary had been doubled to $120,000 per year.

Even if you only make $15 an hour right now, by having a high financial IQ, you can enjoy greater economic freedom than 99% of your peers. Conversely, a lack of financial IQ can crush your net worth, even if you're making millions of dollars per year. This is why you hear of so many famous sports players, movie stars, and musicians file for bankruptcy (disregarding Chapter 11 filings, which are used strategically to reorganize liabilities).

Likewise, you may know or have friends who know of people with seemingly lower-wage jobs like high school teachers, plumbers, or garbage truck drivers who retired in their early forties and spend their time pursuing their hobbies, traveling, or raising their families and homeschooling. Often these individuals had high financial IQs, saved and invested their money wisely, and avoided the common economic traps and pitfalls most people succumb to.

You owe it to yourself, no matter what your current income is, no matter what your future career and income aspirations are, whether they're $40,000 per year or $400,000 per year, to start building your financial IQ today, and to start accumulating and growing your net worth TODAY. The sooner you start employing the strategies in this book and build positive savings and investing habits, the faster your net worth will grow.

The end result will be you having *more freedom*, less stress, and more time to do what you want, including being generous and philanthropic – to be kind to others and give back to humanity and our planet in your own unique way. The sooner you and your loved ones start on this journey, the easier it will be.

READING GUIDE

As you read this book, you will likely come across terms you're unfamiliar with. I'll attempt to define the terms and demonstrate their meaning, but if you're still unsure of its meaning, a simple internet search of the term should help.

CRUNCHING NUMBERS

This book does have some basic math and analysis. Don't be intimidated; none of it is too complicated. Just be patient, and realize crunching numbers is the only way to achieve financial freedom and build wealth.

This book is not intended for accountants or finance geeks; it's for anyone who is motivated to increase their savings and level up in the wealth-building game. There's no way around the fact that in order to build and manage your wealth, you must get comfortable **crunching numbers**. This isn't calculus we're talking about here; this is high school level math at most. If some parts seem intimidating or confusing, that's okay; just be patient and keep going, the math is usually followed by non-mathematical explanations.

Just power through, as difficult as it may seem, life is a lot more difficult without an understanding of personal finance, wasting years of your life because you got taken advantage of by auto dealerships, universities, insurance companies, wall street, credit card companies, financial "advisory" firms, the Federal Reserve, overpriced seminar peddlers, states run by criminals posing as politicians, and the list goes on and on; they come in all different shapes and sizes, all looking to drain you of your prosperity.

It's time to wake up and fight back.

"THE JOURNEY OF A THOUSAND MILES BEGINS WITH A SINGLE STEP."

—**LAO TZU,** TAO TE CHING, CHAPTER 64

CHAPTER 1

SAVINGS...OR HIGHER INCOME?

Before we get into specific strategies to boost your savings, we need to dispel three false beliefs that will, at worst, utterly destroy your savings and future net worth, and at best, set your savings back many years behind where it could be.

FALSE BELIEF #1
SAVING ONLY MATTERS ONCE YOU HAVE A HIGH INCOME

There's a prevailing mindset today that saving only matters once you have a high income and in the interim, you should just spend whatever you need on whatever you want—designer clothes, eating out at restaurants multiple times a week, financing luxury cars, and as many $7 cafe lattes as you need to get you through the day. Once you're rich, you can pay off all that credit card debt you racked up, those car payments, the mortgage, and so on...

What the purveyors of this personal finance theory seem to forget is the fact that if you make $300,000 and spend $300,000, you're no better off at the end of the year than you were at the beginning. On the other hand, the person who made $60,000 and kept $30,000 of it at the end of the year is better off.

Part of the reason I wrote this book is because people would be happier and more prosperous if the habit of saving was revived. This was a skill that people who lived through the 1930s Great Depression were forced to learn by necessity. But it has become largely forgotten; now we've gone to the opposite side of the spectrum where all people are taught about money is consumption, "building credit," loans and payment plans for everything, borrowing from the future to spend today. There are serious hidden and visible consequences to this trend, both for the individual's financial freedom and prosperity, as well as for the economy.

High schools and universities do not teach their students sound financial skills and the importance of savings; they have a strong incentive not to, as the inflation of the costs of tuition, student housing, books, and other educational related fees over the past 50 years has gone parabolic. Case in point, in 1970, tuition at Yale University was approximately $2,550,[3] which, adjusting for inflation, would be $17,106 in 2020. In the 2019-2020 academic year, tuition was $53,430.[4]

This blind spot in academia when it comes to financial education seems to be to academia's benefit, for its students might decide after a semester and some contemplation the degree is not worth the astronomical price. However, because most students and their parents have relied on their high schools and universities for their education and the education of their children... This has enabled the fox to continue guarding the hen house.

---

3 Jeff Muskus, "Ballooning tuition presents challenges" *Yale Daily News* (Apr 13, 2005), "yaledailynews.com/blog/2005/04/13/ballooning-tuition-presents-challenges/"

4 "Cost to Attend Yale University" *CollegeCalc.org* (accessed 9/12/2020), collegecalc.org/colleges/connecticut/yale-university/

Popular culture certainly doesn't emphasize the importance of saving. It's even looked down on, carrying a negative stigma. If you're out at dinner with friends and you opt for a glass of water over the $12 cocktail or glass of wine because you want to save money and it's not even the weekend yet, "you're just being cheap, live a little!"

In June of 2018 (before 2020's government forced economic shutdowns), the median American household had only $11,700 in savings, and 29% of households at that time had less than $1,000 in savings.[5] That is a downright scary statistic. It means most Americans are living a few paychecks away from broke, from having to choose between food or paying their rent or mortgage.

Too many people only think about getting higher incomes, yet their financial IQ is absolutely terrible. They're missing the real value of the income they're currently taking in, and due to poor money management skills, when the day comes they achieve that higher income, much of it gets wasted because that is the behavior pattern that's been ingrained.

If you think you're going to have a life of financial freedom and wealth from your income only, you're sorely mistaken. People teach their kids how to fish, how to play baseball, how to swim. But they don't teach them how to save and manage money, what they will work their whole lives for, the very thing college was supposed to prepare them to do.

This is insane. It's akin to if we were in hunter-gatherer times, and a set of parents taught their son how to draw stick figures in the dirt throughout his whole childhood, only then to send him out in the jungle to go hunt lions...which would be cruel

---

5 Kathleen Elkins, "Here's how much money Americans have in savings at every income level" *CNBC* (Sep 27, 2018), cnbc.com/2018/09/27/heres-how-much-money-americans-have-in-savings-at-every-income-level.html

and idiotic. Why the heck didn't they just teach him how to hunt lions instead of draw stick figures?

Most people spend decades pursuing a profession to get to a certain income level, making terrible, self-defeating financial decisions all along the way because they're only focused on increasing their income, on getting that promotion, on leveling up, yet they're completely wasting the income they made along the way.

For demonstration purposes, let's create a hypothetical person named Jane, an aspiring registered nurse (RN). As of this writing, the median salary in the U.S. for an RN is $67,490. Let's say Jane puts off building her financial IQ and focuses solely on the education and training needed to become an RN, which takes a few years. She succeeds and becomes an RN. Congrats Jane! She's now making $67,490 a year after payroll taxes are withheld, but before paying income tax. Now she's in the hustle and bustle of the job.

What are the odds she will immediately start building her financial IQ? Probably low. Chances are, Jane may not start that journey until a few years, possibly even decades after (like most people). Let's say for argument's sake she only waits three years into her RN job before she decides to boost her financial IQ and savings. During those three years, she's saved $20,000 in cash. Jane thinks that's good. And maybe you do too.

But you would be dead wrong. If Jane is making $67,490 per year for three years, that's $202,470 of pre-tax gross income. Having only $20,000 in savings from $202,470 of pre-tax income and three years of hard work is way below what Jane or anyone reading this is really capable of!

Let's assume in our scenario that the income tax rate for the three years Jane worked was 22%. That would mean she had an after-tax net income of $157,927. That means $20,000 of savings is only 12.7% of her after-tax net income! If she had read this book before she started working, those numbers would be much higher.

If our nurse had a strong financial IQ and read this book prior to her first year of work, she easily could have $80,000 or more after lowering her operating expenses, increasing the percentage of income she saved, and investing those savings wisely. That's four times her pre-financial IQ savings. In other words, what would have taken her 12 years to save up (at that rate), now is condensed into three years due to having a strong financial IQ. The cumulative effects of this add up to nine years of work saved. Such is the power of being a Rational Saver.

If you have kids or grandkids you truly love and would like to shave decades of struggle off their life, buy them this book. Heck, if you have to, pay them to read it; tell them you'll pay them $100 if they read the book and quiz them on it. It could be the best investment you make in them and their future.

Conversely, let's assume you read this book, build a strong financial IQ, and you're currently making $10 an hour waiting tables. You should NOT sit back and think, "with this strong financial IQ, I'm fine at $10 an hour, all is taken care of." That's not the point of this book. Yes, with a strong financial IQ, the effects on your net worth at $10 per hour will likely be multiplied. But you should simultaneously focus on increasing your income.

A large percentage of people live in a delusion that they're going to be multi-millionaires through their work alone, not through savings. Why bother saving when your band is going to be ultra-famous, your startup company is going to rake in millions, when your book is going to become an Amazon top 10 best seller? These are realistic dreams, right?

Wrong! The problem with this mindset is you're not playing the odds in your favor. You're risking your financial freedom on a very small chance of creating mega-income down the road. The majority of aspiring movie stars, musicians, founders of businesses, and authors fail, and fail hard. Not trying to be negative here, but I'm here to tell you the truth.

This does not in any way mean you shouldn't pursue big dreams; it just means don't use them as an excuse to be lazy with respect to your personal finances and building your savings along the way. That's like saying you're not going to wear your seat belt because you're an amazing driver and you're positive you won't get into an accident. No matter how amazing of a driver you are, it would be foolish to think that justifies not wearing your seatbelt.

The percentage of people who become millionaires through exploding their income alone (and not savings) is a tiny fraction of the millionaire population. This is just reality. Most millionaires get there through a combination of increasing their income AND a disciplined approach to savings along the entire journey. Moreover, they do whatever they can to increase their PROBABILITY of success.

FALSE BELIEF #2
I DON'T NEED SAVINGS;
I CAN JUST USE OPM

If you're an entrepreneurial spirited person and would like to one day start and grow a business that crushes it, or partake in joint ventures or real estate deals, you most definitely will be in a better position to accomplish those goals by boosting your financial IQ and building up savings. Even if it's only $75,000 or $150,000, your chances of success will go up exponentially.

Of course, the larger the savings, the better. In fact, having sizeable savings may very well be the deciding factor in your entrepreneurial success, even if you're using other people's money (OPM), i.e., investors who provide the bulk of the money needed for the business startup or real estate deal in exchange for partial ownership in the venture.

SKIN IN THE GAME

Imagine you're an investor. You've worked hard for years and saved up $300,000. You're approached by hypothetical Bob, who says he's found a unique real estate opportunity, a small apartment building with great upside potential (potential for increasing the asset's net operating income). The current owner died and his heirs don't want to run it; they just want to get rid of it. The building has been in disrepair and poor condition for some time. The nearby neighborhood apartments are renting for much higher, and if you make some needed repairs and re-brand the apartment complex, you can get higher rents too.

The down payment required to obtain a mortgage and purchase the investment is $300,000. Bob is looking for you to partner with him in purchasing and running it. You ask Bob how much money he is proposing to contribute towards the venture, and he says "well, none... that's why I approached you. You buy it, I'll run it, and we'll be 40/60 partners..."

Now, let's assume in this illustration you're also approached by hypothetical Mary. She has identified an investment comparable to the one Bob found. You ask Mary the same question, how much of her own money is she going to put into this deal?

Mary responds: "I'd be willing to partner 40/60 with you, and put in $100,000 of my own money towards the costs to rehab (perform repairs and renovations) and re-brand the complex, with the remainder of my 40% equity position being to compensate me for finding the opportunity, facilitating the purchase, repair, and re-renting of the units, and handling the general management and day to day operations of the apartment building. All you have to do is sit back and collect the checks."

Who would you feel more comfortable risking your $300,000 with? Bob has no risk other than his time. Mary, in addition to her time, has $100,000 of her own money at stake. Who do you think will have a stronger motive to ensure the venture is successful, especially if things don't go as planned?

Also, why doesn't Bob have any money to put into the deal? Has he not had any business success in the past to enable him to save up even a small sum of money to contribute towards this venture? Or, if he does have money, why isn't he confident enough in the venture or his abilities to put some of his money at risk?

Most successful investors would choose to partner with Mary all day long over Bob. The entrepreneurs who put some of their own cash at risk will increase investors' comfort levels dramatically, thereby increasing the odds of being able to successfully use **OPM**.

"SHOW ME THE INCENTIVE AND I WILL SHOW YOU THE OUTCOME."

—CHARLIE MUNGER, VICE CHAIRMAN OF BERKSHIRE HATHAWAY

TIME KILLS DEALS

Consider that in today's hyper competitive market, investors in the venture capital world have dozens or even hundreds of prospective investments on their docket at any given time, often taking months or years to review them all. And if you're approaching a wealthy family member or friend who has spare capital, but is not accustomed to venture capital investing, that too could take months for them to do their own due diligence and get comfortable with your venture or idea.

There's a proverb in the commercial real estate world that most veteran brokers and investors are familiar with: **"Time kills deals."** I came upon countless examples proving this true during my time working for an international commercial real estate brokerage firm, where our team's mission was to represent clients in acquisitions and dispositions of retail investment assets like grocery-anchored shopping centers, banks, pharmacies, and so forth.

I had the opportunity to speak with real estate moguls on a regular basis, as well as chief investment officers at private equity groups, family offices, and real estate investment trusts (REITs) with hundreds of millions of dollars behind them. A recurring pattern I noticed was the investors that could move quickly on a deal, that is, who had enough cash/savings behind them to make a purchase happen faster, often ended up beating the other prospective buyers on a deal, even if the offer was lower than the competitors.

One of my clients who was a private individual had an unsecured line of credit from a reputable bank of around $20 million just for the purpose of moving faster on deals – that's like having a credit card with a $20 million spending limit. He could underwrite and close on a $25+ million property faster than many people can close on a home.

But even if you're not a commercial real estate investor, and you'd just like to buy a home one day, by having enough savings at your disposal, you can capitalize on unusual opportunities when they arise; for example, a friend or relative of yours wants to sell their home, and are financially well off and like you enough to where they'd be happy to sell the property to you at a discount to market price because of your relationship. By having the ability to take advantage of the opportunity, you may save tens of thousands of dollars.

In the beginning of March 2020, I had avoided having any significant position in the stock market as I believed stocks were way overvalued and ripe for a correction. Nevertheless, I had cash sitting in my money market fund, ready to trade, as I knew the day would come when the market would correct and stocks would go on sale. By mid-March of 2020, stocks definitely went on sale, dropping by as much as 50% or more.

Because I had savings ready to go, I was able to take advantage of those buying opportunities and increase my positions, mostly in junior and mid-cap gold and silver mining stocks, as I had already been bullish on gold and silver for a few years. Many of these stocks just 4 months after the March 2020 crash went up 300% to 400% or more. It was one of the best investment scores I've had since the 2017 crypto-currency bubble.

Lady Luck really does wait for no one. When a window of opportunity arises, you must take it, and having savings at your disposal will significantly increase your ability to do so, whether it's to buy a rental property, a house to live in, a vehicle, or quality stocks after a market crash.

Do you absolutely need to have savings to start a business, buy a rental property, or fund your project? No. But not having them puts you in a position of fighting an uphill battle and lowers your chances of success. You should be doing everything in your power to stack the odds of success in your favor.

"THERE IS NO ONE, SAYS ANOTHER, WHOM FORTUNE DOES NOT VISIT ONCE IN HIS LIFE; BUT WHEN SHE DOES NOT FIND HIM READY TO RECEIVE HER, SHE WALKS IN AT THE DOOR, AND FLIES OUT AT THE WINDOW."

—MONTESQUIEU

FALSE BELIEF #3
YOU ONLY LIVE ONCE (YOLO)
SO YOU MIGHT AS WELL SPLURGE

The premise here is that you only live once and your younger years are your best years. Why bother saving when you can just spend what you earn and swipe your magic credit card to cover the rest? Hereinafter we'll refer to this as the "**YOLO, so Splurge**" belief.

Anyone who has spoken to elderly persons nearing the end, or simply contemplated the reality that we all will die one day and leave all of our worldly possessions and money behind, should conclude that our time is our most valuable resource. For most people, it would be a mistake to spend all their time living like a scrooge, not having the wonderful experiences life has to offer.

The world is full of joy and wonders, traveling, fun memories with friends and family, good laughs, delicious meals, romance, and exciting adventures. You do not want to look back on your life with regret at having not lived it due to excessive frugality and minimalism.

When you're elderly, how much money and material possessions you have is practically meaningless (aside from being able to leave wealth to your children or a business that continues to serve its employees and customers). What will mean the most to you are your memories, how well you have served God on this Earth, and leaving no regrets.

When I was 24, I decided I wanted to learn how to skydive. It probably had something to do with watching the movie *Point Break* as a kid (the original with Patrick Swayze). Being a law student who worked part-time in a library making $8 an hour, this was an expensive proposition. I went ahead anyway and spent the money I had saved from the library gig to progress through the Accelerated Free Fall (AFF) program, which lets you learn while jumping on your own (without being tandem). After completing the AFF program, I went on to obtain the USPA A License. I was hooked, at one point going for a jump almost every weekend.

I remember my first solo jump vividly. We were up in the air and had reached jump altitude which was 13,500 feet above ground level, just a thousand feet below when you might need an oxygen mask, and I was in the middle of the plane's cabin, so I was able to witness skydivers in front of me jump out first, but I also had people behind me who were relying on me getting my butt out of that plane. In fact, it's a safety hazard when someone changes their mind and refuses to jump, as other skydivers will need to go around the chicken jumper and that's how people's rigs (parachutes in skydiver parlance) get rubbed up against each other's, which may induce parachute malfunctions which could manifest when you try to pull your pilot chute.

What was interesting was how quiet it often gets before people start jumping out. There are the veteran skydivers and instructors that jump every day who are joking and laughing, but then a very long lull of silence arises and an eerie feeling creeps into the cabin. It's the kind of silence that sub-communicates a collective yet also individualized hope among everyone that all goes well—that our parachutes open without any catastrophic malfunctions, that no one runs into each other under canopy, that you don't hit any powerlines and find out what 4,800 volts of electricity passing through your body feels like; that you don't make any mistakes during landing that results in broken bones, being paralyzed or death... I witnessed a fellow skydiver die this way in August of 2014 in Zephyrhills, Florida.

Sitting next to me was one of my instructors at the time, a man named Greg, who looked like a 45-year-old Clint Eastwood.

I was only a minute or two away from it being my turn at the door to jump, and I noticed my hand started shaking. It was odd, because my conscious mind was not scared, yet my hand was still shaking. What the heck? Am I some kind of a wimp? It was like my subconscious mind was not happy that my conscious mind was doing this and disregarding the obvious dangers, some of which are completely out of your control.

I looked over to Greg and he yelled, "don't worry dude, that happened to a lot of us our first time. Just be happy you didn't piss yourself, or you wouldn't have the privilege of jumping with me again... I'd pass you off to an instructor I don't like."

It was our turn, Greg went outside the plane, holding onto a handle on top to keep from flying away like a leaf, I gave him the "I'm ready" nod, and we both jumped out. Immediately, you hear a very loud whooshing sound of air, the kind you'd likely hear if you were in a convertible sports car going 120 MPH on the free-way and you stood up on the passenger seat so your head and torso were above the windshield.

Whatever fear your subconscious mind had is replaced with pure exhilaration while your central nervous system is pumping adrenaline into your bloodstream. You never feel more alive than when you're in that space between life and death. It's a very interesting experience because there's no going back, unlike many things in life. Today, people go back all the time, they change their mind about their career, their job, their marriage, their friends, their place of residence, their business startup or the book they started writing... people have so many options now they don't know what to pick and most don't have the fortitude to stick to it.

But with skydiving, there are no choices, there's no going back, when you jump out of that plane, you'd better success-fully deploy your parachute, make sure it's functioning enough to land, and get your butt to the drop zone. You can't go back up into the plane or undue the decision you made. You're forced to simply be in the moment.

I absolutely loved it, skydiving on the weekends became my therapy, it was like it turned life's volume down so you no longer took things so seriously or became as affected by setbacks or when problems occur. They weren't life and death problems, so no big deal, you'll just handle them and keep enjoying living in the present. Those will always be a part of some of my fondest memories.

The point is that *the most memorable experiences in life are relatively cheap*. My skydiving addiction cost around $3,500 for 2 years of jumping regularly. Compare the memories, emotions, and experiences I got from that, with the experience you'd get from buying a $60,000 (in 2020 dollars) luxury SUV or sedan. Sure, you'll get a quick dopamine hit (the neurotransmitter responsible for feelings of pleasure) the day you buy the vehicle, and when you show it off to your friends and family. Maybe over the next week, you'll still have some residual positive feelings.

Then... wham! It will no longer have an effect on you at all. You'll be totally used to it and feel almost the same as you did when you were driving your previous car. Well, that is, except for the luxury car payments that will now be hanging over your head. You will feel weighed down, another responsibility you have on your plate. And I can almost guarantee you that on your death bed, you're not going to remember that time you bought the Mercedes Benz, much less relay that story to your family around you...that would be super lame.

A trip to Europe or South America is even cheaper. Renting jet skis? That's around $70 for two people (in 2020 dollars). Are there more expensive hobbies? Sure. Sailing yachts or daily horseback riding will cost you. But, if you're sociable and good at research, even those hobbies you can partake in for far less than you'd think (or than the prices advertised to the consumers not willing to do more thorough research and creative negotiation).

In reality, the finest things in life don't cost that much, and trying to buy happiness by shopping for homes, cars, designer clothes, jewelry and so on, in order to **"keep up with the Joneses"** is a futile endeavor, it will only put yourself in a self-perpetuating doom loop of frustration and discontent. It will never be enough.

Material possessions are too limited in the fleeting feelings and emotions they provide compared with that of laughing with your best friend; developing a romance built on emotional and physical connection, playfulness and fun; making someone smile; traveling and seeing the beautiful environments and animals our creator has gifted to us; spending time with family; enjoying a delicious meal; the feeling of accomplishment and energy you get after a great run or workout session; playing with your children or grandchildren; or even just meditating and the accompanying feelings of peace and relaxation. Buying expensive material possessions that you don't need will limit the time you can spend on these things that bring us the most joy in life.

When you implement the strategies in this book, you'll discover that even with a disciplined savings regimen, you still can live a life filled with memorable experiences, adventures, and no regrets. So, as you get further into this book and learn hacks and strategies for lowering your living expenses, remember, I'm not at all saying to be a Scrooge McDuck and put off fun experiences. If anything, you'll have more savings to actually go do the things you really want to do without having to worry whether or not you can afford to. Moreover, you'll see in Chapter 3, I'm going to give you a very powerful tool called the **Cost-Benefit Analysis**, which will help you determine if a big-ticket purchase is really worth making.

In addition to the best things in life being relatively cheap, there's a secondary reason the **"YOLO so Splurge"** belief is false. While people have different life priorities, for some it's building and maintaining a happy loving family, others it's walking closer to God and their faith, but the YOLO mindset tends to be that of people who (at their stage in life) prioritize having fun experiences. If that's you, you're still better off being a saver, because in the end *you'll have more fun experiences in the aggregate*.

This is because the YOLO life ends relatively fast. Eventually, the house will win, in this context the house is your creditors. You will only be able to splurge for so long before it will come to a screeching halt, before the credit card bills, car payments, and mortgage(s) become too much to handle – like a ship that has taken on too much water and ends up sinking. The party will be over and you'll be left dumbfounded, wondering why the good times had to end.

As a non-saver (i.e., a **spendthrift**), you will be forced to do things every day you don't want to do because you HAVE to do them, not because you choose to. You will have anxiety, you will lose your power to say no to a job or a boss, or to go pursue a hobby you'd like to pursue if only you had the time and money. That is why having a sizeable savings is such a beautiful thing – you have the FREEDOM to choose, you don't HAVE to take a job you don't like, you're in a position of power. You have choices.

When you have a lot of debt and liabilities, you no longer have control, and *the things you own end up owning you*. By having a disciplined savings plan, you can actually have more fun experiences in the aggregate over the entirety of your life than you could by being a spendthrift.

SAVINGS... OR HIGHER INCOME?

Now that we've addressed the three limiting beliefs that would hold you back, we'll answer the question posed by this chapter's title. Should you focus more on savings or higher income?

The answer is simple. Why not **both**? In this instance, you can have your cake and eat it too! You can focus on savings **and** on working towards earning a higher income by increasing the level of value you provide to the world!

CHAPTER 2

THE NET WORTH STATEMENT

Imagine if you were climbing Mount Everest, but you had no way to gauge whether you're actually progressing up the mountain, or simply going around the mountain in circles. How frustrating would that feel? Well, metaphorically that's quite similar to trying to build up your savings and achieve financial freedom without a **Net Worth Statement** (**NWS**), also known as a balance sheet.

This applies to everyone, I don't care if you have $0 to your name, you must create an NWS if you want to build your savings. This is an essential tool. A universal law (some call it the **Law of Attraction**) is that what you focus on expands! This book in your hand is a testament to this law being 100% true! That's very, very good news for you my friend, so remember that when things get tough or you encounter setbacks on your journey to financial prosperity, by sticking with it and staying focused, *you will win*, it's the law.

Another reason to have an NWS is, without keeping track of how much income you're setting aside for savings and what percentage of your savings is invested in what assets (also called your portfolio allocation), how can you know if you're increasing the percentage of savings you're retaining from your income? How will you know if you're diversified in the placement of those savings, or if you're over-invested in a certain asset type which puts your savings at risk should that asset type experience a drop in value?

Likewise, if you don't keep track of your living expenses (things you *need* to live such as groceries, shelter, gasoline) and your discretionary expenditures (i.e., things you don't need, but are buying anyway, such as expensive coffees and alcoholic drinks, designer clothes, and so forth), how can you figure out how to lower your expenses so you can increase your savings?

In almost every sport, skill, and discipline, the best way to get better is to track your progress. That's what the NWS will do for us. The NWS is now going to be your new best friend. Don't worry, your previous best friend will never know, at least not until they notice you seem a lot more relaxed and less stressed as time progresses, as using this tool will increase the odds of you becoming a successful saver 10 times over.

As you track progress of where you are in the savings game, you'll start to see noticeable improvements, which creates a positive feedback loop. The more your savings and investments grow, and the lower your Operating Expense Ratio (discussed in Chapter 4) becomes through reducing wasteful living and discretionary expenses, the more satisfied you'll feel, the same way when you're learning a new sport or discipline like a musical instrument and experience a breakthrough in your skill level.

HOW TO CREATE A NET WORTH STATEMENT

I'm a big believer in the "**Keep it Simple Stupid**" **(KISS) principle**. We don't want our statement to be overly complex to where it becomes a chore. For those of you familiar with balance sheets and net worth statements, this will just be a basic review, but with some noteworthy twists so hang on.

John Doe's Net Worth Statement

LAST UPDATED: April 18, 2020

Assets	Market Value	Liabilities	Amount
Personal Items		**Loan Balances**	
Home	$ 200,000	Mortgage loan	$ 150,000
Vehicles	$ 25,000	Home equity loan	$ -
Jewelry	$ 1,400	Auto loans	$ 18,000
Artwork	$ -	Secured Personal Loan	$ -
Furniture	$ 7,000	Student loans	$ 25,000
Electronics	$ 5,000	Medical Bills	$ -
Antiques	$ -	Taxes Owed	$ -
Other	$ -	Legal Bills	$ -
Cash or Cash Equivalent		Other	$ -
Savings account	$ 1,400	**Other Outstanding Debt**	$ -
Checking account	$ 2,000	American Express Credit Card	$ 4,000
Life insurance (cash value)	$ -	Visa Credit Card	$ 2,500
Money market account	$ -	Other	$ -
Certificates of deposit	$ -		
Other	$ -		
Investments			
Retirement account	$ -		
Bonds	$ -		
Mutual funds or 401(k)	$ 2,500		
Individual stock shares	$ 5,000		
Real Estate (Investment Property)	$ -		
Other	$ -		
Total Assets	$ 249,300	**Total Liabilities**	$ 199,500

TOTAL ASSETS MINUS TOTAL LIABILITIES = $49,800 (Net Worth)

Your **Net Worth = Your Assets** (What you own) – **Your Liabilities** (What you owe).

If you **duckduckgo.com** search for "Net Worth Calculator Template" there are a variety of free spreadsheets from which you can download. Avoid the websites that have input fields where you have to type into the site and it spits something out. We want to download the actual spreadsheet template to our hard drive, because we're going to customize it and get rid of some of the items that you'll commonly see on net worth statements, particularly those listed under the asset column. Also, this way after each time you update your personalized net worth statement, you can back it up to the cloud or on a spare USB key.

If you value your privacy and want to keep your net worth statement confidential and secure in case it ever gets misplaced, you can put the file in an encrypted file container using freeware such as **VeraCrypt**, using a password known only to you and that you have not ever previously used.

The previous page is a sample free NWS template you might commonly find. They're fairly ubiquitous in format and content with respect to the type of items listed under assets and liabilities.

Once you have a spreadsheet template that looks like this, it's time to make a few modifications. Note John Doe's approximate net worth is $49,800. Why didn't I just provide you with a sample template, say on my website? Because by going through the modification process together, we can see why many of the items commonly found on net worth statements should not be on there and are actually detrimental to your success as a saver (unless you're declaring bankruptcy, then those items would come in handy. But since you're reading this book, that shouldn't occur).

Once you have something similar to the John Doe template, delete the following items under assets:

- Vehicles

- Jewelry

- Artwork (unless you own investment-grade artwork that you know is marketable and have received bona fide written offers on)

- Furniture

- Electronics

- Antiques (unless you have King Arthur's actual frickin sword, or the Holy Grail, hang onto those, you'll need those for later).

Basically, you're getting rid of almost every "personal" item on the asset column found on most mainstream net-worth statements. We're deleting these for three reasons.

First, by seeing those line items under the asset column of your NWS, it will have a negative effect on your subconscious mind that's harmful to saving. We do not want your subconscious to think discretionary consumer purchases are ok because they go on your assets column and add to your net worth. For the purposes of developing a strong savings, we don't consider depreciating consumer goods as assets. For assets, we're looking for things that permanently increase your net worth. You should NOT view purchasing a car as adding to your net worth, or jewelry, or electronics, or furniture, or antiques, or artwork (unless you're a highly-skilled artwork investor who makes money buying low and selling high).

Despite what you may think, buying, leasing, or financing a vehicle will set your net worth back; as will that new smartphone16 (your smartphone15 you just bought a year and a half ago still takes calls and sends texts; do you really need the new cat emo-jis?); or that new big screen TV (when you already have a TV that works perfectly fine); or the nice watch you want to show off (look at your phone for the time); or that new sofa you've been eying (your mum has a spare sofa in excellent condition). This will be the hardest pill to swallow in this book, that discretionary purchases, when not absolutely necessary, and when done incorrectly, are hurting your freedom and keeping you from financial success.

Second, those personal assets are almost always worth a lot less than you think when you go to sell them, *IF you can sell them*, and they require you to be constantly updating the value on your **NWS** due to changes in market value (almost always to the downside), as newer technology pushes the market value of your electronics down, your vehicle depreciates every mile you drive it, and your smartphone loses about 20% every year that goes by. For example, the new iPhone 7, when it was released in 2016, listed at $650 (32GB). By 2020, a used 32GB iPhone 7 is worth about $100, and that's IF you can sell it.

Antiques and furniture, ha! You can't even give a lot of this stuff away anymore. Think of it in terms of demographics – who buys most antiques? Baby boomers and the generations before them. Baby boomers are now in their mid-60s and 70s (as of 2020), they're retiring and downsizing and have already bought all the antiques and furniture they'd ever want. The self-stor-age business exists due in large part to all the antique furniture boomers no longer want in their homes but haven't gotten around to trashing or bringing to a consignment shop. Most Gen-Xers, Millennials, and younger generations buy their furniture at Ikea. They're looking for modern, functional, and inexpensive.

Jewelry, don't even get me started. I'm not saying if you're a female not to enjoy jewelry, but DO NOT ever, *ever* think that they're an "investment" or an "asset." Diamonds are no such thing, unless you're in the diamond business. They're simply another consumer good, and the vendors who sell them make at minimum a 10% profit, more often 20%+, meaning your "investment" loses 10% to 20% immediately the second you step foot outside the store (or click your mouse on the website purchase link).

What do all these personal items have in common? *They immediately start losing value.* Imagine investors in the bond market purchasing sovereign bonds with an advertised nominal rate of return of negative 20%. Which of them would consider that an asset? Obviously, none, unless the bond market is discounting the apocalypse and can't think of anything better to do during the end than to speculate on bonds.... which isn't too far-fetched these days so never say never right?

Third, from a psychological point of view, we don't want you to fool yourself into thinking your net worth is greater than it really is. This will reduce your motivation to lower your discretionary expenditures and increase your savings. This malady afflicts a lot of people. They trick themselves into thinking "hey, I own this big house and this expensive luxury car, this fancy watch and designer clothes, I'm wealthy." No, you're not; those things don't make you wealthy.

They're all depreciating consumer goods that add to the liabilities side of your net worth statement, with recurring expenses such as insurance, taxes, repairs, and maintenance. You're just hurting yourself and your ability to invest your cash, which, if invested wisely, could be multiplying and making wealth while you sleep.

For example, if you found out from your neighbor that they're selling their triplex they currently use as their residence, but you think it would be perfect for renting out to three tenants, and they are willing to sell substantially below market value for someone who has cash and can close quickly, have fun selling your car and your watch and your clothes and your big screen TV and getting anything close to what you paid for them, and doing all of this in time to take advantage of the opportunity before someone else beats you to the punch. How'd those "assets" work out for you? By continuing the "I'm wealthy because of my fancy car and house" delusion, you're only hurting yourself, like an alcoholic who says he's only a social drinker and is wasted every day by 11 AM.

YOUR HOME DISCLAIMER

Regarding the "Home" line item on the assets side, if you have a mortgage, you're going to add parenthesis and the words "not really an asset." In chapter 12, we'll explain this in more detail. For now, although I personally would not consider my home an asset, you can still have it there with that disclaimer if you'd like, as it likely does have market value. If we took that off most people's NWS's, it would make them too sad to finish reading this book. With regards to market value, the only way to *actually* know your home's value, and the absorption time (how long it would take to sell at that price) is to list it on the market and get some qualified offers.

The next best thing to receiving real market confirmation of your home's value in the form of written offers would be to find a reputable residential real estate agent that's familiar with and has sold properties in your market and similar to your property type. Tell them you'd like to get a BOV (Broker Opinion of Value) to get an idea of what your home is currently worth. Many agents will be fine doing this, as part of their business is cultivating relationships with owners.

When you receive the BOV, there should be "sale comp" data with comparable properties that have sold recently, and info supporting the similarities and differences from your property to the properties that have recently sold which support the agent's estimated range of value. You'll want to do this every year or so, without burning through all the real estate agents in your area.

Regarding the value of your home as it pertains to your NWS, what matters at the end of the day is how much you as a seller see on a net basis, in other words, you need to subtract the cost of sale from the market value. Items that fall under cost of sale include:

- the real estate agent's commission;

- any ancillary costs such as documentary stamp taxes or other transaction fees;

- any capital improvement costs you needed to make prior to sale, such as fixing structural issues, HVAC, plumbing, roof, and so forth;

- and any other fees the seller would usually pay in your market, which the real estate agent should be familiar with.

JOHN DOE'S NWS WITH FAKE ASSETS REMOVED

Now that we've taken off the **fake assets**, John Doe's actual net worth is no longer $49,800, it's $11,400. It's ok John, we're not trying to make you feel bad, we're going to help you get back to where you were, and then multiply that by 10 or 20. But in order to do that, we need to shed misconceptions that are holding you back, so you can focus on acquiring REAL assets.

John Doe's Net Worth Statement (Revised)

LAST UPDATED: April 18, 2020

Assets			Liabilities	
Personal Items	Market Value		Loan Balances	Amount
Home (not really an asset)	$	200,000	Mortgage loan	$ 150,000
Vehicles	$	~~26,000~~	Home equity loan	$ -
Jewelry	$	~~1,400~~	Auto loans	$ 18,000
Artwork	$		Secured Personal Loan	$ -
Furniture	$	~~7,000~~	Student loans	$ 25,000
Electronics	$	~~5,000~~	Medical Bills	$ -
Antiques	$		Taxes Owed	$ -
Other	$	-	Legal Bills	$ -
Cash or Cash Equivalent			Other	$ -
Savings account	$	1,400	Other Outstanding Debt	
Checking account	$	2,000	American Express Credit Card	$ 4,000
Life insurance (cash value)	$	-	Visa Credit Card	$ 2,500
Money market account	$	-	Other	$ -
Certificates of deposit	$	-		
Other	$	-		
Investments				
Retirement account	$	-		
Bonds	$	-		
Mutual funds or 401(k)	$	2,500		
Individual stock shares	$	5,000		
Real Estate (Investment Property)	$	-		
Other	$	-		
Assets Total	$	210,900	Liabilities Total	$ 199,500

TOTAL ASSETS MINUS TOTAL LIABILITIES = $11,400 (Net Worth)

HOW OFTEN SHOULD I UPDATE MY NWS?

Most mainstream articles and "financial advisors" advocate updating your NWS annually or quarterly, or monthly. I personally update my NWS every week. Pick a day, I do mine on Fridays. I use the weekly method for the following reasons:

First, only updating your NWS once a month or quarter leaves too much room for you to forget to add assets you've acquired, particularly if you're employing dollar cost averaging to your investment strategy (see chapter 15).

Second, by updating your NWS weekly, this will make sure you're acutely aware of the rate at which liabilities are being incurred. This will help you realize if you're developing any bad spending habits, as well as increase the likelihood of you identifying any fraudulent or erroneous charges.

Third, from a psychological point of view, if you have a goal you want to achieve, in our case to build up savings, obviously, the more you remind yourself of your goal, the more likely you are to achieve it. Thus, scanning over your NWS on a weekly basis, looking to see if your net worth has increased, will increase the likelihood of your behavior being such that your liabilities decrease and your income and investing increase, because your subconscious wants to see the net worth increase, just as you want to level up in your favorite video game.

BE FAITHFUL TO YOUR NET WORTH STATEMENT

When you start saving and cutting back on expenses you realize were unnecessary, you may have a little voice in the back of your head say "just this one more time, it's no big deal, just don't put it on the NWS, next week I'll stick to the plan." DON'T DO THIS. That's like committing to workout at the gym 4 days a week, and on the first or second day skipping and saying "well, I don't feel like it today, I'll go tomorrow." This is why the New Year's gym phenomenon exists. People make their New Year's resolutions to go to the gym, and the first few days or week after January 1st, it's packed. Then after the first week or two gym attendance drops in half, because half the people quit.

The quitting doesn't happen with "I changed my mind I don't want to go to the gym anymore." The quitting happens with a "I'm not feeling it today, I'll go tomorrow." It starts with a little cheating here, a little cheating there. The monster starts as just a little guy, and every time you let the monster out of the magical cupboard, he gets bigger, and bigger, until he's a freaking 1970s Japanese style Godzilla that totally trashes your house and bites your head off.

PAY ATTENTION TO YOUR NET WORTH TREND

Your net worth trend is basically whether your net worth is going up or down. Pay attention to spot it deviating from what should be its natural trend (to go up). If it decreases, you should notice why and fix that little monster before it turns into Godzilla.

WHAT ABOUT A MONTHLY BUDGET?

If you're already very disciplined with using a monthly budget, by all means, continue if it's working for you. But for most people, myself included, these are quite annoying, time-consuming (collecting and recording every physical receipt and credit purchase) and not nearly as helpful as a net worth statement, because you're focusing on what you can't do, i.e., going over the monthly budget amount, as opposed to focusing on a positive goal (increasing your net worth). HOWEVER, in Chapter 4, we will have you create a diagnostic budget, which is invaluable for lowering your living expenses.

By focusing on the positive goal of increasing your net worth, your unnecessary discretionary spending habits will naturally decrease, you'll say no to that expensive luxury car or buying another nice watch when you already own several, you'll naturally want to live below your means so you can invest the additional savings and increase your net worth. It's more fun to play a game than to have to be disciplined, and I look at monthly budgets as requiring discipline, but net worth statements as playing a game.

CHAPTER 3

THE COST-BENEFIT ANALYSIS

The cost-benefit analysis, originally introduced by the French economist and civil engineer Jules Dupuit in the 1840s, is an incredibly powerful tool to use when making life, investment, or purchasing decisions. With regards to investing, although this tool can be useful, one should employ other methods of analysis, particularly when comparing investments, which we'll discuss in Chapter 16. Some examples of decisions this tool is great for include:

- whether or not to attend college or pursue an alternate path;

- whether to move to one state over another;

- weighing various job opportunities;

- adopting a loving sweet dog versus a silly mischievous cat;

- whether to bring on a business partner or get a loan;

- whether to make an expensive home upgrade or save your cash for investing.

There are various ways to perform this analysis. I personally use a custom version of the traditional cost-benefit analysis which includes a probability of likelihood weighting for the anticipated costs and benefits of a certain course of action and an importance weighting for each of those anticipated costs and benefits.

In order to perform the *Rational Saver* version of the cost-benefit analysis, follow the below steps:

1. **Brainstorm the costs and benefits.** Write down all the costs, monetary and non-monetary (time investment, etc.) in one column, and all the benefits you anticipate the action to bring you in another.

2. **Make sure not to duplicate** benefits in the cost section, and vice versa.

3. **Rank the importance** of each anticipated cost and benefit from 1 (least important) to 10 (most important).

4. **Rank the probability** of each anticipated cost and benefit occurring from 1% (least probable) to 100% (most probable).

5. **Multiply the importance of each benefit and cost by their** associated **probability of being true** or accurate.

6. **Compare the total sum of products** in the benefit column to the total sum of products in the cost column. Whichever product is greater is the better choice.

For example, suppose you're an entrepreneur who works from home, and you're considering whether or not to move from your current residence in California to a home in Florida because you're tired of paying state income taxes, over regulation, and find the cost of living in general to be exorbitant.

Below is an example of the *Rational Saver's* **cost-benefit analysis:**

Benefit of Moving to Florida	Importance	Probability	Product
No state income tax	10	100%	10.00
State that respects natural law	10	90%	9.00
Humid weather with less risk of fires	5	90%	4.50
State government not as corrupt	7	75%	5.25
Lower property taxes	7	70%	4.90
Lower overall cost of living	8	80%	6.40
		TOTAL =	**40**

Cost of Moving to Florida	Importance	Probability	Product
Time to sell, move and buy new home	4	100%	4
Approx. $7,500 moving expenses	4	90%	3.6
Approx. $15,000 closing costs	3	80%	2.4
Making new friends	5	100%	5
Learning new area	2	100%	2
		TOTAL =	**17**

In the above example, the total sum of benefit products for moving to Florida is 40, while the total sum of cost products for moving to Florida is only 17. In this instance, the benefits of moving from California to Florida clearly outweigh the costs, and hence is the superior course of action.

The great thing about the *Rational Saver's* version of the cost-benefit analysis is that it allows you to weigh various elements even though those elements may have different levels of importance to you, as well as different levels of probability of being true. By taking into account the importance and probability of the cost/benefit being accurate, you're making decisions in a far more thoughtful manner than 99.9% of people today. Moreover, this method lets you weigh both monetary costs and benefits as well as non-monetary costs and benefits.

If you become comfortable with using the cost-benefit analysis whenever important life decisions come up, you will find yourself making far better choices than you might otherwise have because you're reducing the level with which emotion is dictating your course of actions, and replacing it with well thought out logic, which will almost always trump emotional decision making.

Below are some ancillary concepts to the cost-benefit analysis which are also worth considering when making important decisions.

SUNK COST FALLACY

Imagine you're going to a particular store, and halfway there, you find out the store is closed. It would be illogical for you to then say "well, I've already driven 30 minutes, I might as well drive all the way to the store (another 30 minutes), so that my previous 30 minutes of driving will not have been wasted."

This is a clear representation of the sunk cost fallacy, a cognitive bias whereby one makes a choice not based on what outcome going forward will be best for them, rather, the choice is made based on a desire to not see their past investment of time and/or money go to waste. Of course, it's illogical to drive another 30 minutes to a store you know is closed.

However, that illogical pattern of thinking is quite common in scenarios that are less transparent and more important than our store example. The most common real-world example of people falling victim to the sunk cost fallacy bias would be when people continue to stay in jobs they know are a dead end with little to no room for upward socio-economic advancement, but they stick with them anyway because they reason they've already invested X years of labor into it (their sunk cost).

I chose to not work in law after spending three years in law school and obtaining a law degree, because I knew working in the law would not have been the best path for my future, both in terms of emotional fulfillment as I found it incredibly boring, and financially as there's a major oversaturation of lawyers in the marketplace today. Rather, it would have been a decision made based on not wanting to lose three years of rigorous study and work (a sunk cost).

I am incredibly glad I chose not to work in the law, as that led me to commercial real estate, hard commodities and mining equities investing, and to writing this book, all activities based on my personality type which I find much more fulfilling.

Another example would be if one invested in a stock, and that stock subsequently loses half its value due to its business model being completely disrupted by a new competitor with new technology, like taxi cabs being displaced by ridesharing apps.

In that scenario, assuming there's little probability of the company turning itself around and recouping losses, and great probability of the stock continuing to plummet as the company eventually goes out of business, the wise investor would cut their losses and move on, while the foolish investor exhibiting the sunk cost fallacy would buy more shares hoping the stock price will go back up and he can recoup his losses.

The latter investor is motivated by their desire not to lose their original investment (the sunk cost), the former is motivated by making the most optimal decision going forward based on the reality of the situation. One will have a chance to regain their losses in an alternate and better investment, the other will only increase their losses.

The moral is simple: be cognizant of when you may be falling victim to the sunk cost fallacy and in those instances, consider **CUTTING YOUR LOSSES**.

BURN THE BOATS

Sunk cost fallacy can be a dangerous concept to teach on its own…it can easily be misinterpreted, misused, and cause more harm than good. Some people will use it as an excuse to quit when things get tough. The best achievements in life are usually those that require tremendous effort, sacrifice, risk, pain, and perseverance.

If you want to accomplish a worthy goal, and you are experiencing incredible difficulty and pain, bringing up the **sunk cost fallacy** as an excuse to quit would be a clear example of misusing this concept to your detriment. Therefore, I strongly believe any discussion of the sunk cost fallacy should ALWAYS be immediately followed with a brief talk about burning boats.

The phrase **"burn the boats"** originates from the year 1519, in which the famous Spanish Conquistador Captain Hernán Cortés, upon his warships landing at Veracruz, Mexico, ordered his men to burn their boats, leaving them no choice but to push forward and conquer their enemies, for they had nowhere to retreat to. This strategy proved successful, and Cortés and his campaign are credited with the downfall of the brutal Aztec Empire (pagans who performed human sacrifices and cannibalism), bringing large portions of Mexico under the rule of the King of Castile and converting many of its inhabitants to Christianity.

This is a powerful mind hack – when you have a worthwhile goal, convince yourself into believing that quitting is not an option, that you'd rather die than quit. By removing quitting from even being a remote possibility, your odds of success will go up dramatically, you will reach deep inside your soul and find the strength, tenacity, and perseverance you need to succeed.

This can go beyond just mentally convincing yourself, to taking actions that do in fact burn the boats, things like quitting the job that's holding you back, or ending the toxic relationship, throwing away all the junk food and crap you have in your kitchen if you're trying to get on a healthy diet, taking some sort of action that has irreversible consequences that force you down the path to the success you seek.

This is a great concept to keep in mind whenever you also think about sunk cost fallacy, ask yourself: "is this truly a sunk cost? Or are things just difficult and my willpower is weakening? Perhaps it's time to step up my resolve and burn some boats."

CHAPTER 4

THE DIAGNOSTIC BUDGET

Do you hear that sound? It almost sounds like receipts being ripped up. Oh, wait, that's the sound of you wielding a razor-sharp Japanese katana and slashing your living expenses into itty bitty pieces so you have more currency left over each month to save and invest. Just like a business cannot be profitable unless it keeps its operating costs lower than its revenues, you cannot succeed in building up your net worth if your living expenses eat up all your income, preventing you from attaining any meaningful savings rate.

THE WHAC-A-MOLE METHOD
OF EXPENSE MANAGEMENT

Most people treat their living expenses like a game of Whac-A-Mole, where a mole pops up out of random holes and you have to whack the mole back in the hole with a mallet, but then another one pops up from a different random hole, which you have to hit again really fast, and then another. This goes on until you run out of coins.

That is, they're just reacting to their expenses as they arise, performing a juggling act to make it to the next month, often exacerbating their financial problems by using the convenient little plastic monster.

In addition to the credit card's onerous rate of interest (18%+) tacking on weight to your monthly expenses, it enables people to continue the same level of spending despite having poor expense management, keeping the debtor from seeing the underlying problem of their living expenses being far too high relative to their **net income**. Because they don't see the problem, they don't address it, at least not until they've already gone really far down the debt hole and have to incur major setbacks to their net worth to undo the damage, requiring years or decades of additional laboring.

THE RATIONAL SAVER METHOD
OF EXPENSE MANAGEMENT

Our method will help you organize your mind and consequently organize your money, moving you towards a place of lower living expenses, lower debt and a higher savings rate. The horse has to come before the cart, meaning you cannot lower your debt and increase your savings without first lowering your living expenses.

In order to identify which living expenses you can either reduce or eliminate entirely, you'll need a clearer picture of what's going on. Cue the diagnostic budget, a sort of expense management self-diagnosis which will be invaluable to you in this process. What exactly is a budget? It's simply a spreadsheet of projected future income against projected future expenses. This will help you see exactly where your currency will be going every month.

On the next page, we're going to give an example of what the average young person's (25-34) diagnostic budget would look like if we put their projected income and expenses into a spreadsheet.

INCOME	Jan	Feb	Mar	Apr	May	Jun	Jul	Aug	Sep	Oct	Nov	Dec	EOY TOTAL
-Salary	$ 3,750	$ 3,750	$ 3,750	$ 3,750	$ 3,750	$ 3,750	$ 3,750	$ 3,750	$ 3,750	$ 3,750	$ 3,750	$ 3,750	$ 45,000
-Side Hustle	$ -	$ -	$ -	$ -	$ -	$ -	$ -	$ -	$ -	$ -	$ -	$ -	$ -
-Passive CFlow	$ -	$ -	$ -	$ -	$ -	$ -	$ -	$ -	$ -	$ -	$ -	$ -	$ -
Gross Income	$ 3,750	$ 3,750	$ 3,750	$ 3,750	$ 3,750	$ 3,750	$ 3,750	$ 3,750	$ 3,750	$ 3,750	$ 3,750	$ 3,750	$ 45,000
-Federal Tax	$ (312)	$ (312)	$ (312)	$ (312)	$ (312)	$ (312)	$ (312)	$ (312)	$ (312)	$ (312)	$ (312)	$ (312)	$ (3,742)
-State Tax	$ (171)	$ (171)	$ (171)	$ (171)	$ (171)	$ (171)	$ (171)	$ (171)	$ (171)	$ (171)	$ (171)	$ (171)	$ (2,050)
-FICA	$ (287)	$ (287)	$ (287)	$ (287)	$ (287)	$ (287)	$ (287)	$ (287)	$ (287)	$ (287)	$ (287)	$ (287)	$ (3,443)
Net Income	$ 2,980	$ 2,980	$ 2,980	$ 2,980	$ 2,980	$ 2,980	$ 2,980	$ 2,980	$ 2,980	$ 2,980	$ 2,980	$ 2,980	$ 35,765
EXPENSES													
-Student Debt	$ (375)	$ (375)	$ (375)	$ (375)	$ (375)	$ (375)	$ (375)	$ (375)	$ (375)	$ (375)	$ (375)	$ (375)	$ (4,500)
-Rent	$(1,000)	$(1,000)	$(1,000)	$(1,000)	$(1,000)	$(1,000)	$(1,000)	$(1,000)	$(1,000)	$(1,000)	$(1,000)	$(1,000)	$ (12,000)
-Internet	$ (65)	$ (65)	$ (65)	$ (65)	$ (65)	$ (65)	$ (65)	$ (65)	$ (65)	$ (65)	$ (65)	$ (65)	$ (780)
-Cable TV	$ (40)	$ (40)	$ (40)	$ (40)	$ (40)	$ (40)	$ (40)	$ (40)	$ (40)	$ (40)	$ (40)	$ (40)	$ (480)
-Electric	$ (65)	$ (65)	$ (65)	$ (65)	$ (65)	$ (65)	$ (65)	$ (65)	$ (65)	$ (65)	$ (65)	$ (65)	$ (780)
-Water	$ (20)	$ (20)	$ (20)	$ (20)	$ (20)	$ (20)	$ (20)	$ (20)	$ (20)	$ (20)	$ (20)	$ (20)	$ (240)
-Heating	$ (60)	$ (60)	$ (60)	$ (60)	$ (60)	$ (60)	$ (60)	$ (60)	$ (60)	$ (60)	$ (60)	$ (60)	$ (720)
-Food	$ (500)	$ (500)	$ (500)	$ (500)	$ (500)	$ (500)	$ (500)	$ (500)	$ (500)	$ (500)	$ (500)	$ (500)	$ (6,000)
-Car PMTS	$ (459)	$ (459)	$ (459)	$ (459)	$ (459)	$ (459)	$ (459)	$ (459)	$ (459)	$ (459)	$ (459)	$ (459)	$ (5,508)
-Car Insurance	$ (149)	$ (149)	$ (149)	$ (149)	$ (149)	$ (149)	$ (149)	$ (149)	$ (149)	$ (149)	$ (149)	$ (149)	$ (1,788)
-Gas	$ (140)	$ (140)	$ (140)	$ (140)	$ (140)	$ (140)	$ (140)	$ (140)	$ (140)	$ (140)	$ (140)	$ (140)	$ (1,680)
-Clothes	$ (161)	$ (161)	$ (161)	$ (161)	$ (161)	$ (161)	$ (161)	$ (161)	$ (161)	$ (161)	$ (161)	$ (161)	$ (1,932)
-Entertainment	$ (200)	$ (200)	$ (200)	$ (200)	$ (200)	$ (200)	$ (200)	$ (200)	$ (200)	$ (200)	$ (200)	$ (200)	$ (2,400)
-Gym	$ (33)	$ (33)	$ (33)	$ (33)	$ (33)	$ (33)	$ (33)	$ (33)	$ (33)	$ (33)	$ (33)	$ (33)	$ (399)
TOTAL EXPENSES	$(3,267)	$(3,267)	$(3,267)	$(3,267)	$(3,267)	$(3,267)	$(3,267)	$(3,267)	$(3,267)	$(3,267)	$(3,267)	$ (3,267)	$ (39,207)
$ left for Savings	$ (287)	$ (287)	$ (287)	$ (287)	$ (287)	$ (287)	$ (287)	$ (287)	$ (287)	$ (287)	$ (287)	$ (287)	$ (3,442)
OER:	87%												
Savings Rate:	-7.6%	-7.6%	-7.6%	-7.6%	-7.6%	-7.6%	-7.6%	-7.6%	-7.6%	-7.6%	-7.6%	-7.6%	-7.6%

I used Boston, MA for the city of residence to try to make the numbers as realistic as possible for things like state taxes, heating, etc. We'll call this hypothetical young person Mary.

This is a powerful tool that will help you tremendously, regardless of your current financial situation. We have the gross income at the top, after which we subtract taxes and get our net income for each month. From our net income, we then subtract our living expenses, and what's leftover we can then put into our savings. Also note there are more living expenses not covered; this is just for demonstration purposes of how the tool works.

The cell that says "**OER**" is referring to **operating expense ratio**, an important metric used to track our progress in reducing our living expenses. The OER is your total expenses divided by your gross income, to give you an idea as to what percentage of your gross income your monthly living expenses are eating up. Remember, if you can't measure your progress, you can't improve on it. The OER is a great way to measure your progress in curtailing wasteful or unnecessary living expenditures.

In our example, Mary's OER is 87%, i.e., 87% of her gross income is eaten up by her total living expenses. Also notice that each month Mary has a shortfall also called a net deficit between her net income and her total living expenses of ($287), or a net deficit of ($3,442) per year, meaning she likely had to swipe that credit card to make up for this deficit, adding at minimum $3,442 of liabilities to her NWS every year (more if we included credit card interest), leaving her with a -7.6% savings rate, meaning not only did she not save any currency, but her net worth is being reduced by -7.6% per year.

Mary's financial situation is toxic, but it's also the norm today. Most people are living far beyond their means to keep up an illusion of having a higher socio-economic status than they really possess. Many of the numbers used were averages, for example, the average adult in the U.S. spends approximately $200 per month on entertainment, and the average young person (25-34) spends approximately $161 per month on clothes.[6] We're not including credit card interest because in a second we're going to completely change Mary's situation around so that she'll no longer need to use a credit card to cover her net income and living expenses shortfall.

THE GOAL IS TO REDUCE YOUR LIVING EXPENSES

$45,000 is a pretty modest salary, but let's see how powerful the budget diagnostic tool can be in clarifying one's financial situation and acting as a roadmap for finding ways Mary can fix this disaster she calls her finances.

First, we'll assume given Mary's experience she's stuck at $45,000 salary for now. Mary does not have any side hustles or passive income at the moment. While Mary lives in Boston, her job can be done remotely (or she can secure a similar job for the same salary in another state), and she realizes she's losing $2,050 every year to useless state income taxes, and as she advances in her career this currency drain is only going to get worse. She also likes the sun, so she decides to move down to Florida, which has NO STATE INCOME TAXES. This automatically increases her net income by $2,050.

INCOME	Jan	Feb	Mar	Apr	May	Jun	Jul	Aug	Sep	Oct	Nov	Dec	EOY TOTAL
-Salary	$ 3,750	$ 3,750	$ 3,750	$ 3,750	$ 3,750	$ 3,750	$ 3,750	$ 3,750	$ 3,750	$ 3,750	$ 3,750	$ 3,750	$ 45,000
-Side Hustle	$ -	$ -	$ -	$ -	$ -	$ -	$ -	$ -	$ -	$ -	$ -	$ -	$ -
-Passive CFlow	$ -	$ -	$ -	$ -	$ -	$ -	$ -	$ -	$ -	$ -	$ -	$ -	$ -
Gross Income	$ 3,750	$ 3,750	$ 3,750	$ 3,750	$ 3,750	$ 3,750	$ 3,750	$ 3,750	$ 3,750	$ 3,750	$ 3,750	$ 3,750	$ 45,000
-Federal Tax	$ (312)	$ (312)	$ (312)	$ (312)	$ (312)	$ (312)	$ (312)	$ (312)	$ (312)	$ (312)	$ (312)	$ (312)	$ (3,742)
-State Tax	$ -	$ -	$ -	$ -	$ -	$ -	$ -	$ -	$ -	$ -	$ -	$ -	$ -
-FICA	$ (287)	$ (287)	$ (287)	$ (287)	$ (287)	$ (287)	$ (287)	$ (287)	$ (287)	$ (287)	$ (287)	$ (287)	$ (3,443)
Net Income	$ 3,151	$ 3,151	$ 3,151	$ 3,151	$ 3,151	$ 3,151	$ 3,151	$ 3,151	$ 3,151	$ 3,151	$ 3,151	$ 3,151	$ 37,815

6 Kim P, "Average Cost of Clothing Per Month Will Surprise You" *CreditDonkey* (Jul 2, 2020), creditdonkey.com/average-cost-clothing-per-month.html

Mary's previous place in Boston that cost $1,000 per month was in a trendy part of town with great restaurants, bars, and shops right outside her place. It was the kind of place that she felt good telling people she lived. But the truth is, Mary never actually had any money to eat at those nice restaurants or shop at those nice retailers anyway, only the credit card which further put her in debt. Contemplating this, Mary realized the place she rents doesn't have to be in the hip trendy area of town; it has to be safe of course but she'd rather pay less in rent each month and have more money left over to put into savings. Consequently, Mary found a modest-sized apartment in Florida, in a safe part of town, for $750 per month, saving her $250 per month AND making her a proud practitioner of the **20% Rule of Housing**, as her monthly gross income was $3,750, and $750 is 20% of $3,750.

Mary also realized her cable TV subscription was a complete waste of money, and more importantly, a waste of time. So, Mary decided to get internet only, saving an additional $40 per month. Fortunately, FL heating costs are non-existent, as it doesn't get cold enough for oil heating, just electric, so her normal monthly heating expense also vanished. Regarding food, Mary realized when she lived in Boston, she was eating out almost every day, and this was a big part of her $500 per month food expenses. Instead, she settled on treating herself to a nice meal out once a week. This lowered her dining out expenses by $200 per month.

As Mary looked over her **diagnostic budget**, she realized one of her biggest expenses was her car payments—$459 per month, all so she could get a few fleeting dopamine hits and compliments. It's only been one year and the vehicle has already depreciated by 25%, the MSRP had been $28,300.

Mary decided she was willing to do whatever it takes to get this personal finance thing taken care of. So, she decided to sell the vehicle, avoiding any dealerships because she read this book and knew going to a dealer was a pointless exercise, instead selling directly online. She sold the car for $21,225 (a 25% reduction from what she had purchased it for). She had originally put 10% down and had already made a year's worth of payments at 0% APR for the first year for a total of $5,508, so she owed $19,962 on the car. She used the $21,225 she received from the sale and paid off her car loan in its entirety, leaving her with $1,263 and no more monthly car payments.

Mary was able to find a used Toyota Corolla on eBay Motors that had 130,000 miles on it, from a private seller, for $2,750 + $250 for the mechanic **pre-purchase inspection** and minor repairs, costing her an additional $1,737 to purchase the car after using up her remaining $1,263.

Next was her car insurance. She had been paying $149, but because that car cost $28k new, and now she was driving a car whose market value was no more than $2,750, she was able to find car insurance that ended up being $70 per month with the bare minimum insurance required by law and by pre-paying for 6 months to get the cheapest rate.

Mary also realized online shopping for clothes became therapy for her when she was feeling down or sad. Rather than addressing the issues that caused Mary to feel sad, she would shop online with her credit card to get a quick dopamine hit. She realized the only way to stop this self-destructive habit was to set a monthly clothing allowance, which she wrote on her refrigerator or whiteboard in her room a sticky note that said "January (or whatever month): $50" and once she spent that month's allowance, she'd cross off the $50 and wait until the next month to put a new sticky note up. This cut her spending on clothes from an average of $161 per month to $50 per month.

Moreover, she decided she would focus more on quality over quantity, that it's better to have fewer but higher quality items than lots of different things. If there's something she wanted to buy clothing wise that exceeded the $50, she would wait until the next month and add $50 to her clothing allowance, making it $100. She would appreciate far more the items she ended up buying, which brought her more joy.

For entertainment, Mary had been going to bars on average around two nights a week, blowing through at least $25 in drinks each of those nights, and this ultimately ended up costing her around $200 per month. Mary decided that she would cut back on drinking, and relegate it to one night a week instead, shaving off $100 a month from the entertainment category. If we assume Mary made these changes by the 1st of January, let's see what her budget for the upcoming year will look like now that she's employed the **budget diagnosis tool**, identified ways to lower her living expenses, and took MASSIVE ACTION to make it happen.

Now that Mary has taken massive action and plugged all the holes in her ship that were leaking currency, she went from an annual **net deficit** of ($3,442), to saving $12,459 in her first year alone, boosting her savings rate from -7.6% to 27.7%. Her **operating expense ratio** (**OER**) went from 87% down to 56% just in the first year!

EXPENSES													
-Student Debt	$ (375)	$ (375)	$ (375)	$ (375)	$ (375)	$ (375)	$ (375)	$ (375)	$ (375)	$ (375)	$ (375)	$ (375)	$ (4,500)
-Rent	$ (750)	$ (750)	$ (750)	$ (750)	$ (750)	$ (750)	$ (750)	$ (750)	$ (750)	$ (750)	$ (750)	$ (750)	$ (9,000)
-Internet	$ (65)	$ (65)	$ (65)	$ (65)	$ (65)	$ (65)	$ (65)	$ (65)	$ (65)	$ (65)	$ (65)	$ (65)	$ (780)
-Cable TV	$ -	$ -	$ -	$ -	$ -	$ -	$ -	$ -	$ -	$ -	$ -	$ -	$ -
-Electric	$ (65)	$ (65)	$ (65)	$ (65)	$ (65)	$ (65)	$ (65)	$ (65)	$ (65)	$ (65)	$ (65)	$ (65)	$ (780)
-Water	$ (20)	$ (20)	$ (20)	$ (20)	$ (20)	$ (20)	$ (20)	$ (20)	$ (20)	$ (20)	$ (20)	$ (20)	$ (240)
-Heating	$ -	$ -	$ -	$ -	$ -	$ -	$ -	$ -	$ -	$ -	$ -	$ -	$ -
-Food	$ (300)	$ (300)	$ (300)	$ (300)	$ (300)	$ (300)	$ (300)	$ (300)	$ (300)	$ (300)	$ (300)	$ (300)	$ (3,600)
-Car PMTS	$(1,737)	$ -	$ -	$ -	$ -	$ -	$ -	$ -	$ -	$ -	$ -	$ -	$ (1,737)
-Car Insurance	$ (70)	$ (70)	$ (70)	$ (70)	$ (70)	$ (70)	$ (70)	$ (70)	$ (70)	$ (70)	$ (70)	$ (70)	$ (840)
-Gas	$ (140)	$ (140)	$ (140)	$ (140)	$ (140)	$ (140)	$ (140)	$ (140)	$ (140)	$ (140)	$ (140)	$ (140)	$ (1,680)
-Clothes	$ (50)	$ (50)	$ (50)	$ (50)	$ (50)	$ (50)	$ (50)	$ (50)	$ (50)	$ (50)	$ (50)	$ (50)	$ (600)
-Entertainment	$ (100)	$ (100)	$ (100)	$ (100)	$ (100)	$ (100)	$ (100)	$ (100)	$ (100)	$ (100)	$ (100)	$ (100)	$ (1,200)
-Gym	$ (33)	$ (33)	$ (33)	$ (33)	$ (33)	$ (33)	$ (33)	$ (33)	$ (33)	$ (33)	$ (33)	$ (33)	$ (399)
TOTAL EXPENSES	$(3,705)	$(1,968)	$(1,968)	$(1,968)	$(1,968)	$(1,968)	$(1,968)	$(1,968)	$(1,968)	$(1,968)	$(1,968)	$ (1,968)	$ (25,356)
OER:	56%												
$ left for Savings	$ (554)	$ 1,183	$ 1,183	$ 1,183	$ 1,183	$ 1,183	$ 1,183	$ 1,183	$ 1,183	$ 1,183	$ 1,183	$ 1,183	$ 12,459
Savings Rate:	-14.8%	31.5%	31.5%	31.5%	31.5%	31.5%	31.5%	31.5%	31.5%	31.5%	31.5%	31.5%	27.7%

Did she have to put in time and effort to make this happen? Sure, it took time and effort to move to a state with no income tax; find more affordable housing; sell her ridiculously overpriced vehicle, find a decent used car and a trustworthy mechanic to perform the prepurchase inspection; get new car insurance, and make a few other lifestyle changes. But the returns on what is in actuality not that much work are HUGE and they will keep paying her back for her efforts year after year.

Financial freedom will not come to you if you don't take MASSIVE planned action to get it. But not only is Mary now building up her savings, she's growing her financial discipline muscles, becoming more mindful of where her currency is going. These are positive habits that will help her down the road, especially as her income increases through career advancement.

THE MIRACLE OF PASSIVE INCOME

A year has gone by since Mary made these life changes, she has built up $12,459 in savings. She plans on buying some rental properties in the future when her savings is large enough or she finds someone she trusts to partner with, but in the meantime, she still wants to put that currency to work, so she buys some relatively low-risk public utility stocks yielding an average of 4.6% per year in dividends (year 2020 yields), or roughly $49 per month. That's enough to cover both her monthly gym and water bills right there.

As time goes on and she continues to build savings and acquire cash flowing investments, her expenses will continue to be paid by her passive income, until down the road, all her living expenses will be covered by her passive income. Investment vehicles for producing cash flow will be discussed further in Chapter 16.

HOW OFTEN SHOULD I REVIEW MY DIAGNOSTIC BUDGET?

The great thing about the diagnostic budget is you only need to review it once a week, updating any new projected future incomes and new projected future living expenses, keeping your objective in mind of finding ways to increase your income and decrease your living expenses. Reviewing your budget diagnostic also helps remind yourself where your currency is supposed to go and where it's not supposed to go, lowering the likelihood of you deviating from the path to freedom.

It's easiest if you review your budget diagnostic consecutive to reviewing your Net Worth Statement, getting them both out of the way in the same time window. Fridays are my personal finance review days, and reviewing and updating both should take no more than 10 or 15 minutes.

CHAPTER 5

HACKS FOR LOWERING YOUR LIVING EXPENSES

This chapter will cover mindsets and specific hacks to help you keep a larger piece of your income pie to put towards savings and investing. Employ these hacks and you will be light years ahead of your peers regardless of your age group and current socio-economic status. Obtaining income is only half the battle. The other half is keeping it by being disciplined stewards of wealth.

HAVE AN EMERGENCY SAVINGS FUND

Having an emergency fund might seem like an odd suggestion in a chapter about ways to lower your living expenses, but...it is a surefire method to lower your living expenses because when people do not have adequate emergency savings and an emergency arises (as they always do), such as your vehicle breaking down, your HVAC needing replacement or other expensive home repairs, an unexpected medical expense, legal troubles, and so forth, most people that do not have emergency savings will turn to the **convenient little plastic monster** which comes with that onerous interest rate of anywhere from 18% to 24%.

For example, suppose your HVAC unit dies and costs $4,500 between parts and labor to replace, so you have to put $4,500 on your credit card that has a 24% APR. That's an additional $90 per month (or $1,080 per year) you'll pay in interest on top of the original $4,500. Remember, **bad debt** is the enemy.

With regard to how much should be in your emergency fund, you should have at least 6 months of living expenses in cash savings. This should be your first priority BEFORE investing. You'll want to perform the **diagnostic budget** from Chapter 4 to see exactly what 6 months of total living expenses will add up to.

For those considering keeping cash in their home, they may want to consider getting a heavy-duty safe that can be bolted down to the floor, and keep the cash, deeds, and any other important documents in a fire-resistant waterproof sealable bag. For extra protection, you can put that bag inside a metal ammo can you keep inside the safe.

TAKE ADVANTAGE OF JURISDICTION POWER

What country, state, and part of the state you live in WILL have a huge impact on your personal finances due to:

(a) **taxes**;

(b) **cost of living** (housing, gas, groceries, and other every-day consumer goods and services); and

(c) **over-regulation** which directly affects you should you start your own business or acquire cash flowing investments like rental properties and small businesses. God help you if you buy rental properties in a jurisdiction that subsequently enacts rent controls.

Generally, almost every state with high taxes also has a higher cost of living, because the higher taxes force businesses to pass that reduction in their net income down onto the consumer. Moreover, the most heavily taxed states almost always have the most severe regulatory environment, which also increases costs for businesses which again is passed down to the consumer.

Understandably, some professions require one to live in a not so desirable state from a tax and cost of living perspective. But if you are comparing a job in one state that pays a wage of X to a job in another state that pays a wage of Y, in terms of dollars and cents, the one that's higher isn't necessarily higher.

For example, suppose you currently live in San Francisco, CA and earn $150,000 per year, but you get a job offer in Dallas, TX that pays $120,000 per year ($30,000 less). When you factor in the cost of living and state income taxes, at those income amounts, assuming you're a single filer (as of 2020), the overall cost of living in Dallas is 25% lower than San Francisco. This means that you would only need to earn $112,466 in Dallas to have the same standard of living that $150,000 would get you in San Francisco.

Therefore, even though your job in San Francisco pays $150,000 per year, if the job in Dallas pays $120,000 per year, by moving to Dallas and taking that job that pays $30,000 less, you'd actually end up having an extra $7,534 after taxes and living expenses to put towards your savings and investments.

This is why whenever you think about salary, you want to start thinking about it in **net terms** as opposed to how the average person thinks of income in **gross terms,** i.e., the salary as advertised by the employer looking to attract labor.

There are free cost of living comparison calculators online you can use to do this for you which will save you some time. Just search "cost of living comparison." The calculator should ask you for the income you receive in one city, as well as how many adults and children in the household. The three primary variables the calculator algorithm should take into consideration are: taxes, housing, and food. You'll know if it takes those into account because it will list them and tell you how they calculated their answer.

Living in a market with lower taxes and a lower cost of living enables you to have more **net income** left over after taxes AND a lower **operating expense ratio (OER)**, both of which equal more currency to put into savings and investments.

If the place you live was once an attractive place with respect to taxes and cost of living, but subsequently turns into a highly taxed expensive place to live, the wise move nine times out of ten is to move your residence and business (if you can) to a jurisdiction that is more tax and property rights friendly. This applies to countries just as much as states, localities, and provinces.

VIEW CASH OUTLAYS
IN TERMS OF OPPORTUNITY COST

The definition of **opportunity cost** is "the loss of potential gain from other alternatives when one alternative is chosen," and **cash outlays** are anything that takes money out of our pocket.

This is a crucial mindset shift for becoming a better steward of your wealth, as well as for considering specific cash outlay decisions involving **recurring** and **one-time expenses,** to include discretionary consumer purchases.

We're defining **recurring expenses** as *any expenses or consumer purchase that will occur at least once per year.* These can be subscription or service fees that you can count on having to pay on a defined regular basis (monthly, quarterly, biannual or annual), things like: life insurance, cable or streaming packages, gym memberships, and so forth.

Recurring expenses can also be expenses that seem to occur randomly in any given week or month, but that over the course of a year repeatedly causes you to make cash outlays, such as dining out or getting that overpriced cup of coffee. You may not dine out at all one week, but another you do. These also qualify under the recurring expenses category.

When you're viewing your cash outlays in terms of opportunity cost with recurring expenses or one-time expenses, a great technique to employ is to use a compound interest calculator. There are dozens of free ones you can download onto your smartphone so you have it with you at all times. Search "compound interest calculator app." Make sure the compound interest calculator you use has the following input fields:

- **Principal Amount**: this is the expense if you're making a one-time expense, or if there is a recurring expense that also requires some sort of initial payment or down payment in addition to subsequent regularly defined cash outlays.

- **Monthly Deposit**: This is how much per month the subscription or service fee is. If it's not a monthly fee, but let's say quarterly, biannual or annual, just take the total expense amount per year, divide by 12 for annual, 6 for biannual, or 3 for quarterly, and input that number into this field and that should get you close enough. If you're calculating opportunity cost for a one-time expense, you would input 0 for this field.

- **Period (month)**: This is how long this goes on for. So, one year would be 12 months, 10 years 120 months, 20 years 240 months, etc.

- **Annual Interest Rate %**: This is where you'll input your opportunity cost rate of return. <u>Use a rate that is un-adjusted for inflation</u>, because you're not going to adjust the principal amount and monthly deposits for inflation as that would add too much work for this to become a regular daily habit, and moreover, you don't really know what inflation will be down the road. So, if you believe that you can get an average compound rate of return (un-adjusted for inflation) of 8% over the long term invested in a stock index, then use 8%.

- **Compounding**: this is how often the investment will compound. Usually this is set to annually. This does depend on if the appreciation or cash flow you get every year from the investment gets reinvested, or if you just put it into cash savings or spend it. So, if you're invested in a stock market index and it appreciates 8% in year 1, and you plan on not taking any profits but letting it continue to grow, you'd set your calculator to compounding annually. If the investment doesn't compound, set it to no compounding.

For example, suppose you're considering a standard video streaming subscription service for $12.99 per month. The average mentality is to only look at it in terms of the stated monthly cost, to think "$12.99… that's nothing, I make $3,000 a month, I can afford that no problem." The R*ational Saver,* on the other hand, looks at the long-term **opportunity cost** before making a decision, and as such would pull up their compound interest calculator app and perform a quick and easy calculation.

- In the **principal amount** field, input $0;

- In the **monthly deposit** field, input $12.99;

- Because old habits die hard, if you're paying for a streaming service now, you'll probably be doing it for at least 30 years, if not longer. Most baby boomers, as an example, who watch cable TV have been doing so for 40+ years, so we'll use 30 years to be conservative or 360 months and input 360 in the **period (months)** field;

- If you think you can invest the cash you otherwise would pay for the streaming service into an investment vehicle that yields an 8% compounding annual rate of return (un-adjusted for inflation), you'd input 8% into the **annual interest rate** field; and

- You would set **compounding** to annually.

Hit calculate, and you'll get a Maturity Value of $18,415, meaning the opportunity cost over a 30-year period for the cash outlays required to get that monthly streaming service is $18,415 or the price of two quality used vehicles or a chunk of a down payment for a house or cash flowing rental property. If after mulling this over it is still worth it to you because you just absolutely love watching streaming shows and movies, go for it. At least you'll have made the decision knowing the real cost isn't "$12.99 a month" the way the average consumer thinks.

Or, perhaps you'll be incentivized to come up with a creative solution to still get the product or service you want, but at a reduced cost. In our streaming example, many people only have a few shows they really enjoy watching, yet they pay for a cable or streaming service for an entire year only to watch those few shows. If this is you, perhaps you can just pay for 1 or 2 months a year and then cancel the subscription after you've binged watched your favorite show; instead of sacrificing $155.88 per year on a streaming service, you just sacrifice $25.98 per year (1/6th the cost). Or, if there is an option for multiple logins per account, split the cost with a friend or family member.

Regarding recurring expenses that aren't scheduled and occur more randomly, for example, eating out, you don't need to be exact, just try to come up with a rough estimate as to how often you have been making that expense or are likely to make that expense, and arrive at an average amount per month that you can input into your app.

Be careful not to overlook a new spending habit you may have picked up that does in fact cause you to have recurring cash outlays, for example, you start getting expensive coffees at a place you like and you're doing this weekly.

This requires you to be aware and observe your spending behaviors, more so than 99% of your peers who don't think about their spending habits at all until they're forced to, and they generally only pick up on the big purchases, not realizing that little cash outlays done repeatedly and over time can be just as detrimental.

Regarding one-time expenses, I prefer to only perform an opportunity cost analysis for expenses that are $500 or more. Less than that and you may turn into Scrooge McDuck.

From now on, before purchasing ANY recurring subscriptions, or any one-time purchases of $500 or more, DON'T BE SHY! Pull out your compound interest calculator app and crunch the numbers!

YOUR EGO WILL COST YOU A FORTUNE

An insane amount of money is spent every year for one purpose: feeding peoples' egos. This is why people who aren't actually wealthy go out and buy things like:

- Homes that are way more than their finances can support (violating the **20% Rule of Housing**);

- expensive designer purses, wallets, sunglasses, watches and name brand everything;

- luxury vehicles that do the same thing a quality used vehicle can do;

- fine jewelry, artwork, and furniture;

- the newest thousand-dollar smartphone when your old phone works just fine; and

- high-end gym memberships.

These things are totally fine once you're able to buy them with passive income, i.e., when you've actually made it. But most people who own these things have not made it, and most never will because they think having the **trappings of wealth** means they're wealthy. By trying to put the cart before the horse, people waste their savings keeping up an illusory image of wealth, and ironically, doom themselves to never become wealthy.

Behind closed doors most of these faux wealthy people don't really get to spend much time enjoying the illusory image anyway, as most of their time is spent sweating bullets trying to pay the bills and keep their "safe" job, too scared to take the necessary risks (investing or starting new businesses involves risk) to become wealthy, forever dooming themselves to live paycheck to paycheck.

While most people are busy **keeping up with the Joneses**, borrowing from the future to spend today and maintain this illusory image of success, in contrast, you'll be saving and investing, building REAL financial success so that eventually, you can live like they can only dream.

MONEY VALUE OF TIME

The **Money Value of Time (MVT)**, not to be confused with the more widely familiar **Time Value of Money (TVM)** principle (which we'll cover later in the book), essentially is this: if you have the income you receive by laboring, then your time has a monetary value. This is what Benjamin Franklin's famous "time is money" aphorism represents.

Knowing the monetary value of your time can help you to guard and wisely allocate your most precious resource you have... YOUR TIME! Wealthy people guard their time fiercely; when they're not helping others and being charitable, they're cheap with their time, far more than they are with currency.

To calculate your MVT, we're essentially looking for the market value of your labor net of taxes and expenses. For service providers who bill by the hour, their MVT would be the rate they bill per hour net of business expenses and taxes. So, if you're a chiropractor and your chiropractic group pays you net of expenses $73 per billable hour, and we assume you live in a state with no state income tax and after federal income taxes and FICA your effective tax rate is about 25%, this means every hour you bill, you end up keeping $54.75. That would be your MVT.

For those on fixed salaries, their MVT would be their annual net income divided by the (# of working days per year x hours laboring per workday). So, if one's salary is $100,000 per year, and we assume they live in a state without state income tax and their take-home pay after federal income taxes and FICA is $77,104 (their net income), and they worked 48 weeks out of the year, 5 days a week for 8 hours per day, their MVT is roughly $40 per hour.

How can knowing this be helpful? Let's suppose you own a house with a lawn. Some data suggests the average person with a lawn spends 2.4 hours per month, 8 months out of the year, on lawn care maintenance. This equates to 19.2 hours per year, so if you purchased your home at age 30 and perform lawncare until you're 70, approximately 768 hours of your life would be spent mowing the lawn.

Let's suppose you're the chiropractor whose MVT is $54.75 per hour. If you can hire someone to mow your lawn for $20 per hour, by doing it yourself, you're arguably losing $26,688 over that 40-year period you could have made working ([$54.75-$20] x 768 hours), just from doing your own lawn care maintenance... Additionally, there's the opportunity cost of not having invested that additional income from working.

Of course, real life isn't going to be nearly this precise, but this is to demonstrate the concept. That said, there's a strong argument that in reality, your real opportunity cost for doing the work yourself instead of outsourcing it would be far greater than the above, because many professions have a limit to the hours you can work, especially if you're salaried. However, that additional time, if spent working on growing your business or making it run more efficiently, or doing the extra work needed to help your team accomplish their goals, even though you may not see an immediate economic benefit, over the long run could increase your MVT altogether.

What is the real cost of spending that time mowing the lawn or the day re-painting that room in your house when you could outsource it for $20 or $25 an hour and spend that time growing your business? Increasing locations or affiliate partners to capture more market share? How about taking on a business partner to help scale the operation? Or by socializing with your company's senior management and helping them achieve their objectives, bringing more value to the table, and securing a promotion for doing so?

The major caveat here is if you outsource a job that you could do yourself, say having a room painted or your lawn being mowed, and then waste the time you saved to go do something that doesn't increase your income, like watching shows or relaxing by the pool.

Until you're very wealthy and able to live entirely off of passive income, this isn't using the money value of time principle to your advantage, this is just being lazy. If you're not going to take the time you saved from outsourcing and use it to increase your income either immediately or over the long-term, you would be much better off doing the job yourself and saving your currency.

The main takeaway from the money value of time principle is to be really cheap...with your time! This has a direct correlation to your income. This doesn't just mean outsourcing lower-income tasks so you can spend more time on your work. It also means every day being cognizant of how you're spending your time, and if it's getting you closer to achieving your most important life goals and objectives or not; it means avoiding or limiting time-wasting activities like watching shows, movies, drinking, video games and hitting the snooze button on the alarm and lying in bed for another 15 or 20 minutes.

This will require discipline, but the good thing about discipline is that it's built one small exertion of effort at a time. When you're thinking about watching a show, but instead go put in another hour on a work project or reading a book for self-improvement, or when you skip playing a video game or drinking with friends to lift weights or go for a run, in each of those instances you're increasing the size of your mental discipline muscles.

Being careful with how you spend your time is such a powerful lifehack it cannot be overstated, because time is money, and wasted time adds up fast and can thus become your BIGGEST LIVING EXPENSE!

LESS IS MORE – THE POWER OF MINIMALISM

Ounces equal pounds, and pounds equal pain. This is a popular adage amongst backpackers and some military forces, and for good reason. The beginner backpacker will bring everything and the kitchen sink – they'll pack too much clothing, multiple pairs of shoes instead of one solid pair of boots, all kinds of unnecessary gear and gadgetry for every conceivable purpose, and when they're a quarter way into their journey, they're already fatigued and ready to quit, moving at half the speed of the more experienced packers carrying 1/3 the weight.

The more stuff the backpacker brings on their trek, even little things that only weigh a few ounces and on their own seem inconsequential, the more the backpacker is weighed down and unnecessarily wastes calories and time, making the journey far more difficult. This is why experienced backpackers will go as far as to do things like cut their toothbrush in half to save even fractions of an ounce, they know all the little weight savings collectively adds up to pounds. Their kit is meticulously thought out and as minimalist as possible.

The same holds true with your everyday life and the accumulation of material possessions. Most consumer purchases, just like the extra piece of gear the novice backpacker throws in his pack, on their own don't seem like a big deal, but collectively they add up, weighing down you and your personal finances.

The more things you own, the more they end up owning you, i.e., the more things you have to take care of, repair, maintain, make space for, insure, guard from theft, put in storage or spend time trying to sell when you no longer have room. Additionally, all these material possessions tie people down emotionally to one location, limiting mobility.

This is why the self-storage industry exists and in 2019 brought in $39.5 billion USD in revenue in the U.S alone. People develop unhealthy emotional attachments to material possessions that they then can't let go of, yet they obviously have zero need for since they're leaving it in a storage locker for years on end, likely never to be used again until the day they try to sell them for pennies on the dollar or just discard because there's no buyers.

A relative of mine suffered from this "stuff" affliction. The relative had sold his home and downsized to a smaller house; he and his wife over the years had accumulated all sorts of consumer products, exercise equipment, gadgets, furniture, enough stuff that when he put it into self-storage he was paying around $800 per month in storage fees. In the end, he threw most of the stuff away. By the time he finally decided to get rid of the self-storage unit and its contents, ten years had gone by and $96,000 in self-storage fees had been flushed down the drain (at an opportunity cost of $130,611 at a 6% rate of compound interest).

Ultimately, the stuff was almost worthless as there's not really much of a market for used exercise equipment or expensive furniture these days, as other baby boomers have their own homes and storage units filled to the brim with furniture and consumer products they've bought over the years, and Gen Xers and Millennials just get their furniture at IKEA for 1/5th the price.

This didn't happen to him overnight; the accumulation of

worthless material possessions you don't really need happens slowly, insidiously, and over years. It starts as a little monster and eventually grows into a Tyrannosaurus Rex with frickin laser beams on its head. Don't let this happen to you.

The caveat here is making sure to have what you need in order not to waste time unnecessarily to save a few bucks, such as equipment required to advance income-wise. Let's suppose your business is video graphics design and you genuinely would save thirty minutes every day if you had a higher-end computer that renders faster. In that instance, being cheap and using your old computer that takes you an extra 30 minutes a day and not acquiring an item that will dramatically increase your work output is foolish. Just make sure you're being honest with yourself as to whether that purchase really will increase your output enough to pay for itself in a reasonable amount of time (called the payback period).

The other caveat is having basic emergency supplies and training. You don't want to be so minimalist that you're completely dependent on the system for things like water, food, medical care, and security. Even when things are up and running normally, if you or a loved one is in an accident and the result is a massive arterial bleed on a limb for example, the minimalist who doesn't own (and know how to use) a tourniquet is likely going to bleed to death long before emergency medical services can show up.

Likewise, in the event of a major disaster like a hurricane, which disrupts the just in time supply chains for essentials like food, the extreme minimalist family that only has a week or two worth of food in their home isn't going to fair well compared to the preparedness-minded family with 6 months of freeze-dried food.

Those caveats aside, when it comes to material possessions, LESS IS MORE. Your net worth will also agree; the fewer things you purchase, the more currency you'll have to put into your savings and investments.

BIG TICKET ITEMS...RENT, DON'T OWN!

When it comes to big-ticket consumer goods, it's usually cheaper to rent, especially with things like:

- Vacation homes;

- Planes;

- Sports Cars;

- Recreational Vehicles (RVs).

- Boats (except Jon boats, which are inexpensive).

Most people overestimate how often they're actually going to use these big-ticket items, and purchase without performing a cost/benefit analysis weighing the actual total costs of ownership versus renting. Generally, unless you're going to spend three months or more every year in your vacation home, or go on your boat or fly your plane every week, these items are cheaper to rent and let someone else pay the storage fees, insurance, property taxes, repairs, and regular maintenance costs.

Moreover, even in the event the big-ticket item you're considering purchasing would, over the long run, actually pencil out to being cheaper to own versus rent, there's still the opportunity cost of the cash outlays you're making to buy and maintain the consumer item.

Suppose you're looking to buy a vacation home for $350,000 and you have $70,000 for a 20% down payment. Also consider you can purchase a triplex with paying tenants for $350,000 using that same $70,000 down payment at a 7% cap rate, meaning the triplex is producing a net operating income (NOI) of $24,500 per year (pre-tax) and is paying for itself, building your net worth, while the vacation home will continue to be a liability year after year draining cash out of your bank account.

Which do you think would be the smarter decision?

Obviously buying the triplex that gives you $24,500 per year in passive income. Heck, you could use the **positive cash flow** (the rental's remaining income after debt service and expenses) to fund a trip to Europe or South America every year. Instead of adding another liability to your net worth statement (the vacation home), you have a cash-flowing asset (your triplex), and the rental property could fund your vacation every year. That's **working smarter instead of harder** as my father would say.

Until you can buy your desired big-ticket item with 100% cash originating entirely from your passive income streams (NOT FROM YOUR SAVINGS), as a *Rational Saver* it would be incredibly foolish to buy these items in today's day and age when you can easily rent for a fraction of the cost and invest the difference.

KILLING TWO BIRDS WITH ONE STONE – TASK STACKING

For my first job out of college, I was fortunate to land a position as a legal assistant (basically a runner, spreadsheet jockey, and note taker) for a very successful owner of a law firm in Connecticut that specialized in criminal defense and family law. The firm was in high demand from both private and government clients; the senior partner had special public defender contracts with state and federal courts for more serious criminal cases involving things like organized crime and racketeering. He had other attorneys under him, a secretary, a personal chauffeur, and owned dozens of single-family homes and apartments in the greater New Haven area that created passive income night and day.

I say I was fortunate because, although I was making a little more than minimum wage after graduating from Yale (this was shortly after the Global Financial Crisis of 2008-2009), I was able to shadow this hyper-productive and successful entrepreneur around all day every day, learning valuable lessons on ways to manage your time and business that I would not have learned had I gone right into some large corporate organization where you're compartmentalized and supervised by people one rung up the ladder from you who themselves haven't achieved real success either.

One of the things he frequently stressed, in addition to the money value of time principle discussed earlier, was the importance of killing two birds with one stone, i.e., accomplishing multiple tasks in one action. Every day it seemed he would do this with the way he organized his meetings, trips, management of his real estate portfolio, general errands, and so forth.

When you consider how valuable your time is, you'll realize the power in this strategy for your own life. Heck, who hasn't ever pondered how much more they could accomplish if they didn't need to sleep and had an extra 6-8 hours every day? Well, that's not possible... you need to sleep, but you CAN stack your daily activities, errands, and work tasks in such a way that you give yourself extra minutes or even hours every day you otherwise wouldn't have.

For example, I meditate 20 minutes every day and also like to get at least 20 minutes of Vitamin D from the sun every day as well. Instead of sitting in the house meditating for 20 minutes, and later in the day laying out in the sun for 20 minutes, wouldn't it be wiser to combine the two activities by meditating out in the sun for 20 minutes? Bam! I just gave myself an additional 20 minutes per day I would not have if I performed each activity individually. Over 30 years if done say 5 days a week, that's 2600 hours or 108.3 days of my life saved with that one task stack alone! Holy smokes, Batman!

If you need to travel to another city for business, why not also meet up with some friends in the area as well and strengthen those relationships? If you're traveling a long distance, instead of just listening to music, put on a self-improvement audiobook, or get a phone headset and use the time to make calls.

When you go shopping for groceries, instead of buying small amounts requiring you to make trips every week to replenish your stock, consider buying in bulk (non-perishables) which on a per ounce basis is cheaper anyway. But the real savings isn't in the bulk discount rates, it's in the time saved.

Some data suggests the average U.S. shopper spends 41 minutes in the grocery store 1.5 times per week, which equates to 53 hours per year. This doesn't account for the time driving to and from the grocery store. As a side note, the weekends are the worst days to do your shopping as that's when most people go. The best days are Mondays and Tuesdays.

For demonstration purposes, let's imagine a hypothetical scenario that takes the average grocery shopper above and assume it's a 10-minute drive to his grocery store of choice. That's 20 minutes of driving per grocery store trip. That means in addition to the 53 hours per year in the grocery store, our hypothetical shopper spends 26 hours driving to and from the grocery store, for a combined total of 79 hours per year.

If our hypothetical shopper employed the **kill two birds with one stone** strategy and instead of the average of 6 grocery store visits per month, went once a month and bought in bulk (metaphorically killing 6 birds with one stone), and we'll assume it increased the shopper's time in the store by an additional 30 minutes (to pick out and carry the larger amount of groceries), for a total of 71 minutes per visit, and again 10 minutes driving to the store and 10 minutes driving back, that's 91 minutes per month spent on the activity of grocery shopping total, or approximately 18.2 hours per year.

When we subtract 18.2 hours per year from the original 79 hours per year, our shopper has saved 60.8 hours per year, over 30 years that's 1,824 hours or 76 days... If we assume our hypothetical shopper's money value of time is $40 per hour, that would mean he saved $2,432 that year by being more efficient with his time just with respect to his grocery shopping, which over 30 years is $72,960. This doesn't include the added bonus of savings in gasoline and wear and tear on his vehicle.

This may sound nitpicky, but if you can save $2,432 per year just from doing your grocery shopping once a month and buying in bulk, imagine how much more time and money you'll save in all the areas of your life where you may have been making unnecessary trips or not utilizing your time efficiently by missing opportunities to stack errands and work tasks. These are hidden living expenses and completely unnecessary.

I can 100% GUARANTEE someone like Elon Musk is a wizard at being efficient with his time; his stacking of work tasks to accomplish multiple objectives simultaneously has to be legendary. But you don't need to be Elon or a wealthy entrepreneur like my former boss to take advantage of this strategy today. How do you think those people got there?

From now on, be like the hyper-successful entrepreneurs and develop a sixth sense for identifying ways to save time every day by stacking errands and work tasks so you can get multiple tasks done simultaneously. Of course, there will be tasks that are time-sensitive and do not allow for this, but for everything else... **stack away**!

SOMETIMES CHEAP IS EXPENSIVE

Reading this book, one might get the impression that they should always go with the less expensive option when it comes to consumer goods or services. This would be false, as sometimes the cheaper option is more expensive than the more expensive option.

Once I needed a set of cobalt drill bits for a project that involved drilling into hardened steel, so I purchased some from a nearby home improvement store for about $20 (and 30 minutes between driving and time spent in the store). Within 10 seconds of drilling, the drill bit snapped in half and got stuck in the steel. I looked at the back of the drill bit pack and it said made in China. Go figure. It took me 5 minutes to manually back it out of the steel with heavy-duty pliers, and 30 more minutes driving to the store, waiting in the customer service line to return the cheap drill bits and driving back. After more research, I found that the best drill bits for that kind of project are from Germany, so I ordered a comparable set from Germany that cost a total of around $45 with international shipping. Those cut into the hardened steel like butter and got the job done. In this instance, the cheaper option was not the superior option, as it wasn't sufficient to get the job done and unnecessarily wasted a lot of valuable time.

Similarly, I once bought a cheap $30 blender, the kind where the blending cup is of the type of plastic that you can't put in the dishwasher or it gets deformed. That means after every use you have to spend 45 seconds or so washing it by hand. In 365 uses that's roughly 274 minutes (4.5 hours) of your life spent as a human dishwasher...

If we assume your money value of time (MVT) is $50 an hour, that means in addition to the blenders base price of $30, with 365 uses you're losing $228 worth of time washing a stupid blending cup, whereas with a higher quality blender for $75 you can just put the blending cup in the dishwasher and it does the job for you. Not to mention the cheap blender broke after a year and a half or so, while my more expensive blender is going on 5 years now… Even without the MVT consideration, if I have to replace the cheap $30 blender on average every 1.5 years, that's $90 for roughly 5 years while my $75 blender was $75. Some things really are *buy once, cry once.*

Another glaring example where cheaper can be more expensive is with respect to food. Buying the cheap food that the masses get at your local big box store or fast food restaurant, is going to be more expensive over the long run due to medical bills and a reduction in your productivity from decreased mental clarity and overall health. This is an area where sourcing your fruits and vegetables from local farmers, as well as making sure you get meats that are 100% grass-fed and free-range organic, will pay off over the long run. I personally like butcherbox.com.

The moral here is not to automatically assume the cheaper option is better; sometimes the optimal option can be the ones that give you the most value, which is determined by things like: quality, reliability, lifespan, how much time the goods or service saves you and so forth.

WARNING! Don't let this be a weasel (an excuse) for wasteful spending or choosing more expensive items or services when the less expensive items or services will get the job done. For example, if we're talking purchasing a vehicle to get to work and run general errands, this doesn't apply at all. Cheap is not expensive. A used Toyota or Honda for $5,000 if it passes your mechanic's pre-purchase inspection, is in fact the better option, while the $20,000 or $30,000 new vehicle is, in fact, stupid expensive.

MICRO-HACKS FOR
LOWERING YOUR LIVING EXPENSES

Coffee Shops: The average American between the ages of 25 and 34 reported spending in excess of $2,000 per year at coffee shops.[7] Over 30 years that's roughly $60,000 (without inflation). The **opportunity cost** if investing monthly at a 6% compound rate of interest is **$163,203**! Hope the café latte Grande mocha sprinkles and syrup snowflake drink was worth it... This doesn't even account for all the wasted time standing in line, ordering and paying, waiting for your coffee to get made, and the time in the car if you drove there.

I use a $10 classic drip coffee maker. These can last up to ten years easily. The coffee itself can be bought in bulk, and you can get USDA organic non-GMO verified coffee. According to the Specialty Coffee Association of America, a single pound of coffee should yield roughly 48 x 6-ounce cups of coffee. If we assume you drink 1 x 6-ounce cup of coffee per day, that means you'll need roughly 7.5 lbs. of coffee per year. The organic coffee I get is $18 for 2 lbs., so that's roughly $72 for a whole year...

The lesson here: going to coffee shops is a MASSIVE waste of time and money when you can brew coffee yourself for 1/20th the cost.

Eyeglasses: If you need these, get your eye exam and prescription from an optometrist, but skip actually buying the glasses from their in-house store or any brick and mortar store for that matter. Instead, go online to a Zenni Optical or Warby Parker; you'll pay at least half if not a third of what you'd pay for eyeglasses in a

---

7 Drew Housman, "Millions of Millennials Spend More on Coffee (and Other Things) Than Retirement" *The Simple Dollar* (Aug 13, 2020), thesimpledollar.com/save-money/millions-of-millennials-spend-more-on-coffee-and-other-things-than-retirement/

physical store. I have friends who learned about this trick after having already been duped into paying $600 for a pair of eyeglasses, only to discover that they could get the same or comparable pair for $250 from one of the previously mentioned online retailers. That's $350 in savings.

Toilet Paper (TP): Some data suggests the average U.S. household of 2.6 people uses 409 equivalized rolls of TP per year at an average cost of $0.84 per roll (in 2020 dollars). This means the average U.S. household spends roughly $344 per year on TP. Households with 4 people on average will spend $529 per year on TP. In 30 years, that's $15,870, and if we whip out our trusty compound interest calculator app, assuming the toilet paper is purchased once a month, not taking into account inflation, if we look at those cash outlays in terms of an **opportunity cost** of 6% compounding annually (had we invested the cash outlays), the true total cost for four people is around $43,166!

In contrast, the Japanese and the Italians use bidets. These are not only WAY more economical, they're also more efficient and more hygienic. After you start using a bidet, you'll feel like a caveman/woman if you ever go back to TP only. You don't need to buy a dedicated bidet toilet, the easiest and cheapest way is to just get a quality bidet attachment that goes on your regular toilet, they can be had for $30-$50 and should last you 10+ years. These reduce the amount of toilet paper you use by 90% easily. You will still need to buy toilet paper to use after you're done with the bidet action, but we're talking 1/10th of the TP you would normally use.

So instead of $15,870 for 4 people over 30 years, we're talking $1,587, that's a difference of $14,283 or 2 used Lexus sedans...As a side perk, if there's ever another run on TP like in 2020, you won't be affected.

Alcohol: If you're in the camp of people who have a drink or two every time you go out, say a mimosa here and a Moscow mule there, we're talking at least $10 per drink. If you go out and get two drinks per week, that's $80 per month or $960 per year so you can have two drinks per week when you go out.

If you're in the camp of people who have a glass of red wine every night with dinner, note a standard red wine glass holds 150 mL. The standard red wine bottle size is 750 mL. An average bottle of red wine costs $15.66. Over one year, that means you're using about 73 x 750 mL bottles per year, which at $15.66 is $1,143 (without tax). If you and your partner do this, double that to **$2,286** per year to have a glass of red wine with dinner.

If you're someone who has 10+ drinks per week out, and this is becoming very common today, we're easily talking $5,000+ per year in booze. In five years, there's your down payment for a starter home or investment rental property.

If you're a drinker, take some time to honestly assess how many drinks you have per week and what the average cost is, then multiply that by the number of weeks in a year to see what you're really losing. Then perform an opportunity cost calculation on what that lost money could do if invested. Perhaps you'll realize it's time to cut back (or quit entirely) if you want to win the game of personal finance.

Eating Out: This is a big one because the cost to eat out has risen to the point of absurdity. Even if you only eat lunch Monday through Friday, you'll likely spend around $10 per meal, that's over $2,500 per year. Over 20 years, your opportunity cost at 6% compounding interest (without inflation) is $91,129, just to go out for lunch...

If you add on top of that eating dinner out three times a week, or breakfast once a week and dinner twice a week (very common), at $20 per meal, add $3,120 to your annual eating out expenses, for a total of $5,620, with an opportunity cost of $200,484...Ouch. This is all just for one person eating by themselves, very sad. Two people at those numbers turns that into over $10,000 per year eating out with an opportunity cost approaching HALF A MILLION DOLLARS over just 20 years.

What's the solution? Make your own lunch, i.e. meal prep for the week. This will not only save you a CRAZY amount of money every year, it's usually healthier. Regarding eating out, how about scaling it back to once per week.

Part of the reason the cost to eat out has gone up so much over the past 50+ years has to do with rising commercial real estate prices. As properties are bought and sold, new purchasers always look for upside (as all investors do, otherwise there's no point and properties would just fall in disrepair) and among other things will try to raise rents or get new tenants that can pay higher rents. As rents go up, restaurant operators (and other retailers) are forced to pass the rising costs down to their consumers in the form of higher prices just to stay in business.

Why did commercial real estate prices rise in the first place? Central banks setting interest rates (interfering with the free market's price discovery mechanism as it relates to the cost of debt, a textbook example of socialism), which as of this writing the long-term trajectory has been lower and lower interest rates, which inevitably leads to asset price inflation (stocks, real estate, and bond prices go up, up and away!). Don't like how expensive it has become to eat out? Until we go back to free market capitalism and sound money, this will only get worse.[8]

---

8 EndTheFed.org

Watches: Do you really need a watch in today's day and age when your cell phone has the time? Even the smart watches are an overpriced scam. There's nothing you can do with a smart watch that you can't already do with your smart phone. If you have a nice outfit for business or social affairs and think a watch completes the look, having one nice watch for that is understandable. But spending more than $300 (in 2020 dollars) on a watch is foolish. There are some very highly engineered and stylish German, Swiss, and Japanese watches for under $300 that should last you a lifetime. Buying more than 1 watch or spending more than $300 before you've made it (can live off of passive income) is like setting your cash on fire. If you've already bought multiple watches and after thinking about it realize you only need one, as long as they're marketable, why not sell them on eBay and boost your savings?

Animals: If you already have animals, skip this, unless you're thinking of adding more. If you don't, before you go get a dog or a cat, make sure you realize the largest costs are not the annual food expense ($250 to $750 or more per dog, or $188 per cat), or the annual veterinarian expenses ($200 to $400 per dog, $90 to $200 per cat), and boarding or pet sitters for your cat or dog when traveling ($300+ per year), the largest costs are in the time spent feeding, cleaning up after, playing with and taking for bathroom walks every day. It's recommended to walk your dog at minimum 30 minutes a day, most people break that up into multiple walks.

Let's just say between taking your dog(s) for walks, feeding them, and cleaning up after them you spend an average of 45 minutes per day; if your **money value of time** is $40, that means your true cost in **MVT** terms is $10,050 per year, on top of the cash outlays for food, vet and boarding (at minimum $750+ for dogs, $578 for cats). Cats are of course easier on both your cash outlays and your MVT because they don't require you to take them for walks outside. If you have children old enough and responsible enough to make sure to feed and take your dog(s) for walks every day, that can make a big difference in cost.

Subscription Services: As a rule of thumb, be wary of taking on subscription services; monthly fees can be quite insidious and slowly siphon off your financial freedom. $10 a month doesn't sound like all that much because most people don't consider what it adds up to over time. $10 a month in 10 years is $1,200…and when we view that recurring cash outlay in terms of opportunity cost, at 6% compounding interest your opportunity cost over that same 10 years comes out to $1,633. If after realizing your true cost is more like $1,633, you still think the subscription is worth the cost, great, you made the decision fully aware of the true cost. Filtering subscription services in this manner will have an amazing impact on your financial prosperity over the long run.

Cable/Dish TV Cutting: Chances are you've already done this, but in case you haven't, please stop paying for cable TV or dish TV. Just stop. In 2018, the average total monthly cable bill in the U.S. (base price + all kinds of miscellaneous fees + government fees and taxes) was $217 per month or $2,604 per year.[9] If you have multiple homes, multiply that by the number of homes you have. In 30 years, just for ONE cable TV subscription, that's $78,120 (not accounting for inflation), and if we assume a conservative 6% annual compound interest opportunity cost, we're talking $212,499 or a starter home.

There is no legitimate reason now that we're well into the

9 Jon Brodkin, "Cable companies use hidden fees to raise prices 24% a month" *Ars Technica* (10/3/2019), arstechnica.com/information-technology/2019/10/average-cable-bill-includes-50-in-hidden-fees-and-taxes/

21st century to be flushing currency down the toilet on monthly TV bills when all you need is an internet connection and you can stream almost any movie or show on Earth for a fraction of the cost. Today, there's nothing worth watching on TV that you can't get through the internet and stream to a smart TV/monitor via a Chromecast, Roku, or similar device, and SAVE A FORTUNE.

E-Retailer Selection: In today's day and age, the top e-commerce retailers give a reasonable time window to return your item for any reason, as opposed to those that only let you return an item if it's broken or defective. By going with vendors that basically have a no questions asked return policy, you'll save money over the long run returning items that either weren't what you expected them to be or that you came to realize were not worth the price, before having to resort to eBay which takes a fee and you have to list for below market value (otherwise most buyers will just buy straight from the vendor new).

Amazon Price Hack: As of this writing (2020), there's a price hack I've been using now for the past few years when I purchase goods on Amazon. Use the list function, and whatever items you're considering, add them to the list and check back in a week. More often than not on at least a handful of the items get price reductions by 15% or more.

Carwashes: These are a waste of money. As of 2020, the average car wash is around $15 for a regular cleaning. If you go once a month, you'll have $180 less each year to invest. If you live in a suburban or rural home with a hose line, you easily could have washed your car and be done long before the time it would take you to drive to the car wash, pay, and drive back. Likewise, if one lived in an urban complex, theoretically one could buy a four-way silcock water key, which would let them use the water lines in their complex's garage to hook up their own hose and wash their car, saving time driving to the wash AND currency.

Home & Auto Insurance Hack: There are several third-party companies that will compare home, auto, renters, landlord, and a variety of other insurance policies for you to find which configuration can save you the most money. If you can save even $500 or $1000 per year for spending 20 minutes of your time using one of these companies (free of charge), that's like earning between $1,500 to $3,000 an hour (in just the first year of savings). One site I use is gabi.com

Bottled Water: The average American spends over $100 per year per person on bottled water. With a family of 4 that's $400 per year that could have gone into savings. A cheaper AND HEALTHIER alternative is to get a Big Berkey water filter. This lowers the risk of synthetic compounds like Bisphenol A (BPA) seeping out of the plastic and causing long term health issues like high blood pressure, cancer, obesity and diabetes. If you forego bottled water for tap water without adequate filtration, be aware tap water is traveling through all sorts of old pipes which may also be giving off all kinds of dangerous synthetic compounds or heavy metals, regardless of whether it's city or well water. Why not avoid all this nonsense and use a Big Berkey? As of 2020, the whole Big Berkey system can be had for around $400 (with fluoride filters). The filters can last for years without needing replacement. This is a case of an initial investment that may seem expensive at first, but will pay off in spades over the long run financially and health-wise.

Gym Memberships: The cost for gym memberships can vary widely, anywhere from $9.95 to $100+ per month and possibly additional annual fees depending on the membership. What are some ways to pay less?

1. Pick a gym whose monthly fees are closer to the $9.95 per month end of the spectrum over the more expensive ones – yes these will have more people, but if you avoid peak times you won't notice it. Get to the gym when it opens in the morning shortly after the staff gets there.

2. Pay for the least expensive base monthly membership. These will usually only let you go to one gym location, but how many people actually need to use more than one gym location on a regular basis?

3. Be aware they will try to sell you on premium memberships by enticing you with additional "perks" or "benefits" which for the most part are nothing-burgers. Things like group fitness classes, online classes, nutrition plans, all information you can get FOR FREE on YouTube University that will likely rival or exceed their quality of instruction, instead of an additional $10, $20, or $30+ a month. Of course, something like a sauna if the base plan doesn't include it may be worth it.

You don't have to pay monthly fees to run and lift weights. You can get a good new pair of running shoes for $50 and buy a workout bench for around $70 on eBay and dumbbell set for around $100 to $200. Supposing you spent a total of $320 on all three, and the monthly membership fees you would have paid to your local gym are $20 per month, in 16 months (the **payback period**) the bench, shoes and weights will have paid for themselves, and every month after that you're saving $20. In 5 years, that's an extra $1,200, plus the time saved that otherwise would have been wasted driving to and from the gym. This is an ultra-savings power move.

Tanning Beds: These usually involve some sort of "startup fee" and cost around $15 to $30 per month. If you live somewhere warm like below the 37th parallel north latitude in the U.S., paying $180 per year for something that's free (sunlight) doesn't make a lot of sense. Likewise, letting this additional gym membership "perk" cause you to pay for a higher gym membership level is also silly (if you live in a warm climate).

Dollar Stores: Dollar stores can be great for things like dish soaps, cotton pads, greeting cards, gift wrap, and other paper goods. You'll find some of these items, like greeting cards for example, you can get these for 1/5 the price that you'd pay for comparable quality greeting cards at big box stores.

Streaming Video/Movie Services: While these are far cheaper than paying for cable or dish TV, you may have friends or family who are already paying for these services and they might be happy to let you use theirs for free.

Streaming Music Services: These are free with short commercials, or you can pay monthly and not have advertisements. Until you're living off of passive income, perhaps a 30 second commercial in between every few songs aren't such a big deal when you consider the $50-$100+ per year you save in fees for the advertising free service.

Smartphone Repair: If you take care of your phone, there's no reason it shouldn't last 5 years or longer. When it gets slow and the system maintenance/device cleaning no longer works, you can take it to an independent cell phone repair store and you'll be surprised what they can do to keep that thing going.

One of my previous girlfriends had her smartphone stop working; it wouldn't turn on at all. We went to the brand smartphone store in the mall, and they pulled out their diagnostic tablet, hooked it up and said something along the lines of "yup, these codes here show it's the chipset, you're going to need to buy a new phone" i.e., drop $500-$1000. I said "we'll think about it" and took her to a third-party cell phone repair store right around the corner.

The independent techie there took her phone apart in front of us and said "look here, there's a water stain, she must have gotten water on it" wiped it off with a cloth, said to put it next to a dehumidifier or in a bag of rice when we get home, and wait 5 hours or so. He didn't even charge us. We went home, put it next to the room dehumidifier, and what do you know, it worked again. If I hadn't gone with her, she probably would have believed the big tech corporate phone store and wasted $500-$1000 on a new phone.

Moral of the story: you're not bound to your smartphone's company store. Find a reputable third-party cell phone repair shop and save your dollars.

How Long Should I Keep My Smartphone? UNTIL IT DIES AND IS BEYOND REPAIR! People waste so much money buying new phones it's ridiculous. These people invariably have one thing in common: they're poor. *"But I need the newer version!"* Do you really? Phones are best for phone calls, text messages, emails on the go and being able to video/take pictures. Even older refurbished versions can do all of these things exceptionally well now. Is having the newest version smartphone really worth being poor?

Buy No-Contract Unlocked Refurbished Smartphones: You probably already have a working smartphone. The day will come when it's beyond repair and you need to buy a new one. If you need a new smartphone, consider buying an older version of that smartphone that's refurbished and unlocked so you can use any carrier. On Swappa.com I found my same smartphone model that cost $800 brand new only two years ago, for $125. By buying a version that's only a few years old, in this instance, you'd save $675. That's $675 more you have to invest.

Ways to Lower Your Cell Phone Bill: Some sources suggest the average person spends around $80 per month on their cell phone usage bill.[10] Over 40 years that's roughly $38,400 (without accounting for inflation). Therefore, lowering your cell phone bill is a worthy quest indeed. Consider doing the following:

- Do not use a payment plan to purchase your cell phone;

- Limit background data usage;

- Always connect to Wi-Fi when you can to avoid unnecessary data usage;

- Shop carriers for the lowest monthly price (which an unlocked phone enables you to do);

- Plan ahead with your cell phone service before traveling outside your home country so you don't get wacked with international fees;

- Avoid smartphone insurance, it's a total waste of money,

10 Jade Scipioni, "This is how much your smartphone really costs over a lifetime" *Fox Business* (Nov 2, 2018), foxbusiness.com/features/this-is-how-much-your-smartphone-really-costs-over-a-lifetime

that extra $10 or $15 a month you're guaranteed to lose to insurance, whereas you could just add that extra $10 or $15 to your savings and draw from that for a new phone in the unlikely event yours is broken or lost. Moreover, like most insurance contracts, they're usually not written in your favor, they're filled to the brim with **exclusions** which can often prevent you from actually using the insurance when you need it anyway;

- Downgrade your existing plan – removing features you don't really use or that don't justify the higher monthly fee, whether that's things like 411, enhanced voicemail, unlimited data, more minutes than you use, emergency roadside assistance, etc.;

- See if your employer has an employee discount for your cell phone service;

- Sign up for paperless billing and automated billing, this may save a small amount of money with some cell phone providers.

The Garfield Experiment: The biggest hit to your personal finances from your smartphone is all the time wasted on activities like:

- Scrolling "social media," which ironically is one of the most anti-social constructs ever devised;

- Texting for hours on end, when you can just call and hear the other person's voice, a far more effective mode of communication that takes 1/10th the time to say the same thing tapping away on itty bitty cell phone keys; and

- Searching for random information not pertinent to anything that will advance the time waster's career or personal life. Some sources indicate millennials spend an average of 5.7 hours per day on their smartphones.[11] Gen Z appears to be as bad or worse.

Let's perform a creative experiment and pretend we have a Gen Zer named Garfield and a time machine that lets us travel 20 years into the future to discover what Garfield's average money value of time will be over 20 years. Based on tax receipts, it averages out to $50 an hour (well assume no inflation for demonstration purposes). Let's also assume Garfield kept his bad habit of wasting 5.7 hours per day on his smartphone.

That means from a money value of time perspective, over that 20 years, Garfield's opportunity cost to scroll his smartphone, just in terms of lost potential income (not even taking into consideration if that income was invested), would be $2,080,500...

"But... I'm using my phone to build my personal life, strengthen friendships and relationships!" BS. You strengthen your social bonds with people by hearing their voice and seeing them in REAL LIFE, having interesting conversations, sharing meals, going to do fun physical activities like hiking, camping, hunting, or whatever other activities you have a common affinity for. You can text someone for years on "social media," meet in real life and completely not vibe.

Try to Repair before Replacing: While there are certain things that wouldn't be safe to try and repair or would be a waste of time, generally speaking, it's always a good idea to see if you can repair

---

11 Jovan Milenkovic, "How Much Time Does the Average Person Spend on Their Phone?" *Kommando Tech* (Feb 11, 2020), kommandotech.com/statistics/how-much-time-does-the-average-person-spend-on-their-phone/

something before replacing it (as long as repairing is cheaper).

Laptop died? Before dropping $500 to $1,000 on a new one, take it to your local computer repair shop, perhaps it just needs a replacement part that's only $100 and $45 for the labor. $145 is a lot better than $500 or $1,000.

Sofa showing obvious wear and tear? Instead of buying a whole new sofa for $500+, what about getting creative and using a nicely designed sofa slipcover that adds some zest to your room? You can get these for less than 1/25th the cost of a new sofa. If your partner says *"a sofa slipcover! You're just being cheap!"* You say: "Every time you call me cheap, I get a little turned on." Then show her the new slipcover.

Money-Back Guarantees: Many products and services have money-back guarantees (usually 30-90 days) as part of their value proposition to entice you to buy. The vast majority of people are too meek to actually exercise them, even when they're genuinely not satisfied with the product or service. From now on, set an alert on your calendar or phone alarm for a week before the money-back guarantee deadline; it's your right to exercise these if you're not satisfied.

DON'T BE A WIMP - NEGOTIATE! Every year I call up my internet, phone, and any other service providers taking cash from me and tell them I'm thinking of switching to another provider because their service is too expensive. Then go silent and see if they say something along the lines of "we have a special retention price" which are usually for one year, after which they raise the prices up again, hence why every year you need to keep calling.

If they don't offer to lower the price and start going through the process of cancelling – you can say "let me call you back." Then shop other services and carriers to see if you can save money by switching. Often times you can, because the industry model seems to be to attract new customers by offering the lowest rates the first year or two of service and then raise them. The smart consumers call every year and are willing to switch every year so as to always benefit from this industry hack and have the lowest monthly fees.

Negotiating is one of the highest paying activities you can do. As an example, my friend called up his internet/phone provider just the other day and used this very hack on his primary residence and got the provider to give him a special retention price that lowered his monthly phone and internet bill by $30. That's an extra $360 per year that can now go into his savings.

Some folks might say to themselves "I'm not going to haggle every year just to maybe save $30 a month." Those people would be dead wrong. The call my friend made took him 20 minutes. He was basically getting paid $18 a minute or **$1,080 per hour to negotiate**. Are you beneath working for $1,080 per hour? Even if you only save $10 a month, a 20-minute call to save $120 a year is like working for $360 per hour.

Negotiate whenever you can. Obviously, you're not going to go into a big box retailer and negotiate with the cashier. But anything else where there's opportunity to get the service provider or vendor to lower their prices for fear of losing your business to a competitor, negotiate! Stop being a sheep and start being a wolf!

Make Friends with your Freezer: Studies suggest that U.S. households waste around 1/3rd of the food they purchase every year, with the total annual cost estimated at $1,866 per household (in 2020 dollars).[12] Researchers noted that higher-income

12 Lana Bandoim, "The Shocking Amount Of Food U.S. Households Waste Every Year" *Forbes* (Jan 26, 2020), forbes.com/sites/lanabandoim/2020/01/26/the-shocking-amount-of-food-us-households-waste-every-year/

households are more likely to have healthier diets with more perishables like fruits and vegetables, and thus may waste more food than lower-income households. A bag of potato chips or a box of Mac n Cheese doesn't expire for years, but fresh fruit and vegetables can go bad in days or a few weeks.

Because you're reading a book on how to increase your savings, odds are you're also the kind of person that believes in healthy eating, so you likely buy more fruits and vegetables at the grocery store. What are some ways to combat this?

1. Buy more frozen vegetables. Things like broccoli, asparagus, peas, carrots, brussels sprouts, butternut squash, cauliflower, spinach, green beans, kale, edamame, are all great things to get frozen and they retain their nutrients.

2. Buy more frozen fruit. Things like blueberries, blackberries, acai berries, strawberries, raspberries, pomegranates, peaches, cherries, pineapple, are all perfect for this. You can also freeze grapes and eat them almost like popsicles, they're delicious.

3. If you use bananas or apples in your smoothie, you can buy those fresh, remove the peel or skin and put them in plastic Ziploc bags or containers and leave them in your freezer for when you want to make a smoothie.

You'll still want to eat your frozen fruit and vegetables within 6 months or so, as after a year they can lose their nutrients. Even if you save an extra $900 a year (half the national average), that's $900 more you can put into your savings and invest. **Less waste = more savings**.

Un-necessary Home Upgrades & Replacements: There's a prov-erb from southern culture in the U.S. that goes something like "*if it ain't broke, don't fix it.*" Too many people are way too quick to replace things that are just fine. Don't be so quick to buy a new toaster, or trash can, or carpet, if the ones you have work just fine and appear normal. Oh, there's a tiny stain in the corner car-pet. Big deal. Is that worth $1,600 to put in a whole new carpet or vinyl flooring? You could easily steam clean it for a fraction of the cost.

In 2015 my HVAC system died, and the HVAC repairman said my unit was from the early 2000s and was on its last legs, it was ready for replacement. That would have cost about $4,500 or so between the unit and labor given they would have needed a crane to get it off the roof and install the new one.

I said what are my other options. He said "well, we could use Leakstop in the lines, that might buy you more time. It's about $800 between parts and labor." I said do it. Five years later, my HVAC is STILL running strong. What the heck do I care if it's an old unit, it works and instead of spending $4,500 it was only $800, a savings of $3,700. That's an extra $3,700 to invest. At 6% com-pound interest over 5 years that $3,700 becomes $4,951.

Don't be so quick to make un-necessary home upgrades and replacements; metaphorically speaking you're just wrapping more chains around your arms and ankles.

AN OUNCE OF PREVENTION IS WORTH A POUND OF CURE

Health Maintenance: Medical bills can be extremely expensive. Prevention is far cheaper than treatment. We all have heard before about so and so who worked out every day, ate extremely healthy, did everything right and died a young death. And then another person who smoked cigarettes, drank like it was going out of style, ate fast food, and lived to old age. There are always anomalies, but smart people know that there are always outliers in any statistical data set. I like to play the odds, and the odds are not in my favor unless I make a concerted daily effort to maintain my health.

For me, this involves things like adequate hydration (filtered water that has had harmful chemicals and metals removed), eating enough fruits and vegetables, avoiding too much sugar, alcohol, and high fructose corn syrup when possible, limiting sweets, daily exercise, consistent and adequate sleep, enough sunlight, adequate vitamin intake, meditation, and so forth.

I'm extremely cautious when it comes to big pharma and the influence they've had on medical practitioners; it's concerning how quick doctors are to prescribe all sorts of medications that treat the symptoms and not the underlying problems. A great information resource I use is Dr. Mercola (mercola.com). "Mainstream" media hates him because he isn't going along with the big pharma program. I've lost relatives who went along with that program and didn't seek out alternative information; in contrast, my grandma had cancer and was told she had less than a year to live and she needed to undergo intense treatment right away, treatment that she'd have little chance of surviving, and she said, "no thanks," sought out alternatives, and lived over 15 years longer than the "experts" said she would.

Dentistry: I make it a point to brush my teeth after every meal, and definitely after having coffee or anything sugary, which consequently causes me to think twice before having sweets. This allows me to go to the dentist far less frequently than most people, saving money and time, and when I do go every few years the dentist is always blown away by my dental hygiene and says some variation of "wow, you really take care of your teeth. Guess we'll just be doing a cleaning" and a sad face because the bill is limited to cleaning work. The average cost per cavity dental filling is around $200 (in 2020). I haven't had a cavity in over 10 years.

Home Maintenance: With home ownership comes all sorts of added tasks to extend the life of your home and appliances that you would not have to do if you rented. Some quick examples are things like: draining sediment from your water heater once a year; keeping your roof clean or else water trapped by debris can cause your roof to deteriorate prematurely (and paying for a new roof is expensive); test your sump pump regularly if you have a basement; check for high water pressure regularly; lubricate garage door springs, and so forth. There are some great resources online, like thefamilyhandy-man.com that go into more detail on all the different home main-tenance tasks one should regularly perform (or have performed) in order to save serious money on expensive damage and repairs

Auto Maintenance: A lot of the costly auto problems people experience can be avoided by proper preventative maintenance: changing the oil at the recommended mileage intervals; having the tires rotated; having transmission fluid replaced. These things are easier to do if you go to an auto shop that keeps track of when the last time you had these things done in their computer systems. Keep records for yourself as well to be sure they're not "over-servicing you" to your financial detriment...

Also, check the tire pressure every few weeks (they make quality tire air gauges for $20). One of the most common mis-takes, particularly by younger auto owners, is not checking the oil levels enough. Many people don't realize how fast their vehicle burns oil (especially in warmer climates) and end up damaging their engine by driving on low oil.

I've met people who believe they only need to get their oil changed, and have never actually opened up the hood of their vehicle and used the oil dipstick to check their oil levels. Then they wonder why their car breaks down. I check my oil levels every few weeks.

IT'S THE LITTLE THINGS THAT COUNT

As you can see from many of the living expense hacks, often times we're looking at the little things, small savings here and there that on their own and from a short time horizon seem insignificant, but in aggregate and over a long-time horizon, will make a HUGE difference to your financial success and freedom.

"NO PERSON HAS THE POWER TO HAVE EVERY-THING THEY WANT, BUT IT IS IN THEIR POWER NOT TO WANT WHAT THEY DON'T HAVE, AND TO CHEERFULLY PUT TO GOOD USE WHAT THEY DO HAVE."

—SENECA

CHAPTER 6

THE 50% RULE OF SAVINGS
& WHY THE RICH BARBER IS DEAD

If there's one thing you get from this entire book, let it be the **50% Rule of Savings** (the **50% Rule**). This rule is an absolute game changer and will turbo-charge your long-term savings and wealth.

Using the 50% Rule could allow you to retire 10 or 20 years earlier and pursue your unfulfilled dreams and ambitions. It could mean the difference between having enough savings to take advantage of opportunities like market crashes or housing downturns and you being crushed by those crashes and downturns. It could be the difference between your marriage working out or ending in messy divorce (some surveys indicate 21% of divorcees cite money as the primary cause of their divorce).[13] It could mean you have enough saved up to help a loved one with an unexpected expensive medical issue.

By the end of this chapter, you will understand this rule, its power, and why you NEED to employ it in the 21st century. Fortunately, your life will forever be changed for the better because of it. I only hope that after you let it change your life, you pay it forward. Spreading positive, empowering knowledge benefits the giver as much as it does the receiver. But first, this barber guy...

13 Deb Hipp, "6 Money Conflicts That can Lead to Divorce" *Debt.com* (Dec 11, 2019), debt.com/news/divorce-over-money/

THE WEALTHY BARBER'S 10% RULE

When I was 14 or so, I was perusing the personal finance section of the local Barnes and Noble when I came across a book titled *The Wealthy Barber* by David Chilton. It was in this book that I first encountered the 10% rule. The wisdom giver character in the book, a local barber, obtained his wealth by being disciplined with his spending, saving and investing, and reveals how he did it on a barber's income. The main financial takeaway from the book is to save and invest 10% of your gross income, and with the power of compound interest, it's supposed to grow into sizeable savings.

I heard this advice in subsequent civics classes in high school that briefly discussed personal finance. Astonishingly, high schools and colleges today that even touch personal finance are still teaching this outdated 10% rule of savings.

Why the 10% Rule Forced the Barber to Retire in a Trailer Park

Before I show the fatal flaw with the 10% rule in modern times, I still want to thank David Chilton for coming out with that book, as it got me thinking about saving at a young age. I'm convinced that the adoption of the saver mindset from an early age helped motivate me to save and invest in adulthood.

The book *The Wealthy Barber* was published in the year 1989. That same year you could walk into your local bank branch and purchase a 1-year U.S. Treasury bill that yielded 8.54% interest, in an economy with 4.82% inflation (reportedly). Assuming that inflation rate was true, your real interest rate (how much your savings grew in terms of purchasing power), which equals your nominal interest rate (8.54% for the 1 year T-bill) − inflation (4.82%), would be 3.72%, meaning those who bought and held the 1 year U.S. T-bill that year grew their real purchasing power by 3.72% (before tax). Certificates of Deposit (CD's) were even higher at that time, yielding around 10% in nominal terms and 5.18% in real terms. Those returns required the investor to take virtually no risk.

If our barber in 1989 made $70,000 per year and began investing at a rate of 10% of his income per year in 1-year U.S. T-bills and re-invested each year for 20 years, and we assume his income remained flat at $70,000, using the real historical interest rates (average closing rate) on the 1-year T-bill for the years 1989 to 2009, in 20 years our barber will have grown the $140,000 of savings he invested over that time frame into $224,875 (pre-tax) by the end of 2009. Even in 2009, retiring for the rest of your life on $224,875 would be pretty tight, like living in a trailer park tight.

The DeLorean Time Machine

If we call up our old friend Doc Brown and hop in his DeLorean time machine to travel back to the year 1989, we'd tell our barber friend about what us *Rational Savers* in the future use, which is the 50% Rule of Savings. According to this rule, the target goal for our savings rate is 50% of our gross income.

Of course, most people are not able to presently save that much of their gross income, but that is the destination. In the meantime, the goal is to hit savings milestones, so if our present financial situation only allows us to save 10% of our gross income, we work towards extinguishing our debts (see Chapter 8), lowering our living expenses (see Chapter 5), and increasing our income, with the goal of getting to 20%, then 30%, then 40%, and ultimately the holy grail of gross income savings, the 50% savings rate constant.

Now that we've traveled back in time to inform the barber, he decides instead of 10%, to save and invest 50% of his $70,000 per year income in the same 1-year U.S. T-bills, starting in 1989 which was at 8.54% interest, re-investing each year for the next 20 years.

Using the real historical interest rates for those T-bills for the years 1989 to 2009, our barber will have saved and invested a total of $700,000 from his income over time, and grown that into close to $1.1 million (pre-tax) by the end of 2009. Such is the power of compound interest when combined with the 50% Rule.

Note: while the average annual inflation rate between 1989 and 2009 was reportedly around 2.78%, even with inflation, our barber has significantly increased his purchasing power due to the positive spread (meaning higher rate in the T-bill holder's favor) between the varying annual rates of inflation and the varying annual yields on the 1-year Treasury Bills.

Why the 21st Century Prohibits the Barber from Retiring on a 10% Savings Plan

In May of 2020, the 10-year U.S. Treasury note was 0.661%, or down 92% in nominal terms from where it was in 1989, and the 1-year U.S. Treasury Bill was 0.17%, or down 98% in nominal terms from where it was in 1989. The average CPI (inflation rate) the government has reported in recent years is around 2%. If this is true (many independent economists believe it's much higher, see Chapter 15), the real interest rate of a 10-year U.S. Treasury today (in 2020) is -1.34%.

A buyer of this instrument would be tying up their money for 10 years on the promise of losing their original real purchasing power at a rate of -1.34% per year. Investing in anything with guaranteed losses in real purchasing power is generally a bad idea and would completely prevent our barber from retiring at all.

The only buyers for these guaranteed to lose bonds are the Fed in their regular course of market manipulations, and speculators hoping that nominal interest rates go lower so they can sell their higher nominal interest rate bonds at a profit to the next speculator looking to repeat the same trade, because as (or if) interest rates on new bonds go down, the market value of older bonds with the higher interest rate goes up.

That is a classic **Ponzi scheme** structure, and usually Ponzi schemes eventually unravel when the flow of new investors dries up and there isn't enough capital to make the last wave of suckers who bought into the scheme whole again.

If U.S. interest rates continue their descent into negative territory, the end result could be a bursting of the hyper-inflated bond bubble, or the Federal Reserve coming in and engaging in plunge protection practices (interfering with the free market) at unprecedented levels that could have a laundry list of unintended consequences worse than the bubble bursting. Either way, that scenario could be very bullish for gold and silver, as sovereign bonds have been a major competitor for capital against precious metals for hundreds of years.

Note the U.S. Federal Reserve System (the "Fed") will come up throughout this book because it directly affects us as *Rational Saver's* working to build wealth and get ahead in life. The Fed is a cartel of private banks that lobbied congress through Woodrow Wilson (and other agents of theirs) to pass the Federal Reserve Act of 1913. They succeeded, giving themselves the power to lend money into existence to the government and charge interest on that money, to be paid by the American citizens. This just so happens to be the year the Revenue Act of 1913 was passed which put in place the federal income tax.

The U.S. Treasury prints or types interest-bearing U.S. Treasury bonds, swaps them with the Fed and the Fed deposits federal reserve notes (IOUs) into the Treasury General Account (TGA), and presto! The government can pay its workers and that currency is re-deposited into the banking system, which then lends it out 9 to 1 (or more today), further increasing the monetary supply. This is a very oversimplified summary of an intentionally convoluted and complex system.

It's quite telling that the monied elite who pushed this scheme settled on calling the legislation and the central bank the "Federal Reserve" considering they were not and are not a part of the government; they're a privately held corporation, and they never had any reserves from which they draw on in order to loan the funny money into existence.

Being Told to Lose

Teenagers and young adults today who are lucky enough to have a class in their high school or college about personal finance are still being told to save 10%. Basically, they're being told to lose. You can't get wealthy saving only 10% of your income today with interest rates down 98% from where they were in 1989 (because interest rates affect rates of return in almost all other asset classes).

Low Interest Rates = Low Yields in General

The problem with the 10% rule in the 2020s is this long-term downward trend towards low yields, which started in the U.S. around 1982, and dropped to levels unheard of after the Global Financial Crisis of 2008-2009. It has put significant upward pressure on prices and downward pressure on yields in all investment classes you'd consider putting your savings into in place of sovereign bonds, such as corporate and municipal bonds, real estate, and the stock market.

This is due to supply and demand; when bond yields are low, there is a larger supply of capital seeking out investments that provide a higher rate of return than bonds can offer, high enough to protect against inflation and achieve positive long term growth. That capital competes to acquire those higher-yielding investments, thereby bidding up prices and lowering investor rates of return (also known as **cap rate compression** in the commercial real estate world).

Now everyone and their grand mum are looking for good returns. This makes sense when one considers the size of the U.S. bond market, which as of 1st quarter of 2017 was approximately $39,688,600,000,000, with U.S. Treasury debt accounting for 35% of the market. This is larger than the entire market capitalization of U.S. stocks.[14]

Thus, *Rational Savers* today (and until real interest rates normalize) will have no choice but to invest in things other than treasuries for their portfolio growth. This is a huge deviation from the very common 60/40 investment strategy of 60% stocks, 40% bonds, that's been the bread and butter of financial advisors and mainstream money magazine writers for the past 40+ years.

"But I can't Afford to Save 50% of my Gross Income!"

Most readers are likely not in a financial position to save 50% of their gross income at this point in time given their monthly financial obligations. That's why you have this book in your hand.

The objective is to hit **savings milestones**. Perhaps you may only be able to start at 10%. But as you further lower your living expenses, and as your savings and investments grow, you can soon get to the 20% milestone, then 30%, and if you simultaneously are able to increase your income, soon it can grow even more. Wealth has a snowball effect, particularly when you're investing your savings and it's working for you.

---

14 Kurt Shrout, "The U.S. Bond Market May Be Much Different Than You Think It Is" *Learn-Bonds.com* (Apr 17, 2020), learnbonds.com/news/how-big-is-the-bond-market/

Most Americans Use the Barber's Savings Rate, and They're Broke
According to data from the U.S. Bureau of Economic Analysis, the Household Savings Rate in the U.S. hovered between 5.8% and 8.5% from the years 2013 to February of 2020. When the **pandemic of 2020** hit and stock markets fell, the savings rate spiked up to 13.10% in March 2020, with 30 million Americans filing initial unemployment claims in March, and by end of May, that number hitting 40 million. The data shows a similar spike in the household savings rate during the aftermath of the global financial crisis of 2008-2009, where the rate had also spiked up to 12%.

THE BROKEN EDUCATIONAL SYSTEM

This shows how broken our educational system is, that most Americans only save 5.8% to 8.5% of their annual income during the "good times" and a meager 12-13% after a global financial crash and an economically crippling government forced shutdown.

Some PRE-PANDEMIC stats that prove most American's are broke:

- A 2017 study released by the United Way's ALICE Project found that 43% of U.S. households don't earn enough to afford a monthly budget that includes housing, food, child care, health care, transportation, and a cell phone.[15]

- In the fourth quarter of 2018, the average American household debt was $13.54 trillion, a new all-time record, and the 18th consecutive quarter with an increase, $869 billion higher than the previous peak from the third quarter of 2008. If you divide $13.54 trillion by the number

15 United Way's ALICE Project, Research Center, 2017 report, unitedforalice.org/all-reports

of American households in 2018 per the U.S. Census Bureau (127.59 million), that puts the average American household $106,121 in debt.[16]

- In 2019, America's collective student loan debt was over $1.5 trillion, a staggering figure, with over two million Americans owing over $100,000 in student debt.[17]

As of June of 2020, one-third of homeowners had less than $500 in savings, leaving them woefully unprepared to even handle the cost of a home repair, such as fixing or replacing an HVAC system which can easily cost up to $5,000. Moreover, approximately 25% of all Americans had NO emergency savings at all.[18]

DO NOT TRUST your children's high school or college to successfully teach them the personal finance knowledge they need as adults. The data and evidence are clear: those institutions have failed multiple generations of Americans, and there's no indication they're not going to continue that failing trend. No, academia has more pressing things to cover, like why there are 53 gender pronouns.

This is true regardless of what university your child gets into. I attended Yale University as an undergraduate and obtained a B.A. in history. Like most liberal arts universities, you don't just take courses pertaining to your major; you take all sorts of core requirements, which should be a good thing.

---

16 Federal Reserve Bank of New York's Center for Microeconomic Data Quarterly Report on Household Debt and Credit, newyorkfed.org/medialibrary/interactives/householdcredit/data/pdf/HHDC_2018Q4.pdf

17 Tucker Carlson, "Tucker Carlson: Congress must address the student loan debt problem and stop colleges from scamming our kids," *Fox News* (March 19, 2019), foxnews.com/us/tucker-carlson-congress-must-address-the-student-loan-debt-problem-and-stop-colleges-from-scamming-our-kids

18 Quentin Fottrell, "Nearly 25% of Americans have no emergency savings," *Market Watch* (June 9, 2020), marketwatch.com/story/nearly-25-of-americans-have-no-emergency-savings-and-lost-income-due-to-coronavirus-is-piling-on-even-more-debt-2020-06-03?mod=home-page

At Yale, some that I can recall were under umbrella fields like quantitative reasoning, science, English, and foreign language. Interestingly, I never noticed a single course available that had to do with personal finance (or capitalism). I learned about planets and stars, gender studies (a total nothing-burger course), Mesopotamian literature, and a hodgepodge of other practically useless subjects when it comes to preparing for the real world, or even just becoming an informed voter.

If I could go back to my younger self, I would not have sat through so many classes covering completely useless information. Mesopotamian literature and the *Epic of Gilgamesh*? No thanks. At that age, you think you've all the time in the world. You don't value your time as much as a rational saver values his or her time. You don't realize what an extra 4 years of learning personal finance, working on your career, saving, and investing can do for your net worth.

Personal Finance Works Best When You Start Early

Because of our completely broken educational system, friends, and family you care about, if left to the guidance of the system, will not get the empowering personal finance knowledge they need to succeed. If you have children, grandchildren, nieces, nephews, cousins, or friends who are young adults that you care about, getting them a copy of this book could be the best gift they've ever received. The principles in this book could save them tens of thousands or even millions of dollars over their lifetime. It is also the best roadmap you could buy them to ensure they have the ability to make it through hard times and economic downturns.

Even if your younger relative or friend doesn't read it right away, perhaps in a few years when there's something they want and realize they'll need to start saving, they'll pick up this book for a few pointers and read it then.

The return on their time reading this book will easily be thousands of times greater than any other educational course they'll end up taking, because it's actually relevant to what they'll spend a majority of their adult life doing, trading their time and labor (economic energy) for units of currency in order to acquire goods and services needed to live and have a family.

CHAPTER 7

DEBT IS MODERN DAY SLAVERY

"THE RICH RULETH OVER THE POOR, AND THE BORROWER IS SERVANT TO THE LENDER."

PROVERBS 22, VERSE 7, KING JAMES BIBLE.

There is much wisdom in this verse. Ask yourself: do you want to be someone's servant? Or your children to be servants? Some synonyms for servitude are "enslavement" and "serfdom." If you want that, keep swiping the credit card and financing everything.

HOW TO OVERPAY FOR BIG TICKET ITEMS

If you want to overpay for a house or a vehicle, just use debt, usually called "credit" or "financing" by the real estate agent or car salesman to sound more palatable. Take the purchase of a house, which we consider a consumer good (see Chapter 12) if it's to be your primary or secondary residence as opposed to a rental property.

Most people realize they're making interest payments over the term of the loan on top of paying back the initial principal. However, you'd be surprised how few people actually amortize it out and see by how much they're overpaying when the total interest paid over the term of the loan is taken into consideration.

For example, suppose hypothetical Bob buys a house at a purchase price of $226,800 (2019 median U.S. home price), and at this point in time the interest rate for a 30-year self-amortizing fixed mortgage is 3.5% (not including broker fees, discount points, and closing costs). Bob puts down $45,360, or 20% of the purchase price which is an 80% Loan-to-Value (LTV) ratio in order to avoid having to also pay private mortgage insurance, which is just insurance for the lender and an added expense for Bob. This leaves the loan amount (the **principal**) at $181,440. Below is Bob's loan amortized for all 30 years of the loan.

Year	Beginning Balance	Interest	Principal	Ending Balance
1	$181,440	$6,295	$3,482	$177,958
2	$177,958	$6,171	$3,606	$174,352
3	$174,352	$6,043	$3,734	$170,618
4	$170,618	$5,910	$3,867	$166,751
5	$166,751	$5,772	$4,005	$162,746
6	$162,746	$5,630	$4,147	$158,599
7	$158,599	$5,483	$4,295	$154,305
8	$154,305	$5,330	$4,447	$149,857
9	$149,857	$5,172	$4,605	$145,252
10	$145,252	$5,008	$4,769	$140,483
11	$140,483	$4,838	$4,939	$135,544
12	$135,544	$4,663	$5,114	$130,429

13	$130,429	$4,481	$5,296	$125,133
14	$125,133	$4,292	$5,485	$119,648
15	$119,648	$4,097	$5,680	$113,968
16	$113,968	$3,895	$5,882	$108,087
17	$108,087	$3,686	$6,091	$101,996
18	$101,996	$3,469	$6,308	$95,688
19	$95,688	$3,245	$6,532	$89,156
20	$89,156	$3,013	$6,764	$82,391
21	$82,391	$2,772	$7,005	$75,386
22	$75,386	$2,523	$7,254	$68,132
23	$68,132	$2,265	$7,512	$60,620
24	$60,620	$1,998	$7,779	$52,841
25	$52,841	$1,721	$8,056	$44,785
26	$44,785	$1,435	$8,343	$36,442
27	$36,442	$1,138	$8,639	$27,803
28	$27,803	$831	$8,947	$18,857
29	$18,857	$512	$9,265	$9,592
30	$9,592	$182	$9,595	$0

Total Interest Paid: $111,867

Notice the total interest paid is $111,867.

Assuming the purchase price Bob settled at was close to the market price, Bob has essentially paid $111,867 above the market price for the home by using a mortgage to finance the purchase. Bob ends up overpaying by almost **49%!** This means if Bob had purchased the home outright, over the long run he'd save $111,867.

COMPOUND INTEREST AND OPPORTUNITY COST

That's an additional $111,867 over the 30-year term of the loan that could have been regularly invested and grown using the **law of compound interest**. Note our example is using a historically low interest rate of 3.5%. If you purchase a home with a mortgage in the future and interest rates have risen, expect the amount of interest you'll pay to be even greater.

Assuming the interest portion of Bob's monthly debt service payments (using the $111,867 interest figure) were instead allocated into an investment or set of investments collectively yielding 6% annually and allowing for reinvestment at that rate, over that same 30 years, Bob could have grown those 360 interest payments he saved by buying his residence outright into **$373,502!**

Remember, the definition of opportunity cost is "the loss of potential gain from other alternatives when one alternative is chosen." So not only has Bob overpaid by 49% to purchase the house now, he's foregone the opportunity to grow that $111,867 in interest payments over the term of the loan into $373,502 (assuming an investment rate of 6% compound interest).

The opportunity cost filter is a powerful way to view purchasing decisions. This is how the rich make purchase and investment decisions. Granted, they're looking at much bigger numbers, but the concepts still apply and can be just as empowering for everyday people as it is for the wealthy.

Over the long term, would it have made more sense for Bob to rent or live with family or friends for a few extra years and work harder in order to save up to buy his residence outright?

PAYING A PREMIUM
TO OBTAIN CONSUMER GOODS NOW

But hypothetical Bob wanted the home now, as do most people. Most people want to have the latest fashion, the big house, the fancy car right now, not when they have actually saved up enough to afford it. This is why credit card companies exist. They feed off people's difficulty in delaying gratitude and their need for approval from their peers.

By using financing or "credit" to purchase big ticket items like homes, boats, RV's, cars, jewelry, furniture, household appliances, cruises, wedding dresses, mattresses, and so forth, you're essentially borrowing money from your future to spend today; you're paying a premium to obtain that good now as opposed to waiting to save enough money to buy it in the future.

Not only is this a terrible strategy from a financial standpoint, it also takes an emotional toll on people that could shave years off of your life. It's been proven that stress and anxiety can shorten your lifespan and lead to all sorts of medical ailments. By having a mortgage or car payment, you're now working for your lender, and if you default on your loan, all your past time and labor you traded for currency which you put into that house or car would vanish. The lender is now your master. That has a psychological cost, knowing you HAVE to work and make payments in order not to lose your home or your mode of transportation. Compare that to the peace of mind one feels when they have zero debt and own their house and their car outright.

THE RENT COUNTER-ARGUMENT

There is a reasonable counter-argument regarding the lost money to mortgage interest: If Bob rents, that rent money is lost while Bob is saving up to buy the home outright; he's better off just getting a mortgage to purchase his home and building up equity from the principal portion of his debt service payments.

First, Bob could get creative and live with family or relatives while he saves up to purchase a home, saving substantially. Or, he could link up with friends and they could collectively buy a house to live in, or rent together, which can be a very cheap option.

Second, if Bob does not have friends or family he can live with, then yes, if he rents, those rent payments are gone forever, but if he buys with a mortgage, he will also lose money forever. The money will go toward:

- **monthly interest payments** on the mortgage and can be as much as half or more of what Bob would spend per year simply renting (depending on his location);

- **property taxes**;

- **homeowner's insurance** policy payments;

- **private mortgage insurance** policy if the down payment is under 20%;

- **costs for repairs and maintenance** of things like the roof, HVAC, plumbing, water heater, washer, dryer, dishwasher, electrical, and normal wear and tear of cabinets, floors and other parts of the home, and structural and foundational repairs if Mr. Murphy is really pissed;

- **costs for landscaping**, tree trimming, and lawn maintenance if he's in a suburban or rural area.

Finally, there is the potential for a **LOSS of the equity** Bob thinks he's building from his principal payments if the market value of his home drops subsequent to purchasing (yes, real estate absolutely can go down and stay down for long periods of time, erasing the supposed equity you were building from your principal payments ...see Chapter 12).

So, there are a few factors to consider when deciding on whether to rent or purchase your home, and these are discussed in further detail in Chapter 13.

THE CONVENIENT LITTLE PLASTIC MONSTER

Credit cards are convenient. Swipe, insert, or type, and presto! The item you had your eye on appears. The problem for us *Rational Savers* is, the onerous interest rates that credit cards charge will SERIOUSLY hurt your savings. What's worse, most credit cards these days compound your interest daily!

What does that mean? It means that hypothetical Jane who has a $10,000 credit card balance, on a credit card with an advertised APR of 18%, doesn't just pay $1,800 per year in interest (which would be her interest payment if it was simply compounded annually). Rather, the interest on Jane's unpaid credit card balance is calculated every day, which is the credit card's annual percentage rate (APR) divided by either 360 or 365 depending on the issuer, and the interest is compounding, meaning Jane's paying interest on interest.

Thus, if Jane maintained that $10,000 unpaid balance for one year, she would actually end up paying $1,972 in interest, which on an annual basis is actually an effective annual interest rate of 19.71%. Most millionaires would laugh at the thought of paying 19.71% interest to purchase consumer goods you can buy with cash or a debit card for 0% interest. Millionaires earn interest, they don't pay it...

If we then pull out our opportunity cost lens from our *Rational Saver* toolbox and assume Jane loses $1,972 per year to credit card interest payments on a $10,000 balance (for demonstration purposes, many people end up building much higher balances if they don't escape the credit card habit), and we assume she does this for five years, and alternatively could have invested that $1,972 at a compounding annual rate of 6%, her total sacrifice is actually $11,474. If this goes on for 10 years, it's $26,829; if Jane is really self-abusing and maintains an average credit card balance of $10,000 for 20 years, her opportunity cost is $74,876!

If we increase the balance (there are people who on any given year have $20,000, $30,000 or more in credit debt...), or the length of time Jane holds the balance, or both, you can only imagine where it goes from there...you might as well be a cartoon villain pouring a can of gasoline on a pile of cash you stole from mob bosses, only you didn't steal that cash from mob bosses, you traded years of hard work and sweat for it.

Credit Card Use = Increased Spending By 100%

In 2001, researchers at the Massachusetts Institute of Technology (MIT) published results of their research on credit card spending and found that shoppers spend up to 100% more when using their credit cards to buy things instead of cash.[19]

This is because of the psychological impact of tangible currency like cash, when you spend it, you actually witness it disappear. With credit cards, you only have to face the reality of your

---

19 Drazen Prelec and Duncan Simester, "Always Leave Home Without It: A Further Investigation of the Credit-Card Effect on Willingness to Pay" *Sloan School of Management, MIT* (Apr 25, 2000), web.mit.edu/simester/Public/Papers/Alwaysleavehome.pdf

loss of currency when you look at your credit statement, long after you've pulled the trigger on the purchase.

In other words, credit cards separate the dopamine hits we get from purchasing things from the pain of having to pay for them, a pain we'd otherwise feel using cash. This is also why credit cards are very dangerous when it comes to enabling impulse shopping to alleviate unhappiness or anxiety.

"But I pay it off right away, really..." Do you always? Well if you do, great! There's no need for you to have a credit card. For day to day transactions just use a debit card or cash.

The problem with keeping a credit card in your possession is that it's like putting a big bottle of gin on the nightstand next to a recovering alcoholic (metaphorically we're ALL like alcoholics when it comes to spending money on things). Sure, he may be doing very well, and can ignore it for some time, until that one late night where he's not feeling good, or in a weakened emotional state, and gives in to the temptation. Why put the temptation there in the first place?

"But I just keep it for emergencies." That's what an emergency fund is for, which we discussed in Chapter 5. Moreover, if an emergency arises that exceeds your emergency fund, you can always walk into a bank and get a credit card. Banks are practically foaming at the mouth to give you a credit card. They'd give credit cards to six-year-old children if they could get away with it.

"But I get points and free stuff when I use the credit card." Yeah, you're not going to become a millionaire or gain financial freedom by paying onerous interest rates to get some free airline miles or small cashback rewards. That's like thinking you're going to have a bigger meal by trading a large chunk of your steak for a few bread crumbs...

For people who have said this or still believe this, do you really think you're getting one up on the credit card company with free miles and points? If you believe this, you must also believe when you go to the casino, you're getting one up on them because they're giving you free drinks while you're gambling your savings at the roulette table.

"But what if my debit card is stolen or compromised?" Fortunately, in modern times your debit card is just as safe as your credit card when it comes to fraud protection and zero liability policies. For example, my VISA debit card is covered under Visa's Zero Liability Policy the same as their credit card. Thus, if the card is ever lost, stolen, or fraudulently used, online or offline, I'm protected and not held responsible for the unauthorized charges made.

You Need to Build Up Your Credit Score
Before We Put the Big Shackles On

You may have heard this sentence uttered by one person to another (usually to a younger person): "You should get a credit card so you can build up your credit score so you can buy X (a house, a car, etc.) one day."

This has been a terrible lie told to Americans, originated by the lenders and proliferated by the auto and real estate industry salespeople trying to drum up transactions. Guess what a credit score is good for? Buying things with credit. Do you think a seller of a home is going to care what your credit score is if you're paying the full amount in cash? No.

Unraveled and unpackaged, this false belief implies that you should use debt to finance consumer purchases and lose money to interest on those purchases so that you can build up your "credit score" in order to finance even bigger consumer purchases where you'll lose even more money to interest payments...do you see the lunacy in this? Of course, this is great for banks and credit card companies, not so good for you. This is why they give you points and flyer miles for using the credit card, also known as "bait" to lure you into their financial trap.

As *Rational Savers*, we know buying consumer goods using "credit" is a terrible idea. So, the credit score is useless to us. But it's understandable why this myth continues to be proliferated. Heck, college campuses are filled with credit card company brochures and advertisements. They pray on the late teens and early 20's college students, and most campuses let them.

Moreover, the banks, credit card companies, and auto industry collectively spend hundreds of millions of dollars every year on clever advertising devised with human psychology and herd mentality in mind; they've done this for over half a century, year after year, decade after decade.

No wonder so many people couldn't even conceive of purchasing a home without a mortgage, or a car without car payments, or living using cash and a debit card. You need a credit card to build up your credit score! Right?... Please. If you still believe that, you've fallen hook, line, and sinker for their scam.

Credit Security Freeze

As a *Rational Saver*, I have no use for a credit score, so I've placed a credit freeze with all 3 credit agencies (Equifax, Experian, and TransUnion) on my credit score to lower my risk of identity theft, and I ensure they stay frozen. I've been doing this for years now. It's not hard, it's free, and it's far superior to wasting your hard-earned money on service fees to pay some "credit monitoring/identity theft prevention" company. After all, the Economic Growth, Regulatory Relief, and Consumer Protection Act of 2018 specifically gives consumers in the U.S. the right to place a security freeze on their credit reports for free, as many times as they'd like.

This is a wise practice not only if you're in the process of becoming debt-free, but to remain debt-free. It would be a shame if you finally paid off your debt, only to have a huge ballooning debt for things you didn't even purchase due to becoming a victim of identity theft.

If you ever need access to your credit score, say for good debt on an investment property, you can always unfreeze it and refreeze it when you're done.

Debt Makes You Defenseless When Mr. Murphy Comes Knocking

As I'm writing this in the Spring of 2020, the majority of the world's economies have been in shut down by the order of our governments (with the exceptions of Sweden and South Korea), ostensibly in order to combat the spread of a virus. This is causing serious economic hardship on individuals, families, small businesses, and corporations that aren't getting a "bailout" and thus collapsing into an economic abyss.

Prior to the onset of the "virus," individuals and corporations were so liquored up on debt that a momentary lapse in their expected income stream would totally prevent them from being able to service their debts and turns what would have been a bad scenario into a catastrophe. Being in debt makes every road bump or crisis a financial crisis on top of the underlying issue.

Corporations that should have had sizeable cash reserves to weather unexpected crises and events, whether they be pandemics, lawsuits, labor strikes, industry disruption, and so forth, instead were running on debt fumes; when the "for your safety" forced government shutdowns came around, within two months dozens of major corporations were marching on Washington D.C. demanding bailouts and filing for chapter 7 and chapter 11 bankruptcy.

If you work a conventional office job and your boss calls you in one day and explains that he's been ordered to lay you off due to corporate downsizing, for most people, that's a catastrophe.

How the heck are they going to survive? They have mortgage payments, car payments, student loan debt that can't be relinquished in bankruptcy, credit card debt; if you don't find another source of income and FAST, your car could be repossessed, your credit debt will balloon at the onerous 18% interest rates, and you could be facing foreclosure and lose your home. Your significant other may lose respect for you and it's not uncommon for relationships to fall apart under these circumstances. Your life turns upside down and the stress is dialed up to the max, not to mention the feeling of inferiority and fear.

For people with zero debt and sizeable savings, it's not that big of a deal; you can find new employment at your leisure and take time to really vet out your options and go with the employer that you think you have the best synergy with and will be able to build a mutually enjoyable and profitable long term business relationship with. If anything, it may be an opportunity to accelerate your career! Or, you can even take a little vacation, go do some traveling or work on that project or take up that hobby you've always been interested in.

Notice how different these two responses are? Not because the underlying road bump was any different, but because the one person was a **debt slave**, and the other was free and well-fortified. Warren Buffet on numerous occasions has given his Berkshire Hathaway investors the following wisdom: "You only find out who is swimming naked when the tide goes out."

By this, he means that when adverse economic conditions arise, you get to see which companies and individuals were actually financially resilient and strong, and which were posers, Instagram salesmen and fakes trying to put out an image but really were covered up to their eyeballs in debt.

You know, the guys who pop up on your Instagram feed or YouTube ads with Lamborghini's and mansions in the background trying to sell you the system or product that got them "rich." If they were honest, they'd include in their systems a brochure on how to max out as many credit cards as you possibly can and leverage up to the hilt.

Those people will and are paying the price of putting up that façade, and that price is poverty. You can only pay off your credit card so many times with other credit cards, you can only re-finance and borrow so much; eventually, those people will have to pay the piper.

Moreover, being a debt-free *Rational Saver* will enable you to handle a multitude of other road bumps that are statistically probable to appear throughout the course of your life, whether they be unexpected legal troubles or simply to be able to help a friend in need.

NOT TRYING TO BEAT A DEAD HORSE, BUT...

Debt is like POISON to your financial and emotional well-being. Debt will keep you poor, and if you're one of the very small percentage of people who has made it to the upper middle or lower upper class with car payments, home mortgages, student loans, credit card balances and other shackles of slavery, I hate to be the bearer of bad news, but you've made the banks a LOT of money over the years, and whatever your current net worth is, it likely would be many times greater if you had not been over paying for things and giving your hard earned money to your creditors in the form of interest all of these years!

Remember our house example? For a $226,800 house Bob paid an additional $111,867 with just a 3.5% interest rate! Wait until we address vehicles, student loans, second homes and credit card debt. Collectively, financing all these things is akin to flushing decades of your hard-earned income down the drain and straight into greedy banker coffers.

For example, let's say hypothetical Bob, on top of buying that $226,800 home at the previously mentioned loan terms with 20% down, also has $35,000 in credit card debt at an effective APR of 19.71%, and a $39,270 Jeep he financed with 10% down at an APR of 3.9% and a 6 year term, and $75,000 in student loans at a 4% interest rate. For demonstration purposes, we'll amortize these debts and to be conservative we'll assume Bob pays like clockwork.

Bob pays his credit card debt in 6 years, putting $9,990 every year towards paying down the principal and interest payments (while making all subsequent purchases in cash and not credit, most people never do this, they always maintain a substantial credit card balance). Bob pays off his student loans in 12 years, putting around $7,880 per year towards paying principal and interest on those student loans. Bob's mortgage ends in 30 years, and his auto-loan in 6.

Debt Type	Initial Balance	Term (years)	Principal Paid	Annual Interest Rate	Total Interest Paid	Opportunity Cost of interest during term
Credit Card	$35,000	6	$35,000	19.71%	$24,938	$31,278
Mortgage	$181,440	30	$226,800	3.5%	$111,867	$373,502
Auto Loan	$35,343	6	$39,270	3.9%	$5,121	$6,145
Student	$75,000	12	$75,000	4.0%	$19,557	$31,345
			$376,070		**$161,483**	**$442,270**

Bob has lost a total of $161,483 to interest payments going into bankers' pockets over the various terms of his debts. Had he invested the monthly interest payments he made towards those debts into investments yielding a collective 6% per year compounding annually, he could have turned that money into $442,270, i.e., his opportunity cost of those interest payments.

Remember, Bob also had to pay the principal back (and make the initial down payments on the house and vehicle), which collectively amounts to $376,070. If we then ask what is his opportunity cost of the principal payments (if the down payments and monthly principal portions of his debt service payments were instead invested at the duration and intervals of the various terms of his respective debt obligations), Bob's opportunity cost is $881,895.

If we combine the opportunity costs of his down payments, principal and interest payments, we get a collective total opportunity cost of: **$1,324,165!** Yikes. I hope that Jeep, college degree, $35,000 worth of credit card purchases and the starter house was worth it.

Of course, Bob isn't a monk and needs a vehicle, a place to live, the ability to earn income, and to buy necessities like food, clothing, gas and things for entertainment and fun. But Bob grossly overpaid for that vehicle, he probably grossly overpaid for his education, unless his degree actually significantly increased his income, and many of the purchases he made to accumulate that $35,000 credit card balance were un-necessary and a result of him not reading this book.

If you're a younger reader who hasn't made many or any of these mistakes, awesome, you're lucky, and you've been forewarned. Read on to see what you'll have to go through after your day of reckoning that will inevitably befall you should you fail to become a successful *Rational Saver.* For my readers who have already committed some of these financial sins, please do not feel bad, do not blame yourself, and do not think you should have known. Our educational system is beyond broken and does not teach this stuff.

Congratulate yourself for purchasing this book and waking up. Most people never wake up. The truth is that the past is irrelevant now. All that matters is what you do from this day forward. What matters is that you stop the cycle of self-abuse, because that's what this is. It's self-abuse.

You're not treating yourself when you buy that expensive dress with a credit card; or that luxury car with financing, or when you make a "down payment" on a house...you're abusing yourself, mistreating yourself, not respecting or loving yourself the way you deserve. Same with doing hard narcotics or getting overly drunk; sure, it will feel good at first, but those good feelings are quickly replaced with the bad and the after-effects far outweigh any short-term pleasure.

WEALTHY PEOPLE AND CONSUMPTION

The truth is, wealthy people don't finance consumption. Wealthy people also don't think in terms of consumption during their day to day lives, they think in terms of production. Every day they wake up, they think about how to enhance their production, how to increase the value they bring to the marketplace in the form of a product or service that will better people's lives.

But I only Financed One Car...
and I Only Have Two Credit Cards I Use for Points...
This is like saying "but I'm only going to try heroin this second time, and that's it. I don't have a problem." Well, you will. The monster starts small, but quickly grows into a fire breathing

dragon. We need to smite this monster down immediately, regardless of how big it is.

Good Debt

Before closing this chapter, we must add a caveat about debt. There is such a thing as good debt, in fact, this good debt can be absolutely life-changing in a tremendously positive way, if used correctly. There are two forms of debt which we can consider "**good debt**":

(a) debt that is used to increase your returns on an investment, such as an apartment building; and

(b) if you need more currency than you currently have to build a business which will enable you to repay that debt and create re-occurring annual cash flow.

If used properly and with much precaution, business debt or debt used to increase your returns on an investment can act as an accelerant to your net worth. These are discussed in further detail in chapter 16.

DEBT EMANCIPATION PROCLOMATION

I, _____ (YOUR NAME), HENCEFORTH DECLARE THAT I WILL WORK AS HARD AS POSSIBLE TO END THE CYCLE OF SELF-ABUSE AND BECOME DEBT FREE. I UNDERSTAND IT WILL REQUIRE CHANGE AND SACRIFICE, BUT I KNOW IN MY HEART THAT IT IS FOR THE BEST, I DESERVE FREEDOM, CHOICE, HAPPINESS, HEALTH AND WEALTH. BEING DEBT FREE IS NOT GOING TO BE EASY, BUT IT IS STILL A HECK OF A LOT EASIER THAN BEING A **DEBT SLAVE** FOR THE BANKS AND CREDIT CARD COMPANIES.

"RATHER GO TO BED SUPPERLESS, THAN RISE IN DEBT."

—BENJAMIN FRANKLIN

CHAPTER 8

ESCAPE FROM DEBT ALCATRAZ

Step 1: Solder silver spoon into makeshift chisel and start digging.

Step 2: Arts and crafts time – build paper-mâché dummy for use as decoy and construct raft out of old raincoats.

Step 3: Rendezvous with other escapees on the top of the roof, but be careful to avoid the search lights.

Step 4: Choose between the **Debt Snowball Method** and the **Debt Avalanche Method** for your final escape from debt prison.

THE DEBT SNOWBALL METHOD

With the **Debt Snowball Method**, every month you ensure to make the minimum payments on all your debts so as to not default or incur penalties, then you organize all your debts by smallest balance to greatest balance, and whatever monthly income you have remaining goes towards paying off your smallest debt. Once the smallest debt is completely paid off, you work your way up to the next largest debt and every month again you put the remaining income you have left over after making all your minimum payments towards extinguishing that next largest debt. You do this until all your debts are extinguished. This system does not consider what the interest rates are on your respective debts; it's simply concerned with the size of the balances.

For example, suppose you have $50,000 in credit card debt at an effective APR of 19.7%, $30,000 left in student debt at an APR of 4.4%, and $15,000 in an auto loan at an APR of 3.9%, you would allocate any remaining monthly income you have after making the minimum payments on all of them, towards paying them off in the following order:

1. The $15,000 auto loan first;
2. Then, when the auto loan is extinguished, the $30,000 student debt;
3. and finally, with the student debt extinguished, the $50,000 in credit card debt.

The idea behind this method is it gives the debt Alcatraz escapee emotional boosts when they extinguish an entire debt, such as the balance on a credit card or an auto loan, which will help motivate them to continue down the path of extinguishing their next debt, building up emotional momentum like a snowball rolling down a hill (I've never seen a snowball actually work like that, and as a kid, I was a snowball making ninja, but it's a reasonable metaphorical representation I suppose).

THE DEBT AVALANCHE METHOD

This is also referred to as the "debt stacking method." In this method, you also make your minimum monthly payments on all your debts so as to not default or incur any penalties. Then, you organize your debts by interest rate, and whatever monthly income you have remaining goes towards the debt with the highest interest rate.

Using the previous example of $50,000 in credit card debt at an effective APR of 19.7%, $30,000 in student debt at an APR of 4.4%, and $15,000 in an auto loan at an APR of 3.9%, after making the minimum payments on all your debts, you would allocate any remaining monthly income you have towards paying them off in the following order:

1. The $50,000 in credit card debt first BECAUSE it has the highest interest rate at a whopping 19.7%;
2. The $30,000 in student debt second because it has the second-highest interest rate at 4.4%;
3. And the $15,000 auto loan last because it has the lowest interest rate at 3.9%.

In comparing the two methods to see which will get you debt-free the fastest and save you the most money, consider the following hypothetical: your favorite aunt passes away and left you a $30,000 inheritance. She really liked you! You have two out of three of the above debts (for simplicity sake), the $50,000 in credit card debt at 19.7% APR, and the $30,000 in student debt at 4.4%.

Debt Snowball Method: You would pay off the student debt first because it's the smallest balance. Great news! It's completely extinguished. You have removed that debt completely from the liabilities side of your net worth statement, giving you a nice emotional boost. You've also eliminated the 4.4% interest you would have had to pay that year on that balance, saving yourself $1,320!

Debt Avalanche Method: You would put the $30,000 towards your credit card debt with the higher interest rate of 19.7%, reducing it from $50,000 to $20,000. Your $30,000 student debt at 4.4% remains the same. In this scenario, you would have saved **$5,910** in interest that year AND every single year after. That's 447% more money in your pocket that year by using the avalanche method over the snowball method, or an additional $4,590; by losing less money to interest, that's more money you can apply to extinguishing your remaining debts, thereby getting you debt-free faster, and depending on your debts, this can be by a magnitude of months or years.

The debt avalanche method of paying off your liabilities with the highest interest first WILL get you out of debt faster and with more money in your pocket than the debt snowball. Now, if you think you won't stick to it because you're not getting those emotional boosts from seeing liabilities disappear from your net worth statement sooner, then, by all means, use the debt snow-ball method. It's still infinitely better than the **Do Nothing and Continue to Accumulate Debt Method**.

There was a Harvard study that found that the majority of people who use the debt snowball method finish paying off their overall debt more often than people that use alternate strategies. So, for the majority of people, this method will have a greater success rate, due to it being easier psychologically for people to stick to it, even though it's financially less efficient and takes longer to get out of debt.

However, given that you've made it up to this point in this book (assuming you've not skipped around), congratulations, you're not like the majority of people and you probably don't need to wear the little orange arm floaties when you go into the pool... you're motivated enough to make the more efficient **Debt Avalanche Method** work.

Sticky Note Emotional Booster Hack

But just for good measure, here's a solution I came up with to add some emotional motivation every time you make a payment on your highest interest debt. All you do is take the amount of money you put towards paying off that highest interest debt, multiply that amount by the APR of that debt, and you'll get how many dollars in interest that payment just saved you this year. Write that dollar amount on a sticky note and put it on your fridge or a section of your wall set aside for more sticky notes!

(Payment Towards Principal) **X** (Annual Interest Rate) = **$ of interest saved**

For example, after making the minimum monthly payments on all your debts, if you have $1,500 left over and you put that $1,500 towards paying off your highest-interest debt which happens to be your credit card debt at a 21% **APR**, you'll take the $1,500 payment and multiply it by 0.21, and you get $315 of interest you just saved yourself. Write "+$315" on your sticky note and place it on the fridge.

BAM! Those of you who needed that emotional boost from seeing your progress got it with the more efficient avalanche method and you can stay on the horse and continue slaying debt monsters.

STOP POURING GASOLINE ON THE FIRE

Regardless of which method you use, you must stop adding to your debts, that is, CEASE AND DESIST all credit card use, no additional auto-loans OR leases, which means when the lease is up do not enter into a new lease; no more drawing down from your home equity line of credit (HELOC), and so forth. Ergo, as you're paying off your debts, you should NOT be adding any additional debts, or adding to any existing debts.

You may have to get thrifty and learn to live on less and use hacks to lower your living expenses, which I provided in chapters 4 and 5. This means paying for things with cash, and locking your current credit cards up in a safe to keep them out of your reach. If you can, call your credit card company and have them issue new cards to you with new card numbers. They do this for free if they are lost. When you get the new cards, old subscriptions and things that may have been acting as parasites on your net worth will no longer be able to charge your cards as they have the previous card info. Of course, you'll want to update any that you absolutely need if you don't have the cash in your debit account to cover, otherwise use your debit card from now on for those things.

When your credit cards are paid off, get out your trusty Shredder 3000 and feed them to it, or cut them up into millions of little pieces and spread them across the ends of the Earth. This will help prevent you from sabotaging your efforts and increase your net worth faster. Remind yourself frequently that, as you pay down and extinguish your debts, you're increasing your wealth and net worth.

Spreadsheet Your Debts

In order to utilize the **Debt Snowball Method** or the **Debt Avalanche Method**, you'll need a more detailed spreadsheet than the one on your net worth statement, which just lists the liabilities in terms of their balances. This more detailed spreadsheet will come in handy on your debt destroying rampage and will include the following items:

- **Gross monthly income**;

- **Living expenses** (groceries, gas, utilities, etc.);

- Your **minimum monthly payments** on all your debts;

First, subtract the living expenses and minimum monthly payments on all your debts from your gross monthly income, to arrive at a **monthly left-over income.**

Second, list your remaining balances on your debts and their corresponding annual interest rates. If any of the debts have a term that's different than their amortization schedule, or in other words, any of your debts have a balloon payment you need to make at the end of the term, it couldn't hurt to note the terms and balloon payment, if any.

Third, if you've decided to use the **Debt Snowball Method,** you'll then sort the debts by balance size and put your remaining monthly income towards the smallest balance; if using the **Debt Avalanche Method,** sort debts by interest rate and put your remaining monthly income towards paying down the debt with the highest interest rate.

Gross Monthly Income	Monthly Expenses	$
$3,500	Groceries	$250
	Wireless	$114
	Gasoline	$80
	Utilities	$100
	TOTAL:	**$544**

Debt Type	Unpaid Balance	Annual Interest Rate	Term (yrs)	Balloon Payment	Monthly Minimum PMT
Credit Card	$50,000	19.71%	--	None	$500
Student	$30,000	4.4%	10	None	$310
Auto-Loan	$15,000	3.9%	6	None	$276
Mortgage	$181,440	3.5%	30	None	$815
				TOTAL =	**$1,900**

Gross Monthly Income – Total Monthly Expenses – TOTAL Monthly Minimum PMTS =   **$1,056**

From the sample spreadsheet above, you'll see at the end we have a **monthly left-over income** of $1,056 we can now use to extinguish debts. I've organized the debts in the sample spreadsheet by interest rate, assuming most of my readers would prefer the faster way that leaves more money in their pockets and pays down their debts sooner. Thus, that $1,056 would then go 100% towards paying down the credit card debt at 19.71% interest. If you're not familiar with Microsoft Excel, there are plenty of free and easy tutorials on YouTube.

PRE-PAYMENT PENALTIES — PROTECTING THE LENDER'S JUICE

Some lenders charge pre-payment penalties, particularly with auto-loans and mortgages. You will need to read the **loan agreement** (also called **"loan docs"**) for those debts to see if there is indeed a **pre-payment penalty**, as well as get verification in writing from your lender (mortgagee) as to what those are and how they're calculated.

It's common that the pre-payment penalty declines over time or disappears entirely when a certain year mark is hit, most often after the 5th year the pre-payment penalty disappears. Thus, if you identify this is the case with your mortgage, you'll want to calculate how much interest you'll have to pay while waiting to hit that year in which the pre-payment penalty is lifted, versus what the pre-payment penalty is if you pay it off early, to see which is more economical.

Some loan agreements permit borrowers to pre-pay up to 20% of their loan balance in any one year without being penalized, so long as they inform their lender of their intent to do so and comply with the terms of their loan agreement. This will usually be the most economical choice, but do compare that to all other choices and see which saves the most money.

Note some **loan docs** may have a provision whereby if you received a discount on your original mortgage's posted interest rate, they reserve the right to add that discount to your pre-payment penalty (get reimbursed on the back end).

If you're considering selling or re-financing, the pre-payment penalty may also be triggered. When the penalty applies to both home sales and re-financing, your loan agreement has what's called a **"hard penalty"** in banker jargon. If it only applies to re-financing, it's called a **"soft penalty."**

Penalties for pre-paying mortgages can vary wildly, so you will need to do some work to figure out which avenue makes the most economic sense for increasing your net worth. Again, every loan agreement is different, but this gives you an idea of how to look at it and what kind of things to look for.

Figuring in pre-payment penalties into your decision-making analysis may take a little work, but you potentially could save tens of thousands of dollars for only a few hours of basic arithmetic, contract reading, and written correspondence with your lender.

Confirm Your Additional Payments Go Towards Principal Reduction

If you intend on prepaying any loans, do contact and inform your creditors in writing of your intent on paying above the monthly minimum payments and for those payments to go directly towards principal reduction. This will help prevent them from mistakenly assuming your additional payment was just a pre-payment on the next month's required payment (which doesn't help you reduce the interest).

DANGERS OF DEBT CONSOLIDATION

Using debt consolidation services to get out of debt is generally not a good idea and will only further decrease your net worth over the long run. Yes, the advantage to debt consolidation is that, from a cashflow perspective you're lowering the amount of **cash outlays** (money leaving your pocket) you have to make every month to service your existing debts.

The problem is what you trade in order to do that; you're trading a lower monthly payment for extending the term of your debts, which will cause you to remain in debt for longer periods of time and make a greater number of payments than you otherwise would have, resulting in you paying your creditors MORE over time than you otherwise would have with your original debts. Moreover, the lender may advertise they can lower your collective interest rate, but in the fine print have mechanisms for that only being for a brief amount of time, after which it hikes back up to its previous level, or even higher. Debt consolidation companies, credit card companies, banks and other lenders, are in the business to make money.

For example, let's assume you have a $20,000 unsecured personal loan at 14% and a 3-year term, and a $15,000 car loan at an APR of 4.5% with 4 years of term remaining. The unsecured personal loan monthly payment is $683.55 for 36 months, for a total of $24,608 in interest and principal payments. The car loan has a monthly payment of $342.05 per month for 48 months, for a total of $16,418 in interest and principal payments. Your total monthly payment for both these debts is $1,025.6 per month for the first 3 years, and $342.05 per month for the 4th year, and the total sum of your cash outlays by the time you've paid both debts off is $41,026.

You go to a debt consolidation company (or your bank or credit card company) that promises to consolidate your debts with your creditors, roll both loans into one and reduce your total monthly payment to $718 per month and your collective interest rate to 8.5%. Your monthly payment has been lowered by $308, and your interest rate reduced, great!

Hold on partner, not so fast. It's not as great as you'd think. Here's the trick, they've increased the term from 3 years for the unsecured loan and 4 years for the car loan, to 5 years for the new consolidated loan. Now, by the end of the 5-year term, you end up paying a total of $43,085, which is $2,059 MORE than before the debts were consolidated, therefore your net worth over the long run is $2,059 LESS after bringing in the debt consolidation company, and it will keep bad debt on your balance sheet for an additional 12 months. That doesn't sound like a very good deal.

To add insult to injury, some of these lenders even have the audacity to demand a fee for this generous "service." No thanks.

PAY OFF THE HOME MORTGAGE EARLY OR INVEST?

Congratulations, you've paid off all your consumer debts with the exception of your home mortgage. Now, do we direct our savings towards paying off the home mortgage early, or keep making the regular mortgage payments and invest our additional savings?

As *Rational Saver's* you took an oath to become debt-free. In the end, this stands true and you should want to own your home outright. However, to accelerate your net worth faster, there may be instances in which paying down your mortgage is the slower option (not the wrong option). Similar to the **debt snowball vs. debt avalanche**, both are not wrong, rather, one will increase your net worth faster than the other.

Three helpful considerations when making this decision are:

1. What are the **pre-payment penalties**, if any, and can they be avoided while still accelerating your mortgage principal reduction (such as with loans that allow prepayment up to 20% per year)?

2. Have you **identified investments with a meaningfully higher yield than your effective mortgage interest rate**? Given the increased resiliency that comes with owning your home outright, to simply invest in treasuries (assuming rates normalize…) over pre-paying your home mortgage just to get a 1% or 2% **positive spread** (rate of return higher than your mortgage's interest rate) may not be worth it; however, if you're investing in an opportunity that has a realistic likelihood of say a **7% or greater positive spread with your effective mortgage interest rate**, perhaps it's worth diverting money you otherwise would have used to pre-pay the mortgage. If you're not very knowledgeable about the investments you're looking at, and you would just be gambling, pre-paying the mortgage would be the wiser choice until you've become an expert in that investment class or are investing alongside experts whom you trust.

3. Be 100% honest with yourself…**do you have the discipline to actually invest the currency you otherwise would put towards pre-paying your mortgage?** Or would you be likely to use some of it for upgrades to your home, furniture, vehicles, designer clothes, jewelry, art, vacations, ponies, jet skis, unicorns, anything!? If you think there's even a remote possibility that you're not going to

invest every red cent, you may want to just pre-pay the mortgage. It's a guaranteed rate of return on the interest payment savings, reduces monthly cash outlays, and will give you better peace of mind and resiliency during tough times.

In addition to the 3 considerations above, below are some benefits, risks, and drawbacks to consider when deciding whether or not to pay off your home mortgage early.

Benefit – Guaranteed Rate of Return

You're guaranteed to save a quantifiable amount of money you otherwise would have to pay towards mortgage interest. For demonstration purposes, let's assume you come into a sizeable sum of money from a relative passing away and you decide to pay off the remaining mortgage balance early.

The existing loan is a 30-year self-amortizing mortgage with an original balance of $300,000 at 4.5% interest, and you're 10 years into the loan with 20 years remaining, by paying off your mortgage 20 years early with a lump sum payment of $240,258, you save roughly $124,000 in interest payments (assuming there's no pre-payment penalty) you otherwise would have made during the remaining mortgage term. In this example, that $240,258 early payment had a guaranteed **2.55% annualized nominal rate of return**.

Benefit – Increased Resiliency and Peace of Mind

By smiting down your mortgage dragon early, from a cashflow perspective you've likely removed the largest living expense from your monthly cash outlays and you get to remove it from the liabilities section on your net worth statement. This certainly comes with peace of mind knowing that if the economy goes bust or you enter financially difficult times, as long as you pay your property taxes, you will have somewhere to live and not have to worry about being foreclosed on by the bank, which happens to a LOT of people during financial downturns, especially people who were over-leveraged, liquored up on debt like drunken fools, and completely reliant on that next paycheck. By not having a mortgage on your home, you're more resilient during those hard times.

Risk – Trapped Equity due to Poor Timing

Suppose a hypothetical borrower who had originally purchased his house for $300,000, completely pre-pays his remaining mortgage balance of $240,258. Then, a few years after, his real estate market goes into a prolonged deflationary collapse like that experienced by the Japanese real estate market from the late 1980s to 2003, and the property drops 70% in market value; if our borrower holds out for 7 years and then due to employment or financial reasons needs to sell at end of year 7, his $240,258 early payment would end up losing him **-9.40% per year**, because the sale proceeds were 70% lower than when the borrower purchased his home at $300,000 and we're assuming a 3% cost of sale.

Returns like -9.40% are a fast track towards making grumpy cat even grumpier. Thus, the borrower's currency used for the early mortgage payment are essentially trapped into the home, unless the borrower is willing to take a huge loss either at sale or refinancing.

The risk of loss in market value is not really an issue is if you plan on living in the home forever. Then, realistically our borrower would receive a **2.55% annual rate of return** on the $240,258 early payment, regardless of what happens to the home's market value, because our borrower needs to live somewhere.

Drawback - Opportunity Cost

As discussed earlier, there is an **opportunity cost** associated with the currency you're diverting into pre-paying the mortgage. If you've identified investments that have a high likelihood of paying out a significantly higher yield, you may be foregoing that opportunity if you instead pre-pay the home mortgage. Be sure to read chapters 14, 15, and 16, which cover some basic principles and considerations of investing, tailored for the economic landscape of the 2020s.

Drawback – Diminished Diversification

We've all heard the idiom *"don't put all your eggs in one basket."* This is actually a 17th century Spanish and Italian proverb that appears in *Don Quixote* by Michael de Cervantes, alluding to it being dangerous to put all of your eggs from your hens into one basket should you be as clumsy as my former girlfriend who would most certainly drop the basket and break the eggs all over the ceilings and the walls and places you'd never think it would even be possible for the eggs to end up, making a huge mess in the process.

By taking your additional savings and putting it towards early payment of your mortgage, you're less diversified than you would be if you put those savings in a variety of other things (cash, bonds, gold, stocks, investment real estate, etc.). This limits your ability to **pivot** should the market change and your home become significantly less **liquid** (difficult to sell or re-finance), essentially trapping that additional money you put in it to pay it off early.

Drawback – Loss of Mortgage Interest Tax Write-Off

A common argument for using a mortgage to obtain your home, or for keeping your mortgage alive for the entirety of its term by only making the minimum payments, is the **mortgage interest tax write-off**, which (as of 2020) allows you to deduct up to the first

$750,000 of your primary residence mortgage against your own personal income. For example, suppose a hypothetical mortgage owner spent $15,000 in mortgage interest for the fiscal year and is in the 22% tax bracket. This means they can deduct the $15,000 against their taxable income, saving roughly $3,300 in taxes (22% x $15,000).

However, the **Standard Deduction** was increased in 2018 to $12,000, which nullifies this benefit for a large percentage of the U.S. populace. Thus, you'll want to see if with the $12,000 standard deduction, you would see any tax benefit from the mortgage interest write-off. If you would still see benefit from the mortgage interest write-off, the next step will be to calculate what this tax write-off does to your **mortgage's effective interest rate**. To do this, use the following steps:

Step 1: [**$ in Annual Mortgage Interest**] – [**$ saved with mortgage interest deduction**]

Step 2: [**Answer from step 1**] divided by [**mortgage balance**]

Step 3: Multiply **answer from step 2** by 100

For example, let's assume the previous 22% tax bracket and $15,000 in mortgage interest for the fiscal year, with a $375,000 mortgage balance at 4% interest. If you deduct the $3,300 you saved on your taxes from the $15,000 in interest you paid that year ($15,000-$3,300), you get $11,700. Then, divide $11,700 by your remaining mortgage balance of $375,000, and we get a quotient of 0.0312, which we then multiply by 100 to get an **effective mortgage interest rate** of 3.12% after the mortgage interest tax write-off, which dropped your interest rate almost 1 point from 4% to 3.12%.

Note this is for the first year of ownership. Every year after, the amount of interest you pay goes down slightly as the principal gets paid down, so you'll have to recalculate for each year using a mortgage amortization calculator that separates interest from the principal.

Knowing your effective mortgage interest rate can be helpful when looking at investments as an alternative to pre-paying your home mortgage. As discussed earlier, you don't want to compare your mortgage's **nominal interest rate** to the prospective **yield** of the investment(s) you're looking at, rather, you want to compare the effective mortgage interest rate you'd pay after the mortgage interest tax write-off, to find out what the actual **spread** would be.

THE "INFLATION LOWERS YOUR MORTGAGE'S EFFECTIVE INTEREST RATE" MYTH

There are a few personal finance gurus online, one of whom is a residential real estate guy from California, who have been spreading this myth that the reported **national inflation rate** off-sets your mortgage's interest rate, so your real interest rate is less than you think, making obtaining or keeping a mortgage a more attractive choice.

Their argument goes like this: let's assume the U.S. Labor Department reports the average annual national inflation rate for the duration of the term of a mortgage is 2%, and the mortgage's interest rate is 4%. Under this theory, you can subtract the national inflation rate of 2% from your mortgage's interest rate of 4%, and your **effective mortgage interest rate** is then only 2% (before any tax write-off considerations).

This argument is DEMONSTRABLY FALSE. I'm a big picture macro guy, but this is an instance where big-picture thinking can

157

get you as an individual homeowner in trouble. If you look at the U.S. Bureau of Labor Statistics, between 1967 and 2020, housing as a whole has experienced an average inflation rate of 4.18% per year, per their U.S. prices for housing inflation rate data figure, which is even more specific than the national inflation rate as it just encompasses real estate pricing, while the national inflation rate data figure encompasses a whole basket of pricing for everyday consumer goods and services not related to real estate. Even if we use this data point that's more specific to housing and even higher than the national inflation rate, does that mean your home is going to appreciate? NO.

One market's housing could appreciate 5%, another could depreciate 3%, yet the average inflation rate per the prices for housing data point could be 4% and the national inflation rate could be 2%. The national inflation rate and prices for housing inflation rate data points are both USELESS for gauging appreciation or depreciation of your specific home, and thus, not a logical justification for adding to or subtracting from your effective mortgage interest rate when making any financial decisions related to a home mortgage.

Why is this? Because of the most widely recognized mantra of real estate, understood by every seasoned real estate broker and investor: "location, location, location!" There are many markets that, after going through inflationary booms, have then experienced severe deflationary drops and never fully recovered, or took many decades to recover, regardless of what the national inflation rate or the more specific national prices for housing inflation rate jumped to subsequent to the deflationary drop.

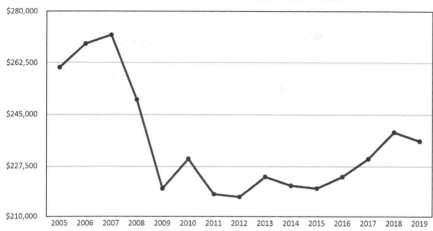

Connecticut Median Home Sale Price

The housing market in Connecticut (CT) is a prime example. In the mid-2000s, homes appreciated significantly and median home sale prices peaked in 2007 at around $272,000. Then the housing bust (deflation) occurred, with homeowners being foreclosed on in droves. At the bottom of the market in 2012, the median home sale price in CT was about $218,000, a 20% drop in value from 2007. In 2019, median home sale prices in Connecticut were $257,163, 5.5% lower than the 2007 peak median home sale prices.

So, if you were a median CT homeowner and you acquired your property at the end of 2007 and you held onto it for 12 years, it only would have depreciated by roughly 5.5%, no big deal, right?

WRONG! The median home price in CT depreciated by 5.5% between 2007 and 2019 in *nominal* terms. What matters more is *real* terms (which adjusts for inflation), because you only increase your wealth by increasing your purchasing power, that is, by how much food, clothes, energy (electricity, gasoline, heating), healthcare, education, transportation, and so on, that you can purchase with your dollars.

A $272,000 home in the year 2007 would have needed to appreciate to $332,670 by 2019 just for your home's equity to have kept up with consumer price inflation and not lose any real purchasing power (taking into account a 3% cost of sale), if we use the average national inflation rate of 1.57% (devaluation) of the U.S. Dollar from 2007-2019 as reported by the government. However, there are strong arguments that the government's methods used to calculate inflation since 1983 have been intended to under-report the true rate of inflation (see chapter 15).

But for argument's sake, if we assume that 1.57% was the actual rate of inflation, this means that the 2019 median Connecticut home valued at $257,163 hasn't just depreciated by 5.5% from the 2007 peak, your equity in that home has actually depreciated in real terms by a total of -22.7%, even though the average annual national inflation rate in this time period was 1.57%.

Therefore, contrary to the finance guru YouTuber's statement that your home will on average appreciate per the U.S. inflation rate, here is a prime example of it doing the total opposite, both in nominal terms and even more so in real terms which is what really matters at the end of the day when it comes to growing or shrinking your wealth.

Note Connecticut isn't an outlier, there are housing markets all over the U.S. and the world that for one reason or another have experienced severe deflationary price drops and never recovered, or if they did recover took multiple decades to do so and often only in nominal terms, with the trapped equity losing real purchasing power due to consumer price inflation.

I had to dispel this myth because tens of thousands of people after listening to these financial gurus are now assuming their home mortgage interest rate is reduced by the national rate of inflation and making mortgage decisions like whether to use a mortgage to purchase their home or whether to pre-pay their existing mortgages, based off this false advice.

"A BANKER WILL BE THE FIRST TO LEND YOU AN UMBRELLA WHEN THE SUN IS SHINING, AND BE THE FIRST TO TAKE IT AWAY WHEN IT STARTS TO RAIN."

—DON POLLARD

CHAPTER 9

POINT A TO POINT B — VEHICLE HACKS

In order to build up your savings and investment portfolio as fast as possible, you should look at a vehicle as a means of getting from point A to point B, nothing more. A lot of people spend a lot of money to impress people at stoplights they'll never meet. That said, there are people who genuinely just love cars. I can sympathize, I love cars too, especially fast cars. But I love freedom and financial success more.

While this chapter briefly covers some specific scams you'll encounter when purchasing and maintaining a vehicle, the biggest scam of all is the insidious idea that an expensive vehicle is better than an inexpensive vehicle, that a Land Rover or a Mercedes Benz is better than a used Toyota, Honda, or Lexus. If you're actually planning a bank heist and need a vehicle with enough speed to outrun the cops, sure, a higher-end vehicle might make sense.

But if you're like 99% of people out there who simply need a vehicle to get from your home to work to the grocery store and so forth, your life will not be meaningfully improved by driving a Land Rover as opposed to a used Toyota, Lexus or Honda you could have purchased for $7,500. Sure, if you buy a $60,000 luxury vehicle, a few friends might go "wow this is really nice." Cool. Hope the few temporary compliments are worth the extra

$52,500 (or more if you used financing or leasing) and the hundreds or thousands of hours worked to save up that currency.

DIGGING INTO YOUR INCOME OR SAVINGS TO BUY EXPENSIVE VEHICLES IS FOOLISH

It's incredible how many people are driving around in luxury cars and SUVs that they had to dig into their income or savings to purchase. Consider that if you make an average of $40 per hour and you buy a $40,000 car (without financing or leasing which will cost you even more in the long run), that's **1,000** HOURS of your life you traded away for a few meaningless compliments!

In the end, people aren't going to want to hang out with you, be your friend, do business with you or date you because of the car you drive.

OPPORTUNITY COST OF BUYING VEHICLES OVER $9,000 (IN 2020 DOLLARS)

Before we even get into leasing or financing, which costs the consumer even more than just purchasing all cash (financing and leases are where auto dealerships selling new cars make most of their money), let's assume hypothetical Bob needs a car, as his current car was driven off of a cliff by Bob's mischievous cat. Cats can be that way.

Anyway, Bob is worried about what his friends, family and/ or girlfriend will think about him depending on the car he drives. Bob decides to get a new Ford Mustang 2020 for $26,670, not over the top luxury by any means, but definitely flashier than a used 2013 Honda Civic for $9,000 total including cost to have an independent mechanic inspect the vehicle prior to purchase and make minor repairs after. What's Bob's opportunity cost by purchasing a $26,670 car instead of a $9,000 car?

The difference between those two vehicle purchases is $17,670. Let's assume Bob is 22 years old. If he had bought the 2013 Honda Civic, and invested the additional $17,670 he was going to dig out of his savings, by the time Bob is 62, at a 6% rate of return compounding annually, Bob could have grown that $17,670 into $181,749 (pre-tax).

Now, if we consider the fact that Bob replaces his vehicle every 10 years, the opportunity cost increases substantially. Supposing Bob makes the same decision at the same prices every 10 years, from age 22 to 32 to 42 to 52 until age 62, investing an additional $17,670 of savings at each 10-year interval, savings that otherwise would have gone towards the more expensive car, by the time Bob is age 62 he would have saved up $371,551 just by choosing the cheaper used car every 10 years, saving and investing the difference.

Imagine if we did this exercise on a $40,000 or $60,000 vehicle? What about when we include leasing or financing, where you're paying even MORE than just the purchase price? What about if you can get more than 6% interest on your investments? We could be talking about an opportunity cost approaching a MILLION dollars...

SPEND (SOME OF) THE INTEREST, NOT THE PRINCIPAL

As *Rational Savers*, we're going to emulate the rich (the ones that stay rich), and not purchase a sedan that costs more than $9,000 used, or an SUV or Truck that costs more than $12,000 used (in 2020 dollars), until we can afford to make such luxury vehicle purchases using currency from our passive income streams ONLY (whether from investment assets or businesses that run without the entrepreneur needing to be there to oversee the day to day operations). Oh, you didn't know? Rich people that stay rich don't dig into their savings OR income to buy luxury and sports cars. They dig into their passive income. And not all of it, a portion of their passive income no matter how rich they are is continually reinvested.

Only middle and lower class people dig into their savings or annual income to buy expensive cars, or rich people who will eventually go broke due to poor money management habits, some extreme and notorious examples being celebrities like Mike Tyson, Nicolas Cage, Stephen Baldwin, Kim Basinger, all of whom made tens or even hundreds of millions of dollars throughout their careers and still went bankrupt. The list of celebrities, sports stars, and trust fund babies who have gone broke due to not understanding the **Spend the Interest, Not the Principal Rule** is a long one.

This is also obvious when you look at all the lottery winners who blew through their winnings and went broke, often in a span of only a few years, many exclaiming winning the lottery was the worst thing that ever happened to them, some even taking their own lives. It wasn't winning the lottery that was the worst thing that happened to them, it was not learning personal finance skills.[20]

Regarding the $9,000 figure for sedans and $12,000 for trucks/SUVs, those are just guideposts, and you absolutely could find a private seller willing to sell a quality make and model sedan or truck for far less, heck I have friends who have bought used Toyota Corolla's (as an example) for $1,500 with under 150,000 miles on them in great condition. There are absolute steals out there.

---

20 Mark Abadi, "20 Lottery Winners Who Lost Every Penny" *Business Insider* (Mar 21, 2019), businessinsider.com/lottery-winners-lost-everything-2017-8

The point is, for the readers who are really motivated to become wealthy as fast as possible, accept the idea that until you're making hundreds of thousands or millions of dollars per year in passive income, a vehicle exists to get you from point A to point B.

"BUT I WANT A 'NICE' CAR!"

Great! Then use that as motivation to figure out how to increase your income, use or even exceed the 50% Rule of Savings, and invest wisely as discussed in chapters 14-16, so you can afford to buy nice cars you want with cash that's 100% from passive income streams, as opposed to cash you dug out of your savings.

Let's say you implement the savings strategies in this book, and 7 years later, you've eliminated your consumer debt, saved, and invested into enough cash flowing assets (see chapter 16) to where you're receiving $50,000 (after-tax) of annual passive income, and you really want to buy that $50,000 luxury SUV. Okay, it's a stupid purchase, and you would have been better off re-investing that $50,000, but at least you're not reducing your current net worth to do it, or trading thousands of hours you've spent working by digging into your savings, rather, you're using passive income (income that comes in even when you sleep) from assets or a business you've built that runs on auto-pilot.

I know it's tough, especially when you're younger, seeing other people your age driving around in new $20,000 and $30,000+ leased or financed vehicles. What you need to realize is that these people have been duped, and like lambs to the slaughter they also noticed everybody else doing it and used that to justify their decision to join in the stupidity. Just because everybody else is doing it doesn't mean it's ok.

NEVER BUY A NEW VEHICLE, It's a Major Financial Blunder!

Shark Tank's Kevin O'Leary has this to say about the matter: "If you're thinking about buying a new car, let me give you a new idea: DON'T!"[21] This point isn't even debatable. One of my former wealthiest clients who is worth hundreds of millions of dollars, even he still only buys used cars. In 2018, car manufacturers globally spent $38.5 billion in advertising to try to sell you a new car. There's a reason they spend this kind of money to sell consumers NEW cars. Never, ever, ever buy a new vehicle.

You're buying a consumer good that IMMEDIATELY depreciates in value by 10% the second you drive it off the lot, 20% after 12 months, and after two years or so, you'd be lucky to get 50% of what you paid for it. After 5 years, new cars typically will have depreciated by about 63%. Those percentages can be higher with German or other luxury cars. For example, suppose you buy a new car for $30,000, the minute you drive it off the lot, it's now worth $27,000. After 12 months, it's resale value will be around $24,000, and after two years, around $15,000. After 5 years, its resale value is around $11,100.[22] I don't know about you, but I call that highway robbery.

The fleecing doesn't end there. Many people just think about price and forget to add on top of that the costs of insurance and car maintenance. Yes, your driving history, level of coverage, age, etc., will affect your cost of insurance. But on average, the cost to insure a vehicle drops 3.4% per year the vehicle ages, meaning a vehicle that is 8 years old is approximately 27% cheaper to insure than a brand-new vehicle, yet another financial advantage

21 Kevin O'Leary, "Experts Agree: Don't Buy a New Car", *CNBC Make It* (Nov 8, 2018), youtube.com/watch?v=mSoNcKMYOfk

22 Charles Khrome, "Car Depreciation: How Much Value Will a New Car Lose?" *Carfax* (Nov 9, 2018), carfax.com/blog/car-depreciation

to buying a used vehicle.[23]

What about maintenance? Well, your average Toyota costs around $259 per year to maintain, or $2,590 over a 10-year period.[24] In contrast, if you buy a luxury German car for example, you'd better be prepared to spend a lot of money, between $1,000 and $1,700 per year (in 2020 dollars).[25] That's $10,000 to $17,000 over a 10-year period just in maintenance costs, or 386% to 656% more than if you had bought a reliable Toyota or Lexus. I am not a Toyota/Lexus spokesperson, but used Japanese cars are just known for quality, reliability, being inexpensive, and having a low cost for maintenance and repairs, all features that *Rational Savers* love.

"But, with maintenance, I can prepay upfront if I buy new..." You're still paying for it, you're just paying for it upfront which is even worse since you're increasing your opportunity cost to purchase the vehicle by reducing the quantity of currency in your pocket with which to invest NOW and grow over time.

This is a concept in finance known as the **Time Value of Money (TVM) Principle**, which states that money now is worth more than an identical sum in the future due to its potential earning capacity. This is because you can invest the money you have in your possession now and earn interest over the time span between now and a point in the future. For example, $10,000 today is worth more than $10,000 one year from now (even if inflation was 0%), because that $10,000 today can be invested, and supposing it's invested at a 4% interest rate, in one year that $10,000 has grown to $10,400.

23 Ava Lynch, "Car Insurance for New vs. Used Vehicles" *The Zebra*, thezebra.com/auto-insurance/vehicles/new-vs-used-car-insurance-comparison/

24 "Toyota Repair and Maintenance Estimates" *Your Mechanic* (July, 2020), yourmechanic.com/estimates/toyota

25 Motor1.com Team, "Average BMW Maintenance Cost: Worth It?" *Motor1* (Apr 18, 2020), motor1.com/reviews/406108/bmw-maintenance-cost/

SUBLIMINAL MESSAGING

Three terms in the context of vehicles will keep you from becoming wealthy quick are "safety, comfort, and performance." This is subliminal messaging used by the auto industry to get you to think you need to buy a new car in order to be safe, to have good performance, and to be comfortable. Nonsense. A 10 or 15-year-old used Toyota, Lexus or Honda is plenty safe, plenty comfortable and has all the performance you'd ever need unless you're towing heavy loads or planning a bank heist.

The "old cars aren't safe" con: There are advertising campaigns and PR pieces released every year to convince consumers they must buy a newer car due to new "safety features." Sure, cars from the '60s and '70s aren't going to have the safety features of modern cars, but a vehicle from a reputable car manufacturer and well-rated model from the year 2000 should be plenty safe.

Actually, buying new vehicles within the first three years or so of their release to the market can be less safe, as car companies are still gathering information and data on their new cars, identifying defects, issues and needed improvements to make them more reliable. You don't want to be their Guinea pig, especially when you have to pay through the nose for the privilege.

"But… if I don't buy the car from a dealer, I can't get the EXTENDED WARRANTY!": These are yet another scam to get more money out of the uninformed buyer and give them a false sense of security, regardless of whether the extended warranty is for a new OR used vehicle. Consumer reports show that in the U.S. 55% of owners who purchased an extended warranty did not use it at all during the lifetime of the policy, notwithstanding the median price for such extended warranties was over $1,200.[26] And of those who did successfully use their extended warranty policies to cover the cost of repairs, the majority still had to spend more for the coverage than they saved in repair costs.[27]

Extended warranties also often come with exclusions by mileage or years of ownership. One wonders if those numbers are calculated very carefully to increase the odds that by the time you actually need to exercise the warranty, it's out of the coverage period. Not saying this is true, just a question worth pondering...

It's not uncommon that the warranty company will claim some insurance exclusion in the contract, for example, that the vehicle had pre-existing damage which triggered a policy exclusion that gets them off the hook and "you should have read the fine print buddy," after hours of wasted time arguing with them of course.

These policies are filled with exclusions, and often times it's who can prove what, the insurance company can simply claim the policy holder didn't change the oil enough or was negligent in maintenance of the vehicle, and you're arguing with an insurance company whose business model is based on this setup, do you really think they'll sell you an insurance policy that results in you getting more value than they do? And what are you going to do, spend tens of thousands of dollars and possibly years fighting their staff attorneys in court? Just save the $1,200 and invest it to get interest and use it when the day comes that you need to make repairs.

---

26 "Extended Car Warranties: An Expensive Gamble – The majority of buyers never use the coverage" *Consumer Reports* (Feb 28, 2014), consumerreports.org/extended-warranties/extended-car-warranties-an-expensive-gamble/

27 *Ibid*

NEVER BUY A USED CAR
FROM A DEALERSHIP OR A CAR LOT!

So, you've decided to save a ton of money buying a used car instead of a new car? Great! Now you're just going to head on down to your local dealer's used car lot and.........STOP! DROP! AND ROLL! Buying a used car from a dealership or used car lot is like being a sheep and walking up to a pack of wolves asking them "what's for dinner?" the answer is YOU!

The used car dealership bought the used car from a private individual and HAS TO sell it for more than they bought it for in order to make a profit. And not just any profit, they need enough profit off of each used car to collectively enable them to cover:

- their monthly lease or mortgage payments for the real estate the dealership sits on;

- taxes;

- electricity;

- utilities;

- business, inventory, and liability insurance;

- legal costs;

- the salaries of their non-commissioned employees or partial commission employees;

- profits for the commissioned salespeople;

- marketing expenses such as radio, internet, and television advertising;

- and enough profits after all these and other expenses are covered to incentivize ownership to continue incurring risk and trading their time managing the business.

Basically, by purchasing a used car from a car lot, you're introducing an army of middle men who need to have the price you buy that used car for increased considerably from what they bought it for. This is why most used car lots will sell their cars anywhere from two to four times what they actually paid for the vehicle, so you're paying two to four times (200% to 400%) more than the used vehicle's actual market value.

Moreover, being professional salespeople who move a lot of product, they know which makes and models sell and are willing to wait until they can get as much as they can, meaning you aren't going to "get one up" on the dealer, no matter how clever you think you are. Also, the used car dealers will have a lot of back-end extra fees they don't tell you about until it's too late. Tax, title, license, extra handling fees like getting the registration in your name, "dealer prep costs," and the list of creatively named hidden fees goes on.

Instead of all this, why not just cut out the army of middle men and buy it from the private individual seller yourself? By purchasing your used car from a private individual, you're doing what the used dealer does, you're taking advantage of the fact that many people who sell their used cars are often in a hurry to get money, as cars are one of the few big ticket consumer items most people own that they can quickly get cash for. It's much easier to do in today's digital economy than in times past, with sites like Facebook Marketplace, eBay Motors, CarGurus, Craigslist, Autotrader, and so forth.

"But... the used car dealer has a Certified used car sticker!": These are useless. I have talked to multiple mechanics on this issue, and they've all found all kinds of problems with "Certified used" or "Certified pre-owned" cars. While this used dealer "certification" is useless, the other sticker they put on the used car that says "As is, no warranty" is not useless, nor is the legal document they have you sign acknowledging the sale is an "As is, no warranty" sale, absolving them of having to help you when your used vehicle starts having problems.

Vehicle History Reports

Any vehicle history reports cannot be relied on when purchasing a used car. I've spoken to a number of mechanics who have all said they've come across many vehicles with all kinds of problems that supposedly had clean vehicle history reports, sometimes becoming apparent when the mechanic puts the car up on a jack and inspects the underbody, noticing obvious collision damage and even parts being ripped off.

One mechanic said he had bought a used car from a collision shop, which the shop admitted it had been in an auto wreck prior to the body work, and he ended up crashing the car himself, sent it to a different collision shop, and after the work had been done, for science he pulled the history report and it said the car had never been in a wreck before!

THE PREPURCHASE INSPECTION – THE ONLY WAY TO PROTECT YOURSELF

Have your own qualified independent mechanic (whom you trust) inspect the vehicle before purchasing. This is the only real certification and vehicle history report you can rely on. The mechanic can put the vehicle up on a jack, inspect the under-body for evidence of prior wreckage, water damage, and rust if the car was in a maritime environment; inspect the engine, look for parts that have been replaced, test to see if it's an oil burner, test drive it (with seller's written permission) to see how it handles, and so forth.

If you don't have a mechanic that you trust, one trick is to go down to your local AutoZone or similar parts retailer, befriend the store manager and ask if he can recommend a mechanic that he trusts and that does good work. Often times the employ-ees of those stores are car guys and will know of a really skilled mechanic who does work for them.

That's how I found my favorite mechanic, and don't be alarmed if the mechanic may have their shop in a rougher part of town, that's inconsequential if they do good work, have good reviews on their business and can be trusted. Often, they will be in a lower-income area to save on rent. Or you can head on over to your local auto dealership sitting on prime real estate and get robbed blind. But seriously, stay far, far away from dealership mechanics.

Pay the mechanic a flat fee for inspecting the used vehicle you're considering buying when you meet with the seller, and make sure to iterate that you'd like a very thorough review of the vehicle the same way the mechanic would inspect it if he was personally buying it for himself to use as his primary means of transportation.

Have your mechanic put in writing (preferably in an email) all the problems it has, take pictures, and the parts and labor costs for any repairs, and which repairs are necessary and which are simply luxury repairs (such as fixing sensors or trivial things that don't affect the vehicles ability to get from point A to point B). One of my previous SUV's four-wheel drive was broken, but

I live in Florida which is pretty flat, so there's no need for that feature, which would have cost around $4,000 to fix between parts and labor.

Yes it costs money every time you have your mechanic inspect a used vehicle you're considering purchasing, but let them know from the onset that you're probably going to look at multiple vehicles, you'll use them each time and for any necessary repairs on the vehicle you buy. Compare mechanics when it comes to the price they charge for a pre-purchase inspection. As of 2020, $100 to $150 is a reasonable range for a very thorough inspection.

If you end up having 4 cars inspected and paying $600, that might sound like a lot, but not if you avoid buying a car that's a lemon or has thousands of dollars needed in repairs (which you may be able to use to **re-trade**, that is, have your mechanic put in writing the repairs needed based on the inspection, and use that to negotiate with the seller to lower their price).

STAY AWAY FROM CAR AUCTIONS UNLESS...

The problem with car auctions is the cars are usually sold "as is, no warranty," and it's not uncommon for there to be lemons and cars with all sorts of problems. Many auctions won't give buyers enough time to have their mechanics perform a thorough inspection of the vehicles prior to purchase. You'll be competing with pros who understand this risk and show up with enough cash to buy five or more cars at a time.

For these pros, because of scale, if they get a lemon or two, they're still making profit because they're selling the other 3 cars for 2-4 or more times what they paid for each unit, and the lemons for scrap, so they can eat two lemons no problem. But as an individual consumer, you're looking for one used car to be your means from getting from point A to point B, you cannot afford this if this isn't a side hustle of yours.

The exception to this rule is if the car auction will allow you to bring your own mechanic and perform a pre-purchase inspection prior to any financial commitment. In that case, depending on the auction house, you can find some amazing deals. My friend Randall bought a Ford Crown Vic with around 120,000 miles on It for $1200, and after repairs and other expenses, paid a total of around $2,300 (in 2020 dollars).

FINANCING VEHICLES IS A COMPLETE RIP-OFF

First off, this shouldn't even be an issue if you follow the previous advice to NEVER buy a new vehicle, and NEVER buy a used vehicle from a dealership or car lot. If you follow those two previous tips, you realistically shouldn't ever be in a position to finance a used vehicle you purchase from a private seller (yes it's still possible if you went out of your way to do this and found a seller willing to accept a note, but this is not realistic for a $9,000 used Toyota; most private individual sellers just need cash).

However, just in case you weren't convinced, financing vehicles is a terrible idea, unless they're for your business, and I don't mean going around looking at houses as a real estate agent and want to impress your clients type of business, I mean like you own a trucking distribution company or something of that nature and need a fleet of trucks for your drivers and it makes more economical sense to lease or finance. But for personal vehicles, it's a no-brainer that financing a vehicle is a form of financial masochism.

By using financing to purchase your vehicle, you're borrowing money from someone who's borrowed money to buy those cars, because most dealers use financing from a bank or a credit union to purchase their inventory, so you can count on paying a higher interest rate than the dealer paid when they financed the car you're now trying to finance...the whole thing is ridiculous.

As discussed in chapter 7, when consumer goods like cars and homes are financed, the buyer is paying more than the purchase price due to interest. And in the case of a vehicle, the buyer is paying interest to own a consumer good that depreciates in value by 10% to 15% per year, and worst of all, at a purchase price that is usually 2 to 5 times (or more) the cost of a reliable used vehicle, when that reliable used vehicle will do the same job of getting you from point A to point B as the brand new vehicle that's 5 times the price.

Don't be Fooled by the 0% APR or Low Financing Interest Rate – these are financing tricks used as a sales tactic to make over-priced inventory more psychologically palatable. They'll simply raise the sticker price of the car to offset the cheap financing, just another way to get suckers to overpay for cars.

LEASING VEHICLES IS A SOPHISTICATED RENT-TO-OWN SCAM

The first part of the leasing (also known as fleecing) scam is when the salesman or PR piece tries to convince you leasing is cheaper than owning, they're comparing the cost to lease a car with the cost to purchase a *brand-new car*. Right there we have a major problem, as we've already seen, it's not a good idea to buy a brand-new car when it's going to depreciate between 10% and 15% per year, and you can buy a reliable used car for a fraction of the price and invest the difference. But let's see an example of what the leasing scam looks like.

After doing some research, I found a 2020 luxury sedan, which has a sticker price of $39,600, and the cost to lease is $358 per month for 36 months with $3,999 due at signing (DAS) and a residual value (how much banks believe your vehicle is worth at the end of the lease) of around 62% (a realistic figure for this make and model sedan). This means at the end of the lease, if the lessee wants to purchase the car, they'll have to pony up 62% of the car's sticker price, in this example 62% of $39,900 which is $24,738.

Let's see what this looks like for people who are continually leasing and upgrading models at the end of their lease (Scenario A), and for people who buy the car when their lease is up (Scenario B), over a period of 12 years. We'll assume all repairs are covered during the lease term and the same terms and prices for each successive lease for demonstration purposes.

Scenario A: Lease New Vehicle Every 36 Months

DAS	$3,999	Year 5	$4,296	DAS	$3,999
Year 1	$4,296	Year 6	$4,296	Year 10	$4,296
Year 2	$4,296	DAS	$3,999	Year 11	$4,296
Year 3	$4,296	Year 7	$4,296	Year 12	$4,296
DAS	$3,999	Year 8	$4,296		
Year 4	$4,296	Year 9	$4,296		

TOTAL COST FOR 12 YEARS $67,548

Note at the end of the 12-year period in Scenario A, **the consumer is left without a vehicle** as her 36-month term was up at end of year 12, and will again need to decide whether to lease or purchase a vehicle, or opt for an alternative mode of transportation such as ride-sharing, and so forth.

Scenario B: The consumer leases the new 2020 luxury sedan and buys the vehicle at the end of a 36-month lease for a residual value of 62% of its sticker price (this means this vehicle depreciated by 12.6% per year, which is a reasonable estimate for this make and model), and we'll assume $0 in maintenance for the 36 month lease period, and an average annual repair cost of $468 (also a reasonable estimate) for each year after that, which comes to a total estimated repair cost of $4,212 (years 4-12), as this sedan is a very reliable make and model that people often own for many decades without any major repairs needed.

Scenario B: Lease and Purchase at End of 36 Months

Year 1 DAS	Year 1	Year 2	Year 3	Lease Buyout	Years 4-12 Repair Costs
$3,999	$4,296	$4,296	$4,296	$24,738	$4,212

TOTAL COST FOR 12 YEARS
$45,837

As you can see, scenario A cost our hypothetical consumer approx. $67,548 over a 12-year period AND left our consumer vehicle-less at the end of the 12-year period, and scenario B only $45,837 and with a vehicle. Clearly, buying the car at the end of the 36-month lease and maintaining it every year after is cheaper than continually leasing. But what about when we compare Scenario B to Scenario C, which is to skip the fleecing all together and buy a reliable used vehicle for a fraction of the price?

Scenario C: I found the same make and model luxury sedan, but used from 2009 as opposed to the newer 2020 version, for sale by a private individual for $9,498 with 72,000 miles on it, and we'll assume you'll have paid your mechanic $500 between the prepurchase inspection and repairs, for a round total of $10,000.

Before you say "yea but it already has 72,000 miles on it so you won't get near the longevity with the 2009 version as you would in Scenario B with the 2020 version" know that this make of car (yes it's Japanese) frequently makes it to the 350,000 mile mark and beyond with proper care and maintenance, so the 72,000 mileage is likely negligible over a 12 or even 20 year time period, unless you do an insane amount of driving.

Scenario C: Buy a Reliable Used 2009 Model

Purchase Price + inspection & repairs	Years 2-12 Repair Costs
$10,000	$5,148

TOTAL COST FOR 12 YEARS
$15,148

Here we see Scenario C is clearly the most financially intelligent way to go and shows why leasing is just another scam to get people to overpay for vehicles, in this case, the consumer in Scenario B overpaid by 303% or by 3 times as much as the consumer in Scenario C who bought this luxury sedan used. The consumer in Scenario C has an extra $30,689 in his pocket to invest, all the while driving the SAME MAKE AND MODEL SEDAN, just older and with some light mileage on it.

Note we haven't even taken into consideration insurance costs, which would obviously be lower for the used vehicle that had a purchase price that's ¼ the sticker price of the new leased vehicle, and would increase the total costs of both leasing options compared to buying used, in which the insurance costs would be significantly less (33% to 50% less). So, if we include insurance costs into the comparisons, Scenario C would be even MORE attractive.

Finally, leases have all kinds of limits and hidden ways to extract additional fees out of the duped consumer, such as **mileage limits** where if you go over the mileage limit for that year, you have to pay an additional amount per mile which can add up. In addition, many leases will say they only allow for **normal wear and tear**, which is subjective and opens the consumer to all sorts of additional repair costs when they turn the car in if they don't go along with the salespersons suggestion to buy the car or lease another one (i.e. if the consumer tries to escape the fleecing).

PICK YOUR USED VEHICLE WISELY

Just about any vehicle can make it to 300,000 miles or more if you don't mind spending a small fortune on major repairs, especially putting in a new engine or transmission. However, this usually doesn't make economic sense. If you have a car with 150,000 miles on it and need to replace the engine and the total cost (parts and labor) will be $7,500. At that point, it will likely be cheaper to just buy a new car with half the mileage on it. In these instances, the vehicle is so worn out it's more expensive to repair than replace.

One way to avoid this is to choose a make and model vehicle that's known to make it to 300,000 miles and beyond without needing expensive repairs like having to put in a new engine or transmission. The longer mileage you can get out of your vehicle and not need such major repairs, the more money you save compared to most people who switch out their cars every 6 to 10 years. If you can get 12-20 years out of your vehicle, you will have saved a boatload of cash.

Top 5 cars known to be able to exceed 300,000 miles without needing major repairs:

1. **Toyota Corolla** – an added bonus with these is that there are so many floating on the market, parts are incredibly cheap.

2. **Honda Civic** – same benefits as the Corolla.

3. **Lexus ES** – These are notorious to get incredible mileage without major repairs.

4. **Ford Crown Victoria** – arguably the most reliable model sedan Ford has ever produced, there's a reason these were/are used by police and sheriff's departments around the U.S.

5. **Ford F150 pickup** – While these obviously burn more gas than a smaller sedan, for those needing a truck for work or towing, they are excellent vehicles known to last for a very long time. The only weak link can be the automatic transmission; however, Ford makes re-manufactured automatic transmissions that are inexpensive, so unlike most vehicles, installing a new transmission on an F150 is more economical than purchasing a whole new vehicle.

LOOK FOR USED CARS WITH ROAD RASH

In order for a car to be able to have a really long useful life without needing major expensive repairs, in addition to regular maintenance and being of a make and model with high-end manufacturing like the aforementioned 5 models, it's preferable if the vehicle had a majority of its miles come from highway driving.

So, when you're looking at purchasing a used car, you want to screen for cars with the tell-tale signs of having been driven extensively on the highway. Specifically, you're looking for vehicle road rash, a mechanic term used to describe scratches and markings that spoil your vehicle's paintwork around the hood and bumper, which appear as nasty looking chips, scratches, peeling, and small little impact dents on the front hood where the highway rocks impacted. The more the merrier.

Why is this? Because highway driving only puts about 10% of the wear that town/city driving puts on a vehicle's engine. Driving at 65 mph gives significantly better airflow to cool the engine than driving at slower town or city speeds, and the oil is lubricating better and prevents buildup in the engine because its burning fast and getting rid of impurities.

What's the main lesson here?

- BUY DIRECT FROM PRIVATE INDIVIDUALS;

- RELIABLE USED CARS THAT ARE KNOWN TO EXCEED 300,000 MILES WITHOUT MAJOR REPAIRS;

- PAY IN FULL, NO FINANCING OR LEASING;

- AFTER YOUR TRUSTED INDEPENDENT MECHANIC PERFORMS A PREPURCHASE INSPECTION;

- AND HOLD ONTO THE CAR FOR AS MANY YEARS AS YOU CAN UNTIL THE VEHICLE IS SO WORN OUT IT'S MORE EXPENSIVE TO REPAIR THAN REPLACE;

- INVEST ALL THE EXTRA MONEY YOU SAVED;

- REPEAT.

ADDITIONAL VEHICLE TIPS

1. <u>Do you really need all-wheel drive (AWD)?</u> You don't need AWD or four-wheel drive (4WD) if you live in an area that doesn't have a lot of snow, is relatively flat and has decent roads. By paying for AWD or 4WD in those circumstances, you're throwing money away, as these vehicles are more expensive, weigh more, have more friction, get worse gas mileage and are more expensive to repair because the mechanic has to move a bunch of stuff that gets in the way of many common repairs, such as repairing the starter.

2. <u>Do you really need a 6- or 8- cylinder vehicle?</u> 4-cylinder engines are perfectly fine if you're not attending illegal street races on the weekends and will save you a lot of money by getting better gas mileage. The only caveat to this is the "turbo charged" 4-cylinder vehicles, I've been told by a trusted mechanic to stay away from those for reasons beyond the scope of this book.

3. <u>If you need a vehicle for towing, consider getting a diesel engine</u>, as these are superior for that kind of work.

4. <u>Spend time researching the used vehicle you're considering purchasing to avoid buying a bad make and model.</u> It's easy to look up on the internet consumer reviews and repair history of the make and models you're considering, to see which ones were well built and during what years, and which ones are going to be repair nightmares. Another part of this is looking at the re-sale value of the car you're considering purchasing. If the re-sale value is

significantly lower than the MSRP, there's a reason for this, it means it's probably a crummy model.

5. Don't fall in love with a particular car – be willing to walk away from a deal with a private seller if after your mechanic completes the prepurchase inspection the purchase price and cost of repairs exceeds what you want to pay (especially if it starts to exceed $9,000 in 2020 dollars).

6. Don't be in a hurry to buy a vehicle – spend some time finding the best deal. In the meantime, if you have no way to get around, consider ride-sharing, borrow a car from friends or family or hitch rides with friends and family until you get the deal you want.

7. Drive your vehicle into the ground – most wealthy people buy used cars and keep them anywhere from 12 to 20 years, keep them well maintained, make repairs when necessary and drive them until the cost to repair no longer makes economic sense and they are forced to buy another used car. In contrast, the average person who is not wealthy changes cars every 6 years.

8. Choose White or Black if you anticipate reselling the vehicle in the future due to moving to an area where you'll need a different kind of vehicle or maybe not need a vehicle at all. White is the most popular car color in the U.S., compromising 35% of all vehicles sold, followed by black with 17% of vehicles sold, thus, those colors will make your vehicle more **liquid**.

9. Don't get suckered into violating the rule of staying away from car dealerships because you want better technology and gadgetry. You can easily have a good independent

mechanic install all the tech and gadgets you could want in your used vehicle, from the LCD screen, front and rear cameras, sound systems, nitrous boosters, license plate rotator, caltrops, machine gun turrets… all for a fraction of what you'll pay when you buy a vehicle from a dealership.

10. <u>Don't get suckered into violating the rule of staying away from car dealerships because of their marketing tricks,</u> such as "huge sales! offers and discounts!" because of "December sales" or "needing to get rid of last year's models" or "going out of business sale!" or whatever. It's all just another trick to dupe naïve suckers into going to the auto dealership and grossly overpaying for vehicles compared to what they could buy them for used from a private individual.

11. <u>AVOID DEALERSHIP/NATIONAL MECHANIC SHOPS</u> — Let's say you need to replace an alternator and the part for your car happens to cost $60 at AutoZone, and the labor costs $75 with your **independent private local mechanic**, a total of $135 (in 2020 dollars). If you walk into a dealership mechanic or big brand mechanic, I've personally found that they'd want to charge me 5 to 8 times that. In that scenario, what would be a $135 repair job between parts and labor costs using an independent mechanic, could end up costing between $675 and $1,080. Don't believe me? Test it yourself next time you have an issue and need a repair, and see what the total price differential would be between the two. You'll be shocked.

12. <u>Take gas mileage seriously</u> – In 2018, the average American spent around $1,968 per year on gas and motor oil, that's

close to $19,680 over 10 years.[28] If you can get away with a small sedan, and say you drive an average of 15,000 miles per year, you can lower your gas costs by as much as 33% from what you'd pay if you were driving a large sedan, potentially saving tens of thousands of dollars over the years. When buying a used car, try to get a model that has the best gas mileage for the intended use. Obviously, if you need a big truck for your work, then work will trump gas mileage and you'll just need to bite the bullet. But many people are driving way more vehicle than they need and losing money to fuel costs, money that could be invested and earning interest.

13. <u>"I'm a man and I'm worried if I don't have an expensive car I won't get an attractive girlfriend"</u> – only gold diggers who you can never trust will care about what kind of car you drive, so this is just another plus as you can filter these girls out by driving an inexpensive used car. Girls worth your time care about how you make them feel when you're together.

14. <u>You're not going to beat the house</u> – buying or leasing a vehicle from an auto dealership, new or used, is like going to a high stakes poker table in Las Vegas and thinking you're going to beat the house. There's a reason they can afford to hire all those employees and pay to keep the lights on and the free drinks flowing. In the end, the house always wins, it has to by design or it goes bankrupt.

---

28 Megan Elliott, "How Much Money Does the Average American Spend a Year? What the Typical Person Pays for Food, Gas and More" *Cheatsheet.com* (Sep 17, 2018), cheatsheet.com/money-career/how-much-money-does-the-average-american-spend-a-year-what-the-typical-person-pays-for-food-gas-and-more.html/

CHAPTER 10

"JUST GET THAT DEGREE"

Education is hands down the most important endeavor you can undertake in your life. Unfortunately, the word education is often misconstrued to be synonymous with a degree from a liberal arts college or university.

Such a "formal" education can end up being one of the biggest financial mistakes of your child's adult life if the degree doesn't actually increase their post-graduation wage-earning ability enough to offset both the tuition expense and the four-year time commitment.

Even if college were FREE, it still may be the inferior life choice in terms of their development as an intelligent self-sufficient adult and their future financial and career success. Whether college is right or not for your child will depend on a number of variables, including their desired career path, which will be discussed further into the chapter.

One of my previous real estate clients came from a depressed area of New York City and he started from the bottom picking up cigarette butts in building parking lots. He ultimately befriended and then apprenticed under one of the building's owners, a successful commercial real estate investor in his time.

This successful investor mentored and taught my client the knowledge and skills of property management and investing, which he used to go on his own and buy, fix, manage and flip small apartments working his way up to large commercial buildings, eventually building a portfolio of apartment complexes, hotels, and shopping centers collectively worth over two hundred and fifty million dollars (in 2019 dollars). Is this fellow uneducated because he doesn't have a college diploma hanging on his wall?

I've also met graduates with finance degrees and MBAs that are one paycheck away from broke. Financially, some of these people are hundreds of thousands of dollars in the hole in terms of undergraduate and graduate student loans.

All the coffee shop baristas, grocery store clerks, ride-sharing app drivers, retail and restaurant workers well into their mid and late 20s and 30s making close to minimum wage who took $40,000 to $100,000+ of student loans to get a diploma from a four-year liberal arts college, as well as graduate degrees, how many of their lives might have turned out differently had they instead apprenticed under a successful business person like my former client?

What about if they attended a trade school to learn a specialized skill in high demand like HVAC, electrician, specialized welder, or plumber, and wisely saved and invested their income?

If you're one of these college graduates with a mountain of student debt, working a low wage job and barely making ends meet, don't worry, as long as you work hard and employ the strategies and hacks in this book, we will undo the damage as quickly as humanly possible.

UNIVERSITY MAY STILL BE A GOOD CHOICE

The point of this chapter is not to say getting a college degree is never a good choice. A college degree may very well be the best choice depending on what the desired career is. Doctors, veterinarians, and some entry-level jobs in STEM (science, technology, engineering, and mathematics) require a college degree. That said, many jobs in technology do not require a college degree, just skill and trade certifications. Oh, and let's not forget, employment in academia requires many academic credentials.

The point of this chapter is to illuminate the truths behind this momentous decision, including the pros and cons, so you can make an educated decision on the matter using the Cost-Benefit Analysis covered in Chapter 3. Remember, wealthy people don't do things because they were told to, or because everyone else is doing it. In fact, they get suspicious when everyone else is doing it. Oftentimes that's a bad sign. Rather, wealthy people do things because they've logically thought through the decision, weighing the costs, benefits, risks, and probabilities.

In order to do that, we must shred the limiting belief that society preaches as incontrovertibly true that you or your children or grandchildren HAVE TO GO TO COLLEGE in order to be successful adults.

Investors and Lenders Love College!

I know this chapter will be a hard pill to swallow for a lot of readers, as it goes against decades of social programming, academic public relations (PR) campaigns and Hollywood propaganda. After reviewing the data, some readers who have already fallen victim to the college trap may feel an emotional jolt, that being the sense that they've been lied to and scammed (they have).

Notwithstanding, I have a moral obligation to present the truth, because the truth will set you free. I won't repeat false narratives promoted by the mainstream media. This narrative benefits the big tax-free business of academia and the lovely folks on Wall Street who profit off of student debt by securitizing and selling it as Student Loan Asset-Backed Securities (SLABS) to investors who are quite comfortable with these debt instruments higher yield in comparison to U.S. treasuries, and with the fact that student loans are extremely difficult to get discharged in bankruptcy, and generally will be carried by the borrower until the day they pay them off with interest and any collection fees, or until the day they die.

Multi-Decade Debt Sentence

The average student loan balance per borrower in the U.S. in 2018 was approximately $35,359.[29] The average length of repayment for student loan debt based on a study performed by the One Wisconsin Institute is 21.1 years.[30] Thus, if you or your children require student loans to pay for college, the average is a twenty or more year debt sentence. A student who graduates when they're 22 is statistically likely to carry that student debt until they're around 43 years old.

These data points indicate that the post-graduation wages available to the average college graduate are nowhere near commensurate with the costs. Do you think real estate investors get rich by retrofitting a building with upgrades (like stainless steel kitchen appliances in the units, for example) that have a 21-year payback period? I don't think so...try a 1- to 6-year payback period maximum.

This means a host of sacrifices on the part of the student borrower; it means for 21 years you can expect to have a large chunk of your income, anywhere from $200-$500 or more every single month, siphoned to pay off the interest and principal on

29 Daniel Kurt, "Student Loan Debt: 2019 Statistics and Outlook," *Investopedia* (Nov 15, 2019), investopedia.com/student-loan-debt-2019-statistics-and-outlook-4772007

30 Mike Browne, "Twenty to Life: Higher Education Turning Into Multi-Decade Debt Sentence," *One Wisconsin Institute* (June 24, 2014), onewisconsinnow.org/press/twenty-to-life-higher-education-turning-into-multi-decade-debt-sentence/

those student loans, money you could have otherwise used to build a nest egg to purchase a home or invest and grow your net worth. It means postponing being able to enter the middle class and, in many ways, postponing being an adult.

In terms of family, it means you and your significant other, who may also be saddled with loans, will have to postpone buying a home or having children, possibly for decades. Student loans are basically structured so they are never paid off in any time-frame imagined by the borrower. The lenders WANT the student borrower to carry that debt for decades. The longer the term, the more money the borrower will give to the lender.

The day you graduate college your loan payment schedule kicks in. For most college graduates, they cannot immediately start paying back the principal and interest payments, so they postpone it, and as an example, if you graduate with $40,000 worth of debt on your balance, it will no longer be $40,000, now that you've postponed, it will be $43,000, and the interest will continue to roll and grow, resulting in the student carrying the debt for much longer and paying more than they anticipated when they (and their parents) signed and co-signed the promissory note.

In fact, the student loan crisis, specifically the massive student loan bubble and glut of college graduates not being able to secure wages high enough to repay those loans, has become so bad that some graduates are fleeing the U.S. in the hopes of starting a new debt-free life elsewhere.[31] Unfortunately, most countries will not help them escape those U.S. loans unless they use cash for all transactions. This is harder to do in today's digitalized economy than many people realize.

---

31 Andrew Pentis, "Can You Really Get Rid of Student Loans by Leaving the Country?" *Student Loan Hero* (Dec 20, 2018), studentloanhero.com/featured/how-to-get-out-of-student-loan-debt-leave-country/

Also, if the student's family co-signed on the loans, the lenders will be able to go after the expat's family for repayment with interest. Moreover, the expat could lose any U.S. financial privileges, including having any wages earned if they moved back to the states garnished, and penalizations by the IRS, destruction of credit score (not as big of a deal if you read this book), and so on.

FIELD EXPERIMENT

I usually make a point when I go to the grocery store, take an uber ride, or get food at a restaurant, to ask the cashier, waitress or driver if they went to college. Many times, these individuals are in their 20s and 30s. More often than not the answer is yes, they received four-year degrees, often from mid-tier universities with expensive tuitions, and in a wide variety of disciplines like business administration, economics, accounting, biology, marketing, graphic design, linguistics, communications, political science, philosophy, etc. Sometimes they'll also have graduate degrees. Try it yourself for the next few weeks when you go out. You might be surprised.

Peter Schiff, CEO of Euro Pacific Capital, Inc., did the same field experiment I do, only he has it on video. In the video, he's walking around Bourbon Street in New Orleans interviewing adults in their 20s and 30s working obviously low-wage jobs, asking them if they attended college, what their majors were, and how much student debt they have.

- One lady's job was to hold a sign outside of a retail store that says "free admission." She has two undergraduate degrees in mathematics and evolutionary biology, and her graduate degree is in evolutionary biology. She stated she had about $25,000 of student loans and that she "lucked out";

- Another lady is a stripper that said she went to a Virginia state university and majored in physical education, and had $90,000 worth of student loans;

- One interviewee is a bicycle delivery man who majored in history and English;

- Another graduated in 2003 in the field of robotics and was working as a strip club bouncer.

- Another lady went to graduate school for neuroscience and now drives a bicycle taxi.

If you search "Peter Schiff: Is a college degree worth the cost? You decide," you'll find the video and can watch for yourself.

"JUST GET THAT DEGREE"

"Just get that degree" or the variation "just get that piece of paper" is an antiquated trope I hear frequently, usually from older people giving advice to their children, grandchildren, younger cousins, nieces, or nephews. The logic goes as follows: if you don't have a degree, because everyone else has a degree, you won't even be considered for employment. "Just get that degree" so you won't be at a major disadvantage from other job candidates.

Riddle me this Batman, if everyone else has a degree, why would having a degree matter? If it's so common it's now become almost inconsequential in most careers.

Wouldn't spending a few weeks studying and practicing sales (Jordan Belfort's book *Way of the Wolf: Straight Line Selling* is an excellent start), or a few months getting trade certified, or finding a successful person to mentor under, exponentially increase your odds for attaining employment in comparison to having a piece of paper everyone else has?

It's helpful to understand where this myth that having a degree is a competitive boost in the job market comes from. It comes from truth. This myth used to not be a myth, it used to be true. In the 1970s, 1980s, and even early 1990s, a college degree actually stood out against competing applicants for employment. Why? Because not everyone and their cat had one.

In 1980, around 49% of U.S. high school graduates enrolled in college after graduation.[32] In 2016, roughly 70% of high school graduates enrolled in college in October of 2016,[33] which is a **43% increase**...

Remember, scarcity is a major factor when determining value. Water has very little value if you live in an area where you can turn on your sink and the water will flow for days; but if you're stranded in the middle of the Sahara Desert, at some point you might literally be willing to trade your left arm for a glass of water...

Do you really think when your child submits an application for employment in today's day and age, the mid-level manager responsible for hiring is going to look at the application, see they have a college degree and go "hey I found one! Hey guys, we have a college grad over here. Finally, let's get him in here pronto

32 Statista, "Percentage of U.S. high school graduates enrolling in college immediately after graduation 1980 and 2009, by income", (November, 2011), statista.com/statistics/222440/us-high-school-graduates-enrolling-in-college-after-graduation-by-income/

33 U.S. Bureau of Labor Statistics, "69.7 percent of 2016 high school graduates enrolled in college in October 2016", (May 22, 2017), bls.gov/opub/ted/2017/69-point-7-percent-of-2016-high-school-graduates-enrolled-in-college-in-october-2016.htm

before another company picks him up. This could really increase our bottom line!"

The same people who say "just get that degree" to younger people, when presented with this obvious fact that everyone having a degree relegates it to becoming almost inconsequential, will retort with something along the lines of "yeah, but that's why you have to have one. Because not having one automatically disqualifies you."

This is mostly false with respect to any kind of job you'd actually want your child to get (other than a doctor and a few other very specific fields). It is true that many menial low wage jobs today are now requiring college degrees, but most higher-income fields with advancement potential would rather see something unique or interesting, like apprenticing and having work experience, or the applicant having started their own business and achieved some success, even if it ultimately failed, but they learned valuable lessons and skills that make them a better worker, salesman and entrepreneur that can add value to the company's operations.

Also, most technology jobs, such as cybersecurity, coding, web design, networking, hardware and server maintenance, and so forth, could care less about a college degree. They care about demonstrable skill and trade certifications.

Be cognizant that some of the people who parrot the "just get that degree" platitude may also be saying this in part due to having the keeping up with the Joneses syndrome, if they're concerned with what their neighbors or friends might think since their children went to college. This is not a valid reason to go into massive student debt and sacrifice four years of your life.

Degree Value Deflation, Cost Inflation
According to a report analyzing 2016 Federal Reserve data, Americans between the ages of 25 to 34 with college degrees

and student debt have a median net worth of *negative* $1,900.[34] Remember, this figure was pre 2020 pandemic madness, when the economy was supposedly in the "good times" and at the "height of the economic recovery."

When this Federal Reserve data figure is considered in conjunction with the significant reduction in the scarcity of a college degree as evidenced by the 43% increase in the number of U.S. high school graduates enrolling in college between 1980 and 2016 (i.e., inflation of the number of degree holders in the marketplace), it becomes abundantly clear that the long term trend for the value of a college degree for one's employment income prospects is deflationary.

Despite this long-term deflation of the employment value of a college degree, the cost has risen precipitously. For example, the average total cost to attend a four-year private university from the years 1980-1983 would have been $72,450 (inflation adjusted to 2019 dollars). The average total cost to attend a four-year private university from the years 2015-2018 would have been $184,730 (inflation adjusted to 2019 dollars), or a 255% increase in real terms.

Likewise, the average total cost to attend a four-year public university from the years 1980-1983 would have been $32,590 (inflation adjusted to 2019 dollars). The average total cost to attend a four-year public university from the years 2015-2018 would have been $84,530 (inflation adjusted to 2019 dollars), or a 259% increase in real terms.[35]

---

34 Jillian Berman, "College graduates with student debt have depressing net worth," *Market-Watch* (April 19, 2018), nypost.com/2018/04/19/college-graduates-with-student-debt-have-depressing-net-worth/.

35 Michael B. Sauter, "Here's the average cost of college tuition every year since 1971", *USA Today* (May 18, 2019), usatoday.com/story/money/2019/05/18/cost-of-college-the-year-you-were-born/39479153

WHY THE MASSIVE RISE IN EDUCATION COSTS?

The real reason for this precipitous rise in the cost of college tuition has to do with something called the Bennett Hypothesis, coined after education secretary William J. Bennett authored an op-ed in the New York Times in 1987 titled *"Our Greedy Colleges"* in which he postulated that federal loan subsidies and the rising cost of tuition are inextricably linked, with an increase in the former necessarily resulting in an increase in the latter.[36]

As usual, more government interference in the free market, i.e. socialism, ends up hurting the very people they promise to protect, as well as the overall economy and the everyday consumer. Renowned American economist Milton Friedman put it best when he stated *"Many people want the government to protect the consumer. A much more urgent problem is to protect the consumer from the government."*

Henry Hazlitt covers this recurring problem of government interference in the economy in more depth in his seminal book *Economics in One Lesson*.

Rather than benefiting the consumer, government subsidizing of student loans really benefits a small minority of the population: academia, Wall Street, and the politicians using education as a speaking point to gain votes. Federal government (taxpayer) subsidizing of education and student loans is the primary reason we've seen ridiculous levels of tuition inflation over the past four decades.[37]

But for government interference, students wouldn't need loans in the first place, a part-time job could cover the cost of

---

36 William J. Bennett, "Our Greedy Colleges" *New York Times* (Feb 18, 1987), nytimes. com/1987/02/18/opinion/our-greedy-colleges.html

37 Preston Cooper, "How Unlimited Student Loans Drive Up Tuition" *Forbes* (Feb 22, 2017), forbes.com/sites/prestoncooper2/2017/02/22/how-unlimited-student-loans-drive-up-tuition/#34308b0652b6

tuition, something previous generations did before socialist poli-cies wrecked that opportunity.

When you subsidize something, you get more of it. More stu-dents apply to college, so schools raise tuition and use that money to attract even more students, hire more administrators, build big-ger buildings, engage in less efficient and more costly activity, all to attract more tax-subsidized money, and the cycle repeats.

Simultaneously, this government interference in academia has also *significantly* lowered the quality of education by taking away the free market monetary loss incentive colleges otherwise would have to provide an education that increases its students post-graduation ability to earn incomes sufficient to repay their loans, as those student loans are guaranteed by the federal gov-ernment (the American taxpayer).

Thus, colleges have no problem offering courses like sociol-ogy of pop culture, Harry Potter in America, film history, gen-der studies, multicultural and diversity studies, and hundreds of other nothing-burger courses that are a complete waste of time and money that do nothing to prepare these students to repay their loans or even be functioning adults in society beyond work-ing as a coffee barista or passing out protest flyers.[38]

Ideological Dangers of our Broken Educational System

The broken educational system neglects to teach two very cru-cial subjects for adulthood: personal finance and our God-given inalienable natural rights as affirmed by the U.S. Constitution. For those interested in this topic, search online for the Cashflow Ninja podcast "092: Edward G. Griffin Individualism vs Collectivism."

The Case Against Socialism by Dr. Rand Paul is another excel-lent bulwark against what's coming, as it's becoming increasingly

---

38 John Stossel, "Jordan Peterson vs. 'Social Justice Warriors'", *ReasonTV* (Jun 19, 2018), youtube.com/watch?v=jnJEEdp6W24

common to hear criticisms being levied against capitalism, especially from professors and their students. They exclaim that capitalism is not working for the masses. Those in the Austrian School of Economics know these people are totally ignorant of real-world economics outside of a classroom, or what capitalism even is.

There is a general consensus among those in the Austrian School of Economics that since 1913, year after year we've slowly but surely been whittling away at free-market capitalism, replacing it with big government socialism or fascism (there's no meaningful difference between the two, they're both different flavors of the same collectivist dog food that inevitably results in big government, loss of individual liberty, and the slow death of the economy).

This big government socialism does indeed only benefit a minority of special interest groups (what some call "crony capitalism") and their puppet politicians. This phenomenon isn't limited to the U.S., the central banking octopus has its tentacles all over the world. Every transaction to buy or sell a good or service involves fiat central banker currency on one side of the transaction.

If you have a Soviet-style central banking "authority" artificially manipulating the cost of debt and consequently the value of currency via what they call "monetary policy" (decree), rather than the cost of debt and value of currency being determined by free-market price discovery, that means half of *every* transaction in the economy to buy or sell goods and services is under socialism.

Politicians will call on their nation's central bank to implement this policy or that policy to affect employment levels and "price stability." This is textbook socialism, not capitalism. In a free-market capitalist society, employment levels and pricing of goods and services aren't manipulated or tinkered with by central planners, they're arrived at by free-market price discovery. This tinkering always ends up economically hurting the lower and middle classes, while benefiting a very small ultra-wealthy and politically connected minority.

So how is it then that capitalism is not working when our entire monetary system is socialist?

Capitalism also means as long as a business isn't infringing on another's person, liberty, or property, they are not forcibly shut down or their customer's behaviors forcibly altered "for your safety" ('Fur Ihre Sicherheit'). Some axioms of wise governance truly are immutable, like the ancient Chinese philosopher Lao Tzu's warning some 25 centuries ago: *"the more laws and restrictions there are, the poorer people become."* – Tao Te Ching, chapter 57.

The inefficient hand of central planners and government interfering with the free market economy (i.e., socialism) **always** has far-reaching unintended consequences that are harmful to the productivity and prosperity of the society as a whole.[39]

Our government has interfered so much in the economy that it has diminished any uplifting effects free-market capitalism could have had on our society. We've simply been masquerading as capitalist, and as a consequence we've discredited capitalism by not practicing it but pretending to, creating tinder for a resurgence of the historically catastrophic failed doctrines of socialism, communism, and fascism (which is just socialism with a capitalist veneer).[40]

If the same university professors decreeing that capitalism isn't working actually understood what capitalism is, they'd be saying "socialism/fascism/communism isn't working! We need more capitalism!" Presently, most people (especially academic professors and teachers) are unaware of the principles of the Austrian School of Economics or what capitalism is, and will continue to

---

39 Dr. Antony Davies & James R. Harrigan, "The Cobra Effect: Lessons in Unintended Consequences" *Foundation for Economic Education* (Sep 6, 2019), fee.org/articles/the-cobra-effect-lessons-in-unintended-consequences/

40 Sheldon Richman, "Fascism: Socialism with a Capitalist Veneer" *Foundation for Economic Education* (Mar 16, 2019), fee.org/articles/fascism-socialism-with-a-capitalist-veneer/

blame capitalism for the increasing disparity of wealth we're seeing today, demanding more socialism as the antidote; metaphorically, this is like trying to put out a fire by pouring gasoline on it.

Ayn Rand was asked in an interview in the late 1970s how she views the issues the U.S. faces. Her response: "the country would be destroyed by its philosophy, specifically by its universities...because they're teaching the kind of ideas that would necessarily have to lead to [its] destruction."

The philosophies she was referring to are collectivism (emphasizing the group over individual rights) and statism—a political system whereby the state has substantial centralized control over social and economic affairs enforced through authoritarian measures, the type of system Ayn Rand escaped from when she fled the Soviet Union in 1926.

"But the Statistics Show College Graduates Have Higher Incomes than Non-College Graduates!"

The general acceptance of this platitude is understandable given the steady stream of PR pieces that are put out every year pushing this narrative. Most people see these pop up on their news feed, briefly read the title or even the whole one-page article, and accept the narrative as truth, without asking any further questions, looking at the important nuances to the claims made, or investigating the primary sources used to support these articles' conclusions.

For example, CNN Business released an article in June of 2019 titled *"College grads earn $30,000 a year more than people with just a high school degree."* [41] Seeing this article, most parents would be left believing that sending their children to college will lead to their children having higher incomes than non-college graduates.

---

41 Anna Bahney, "College grads earn $30,000 a year more than people with just a high school degree", CNN Business (June 6, 2019), cnn.com/2019/06/06/success/college-worth-it/index.html

What they missed by not digging deeper is that the "new research" this article cites as the basis for its conclusion isn't new, it's based on data spanning FOUR DECADES from 1974 to 2014.[42] Of course, a large part of the data used would indicate college graduates have higher incomes; remember, a college degree used to have scarcity in the labor markets of the 1970s, 1980s, and even 1990s.

In addition to this glaring error to account for the scarcity variable, there's another point made in the Federal Reserve Bank of NY's periodical issue which is the basis for the CNN Business author's article, a point which is also not mentioned:

"By analyzing more than four decades of data, we are able to put the recent experience of college graduates-those with either a bachelor's degree or an associate's degree-into historical perspective. Our analysis reveals that the average wages of college graduates have been FALLING for the better part of a decade, with the pace of decline ACCELERATING after the Great Recession."[43]

So, in the Fed's own admission in the primary source that is the basis of that *CNN Business* article, the trend for average wages of college graduates has been FALLING for the better part of a decade.

Hhmmm, didn't see that in the lamestream media article painting college as the path to higher income. This article is just one example, every year dozens come out just like it.

---

42 Jaison R. Abel and Richard Deitz, "Do the Benefits of College Still Outweigh the Costs?" Federal Reserve Bank of New York Current Issues Volume 20, Number 3 (2014), newyorkfed.org/medialibrary/media/research/current_issues/ci20-3.pdf

43 *Ibid*

Jobs at Top Fortune 500 Companies Are
Beginning to No Longer Require College Degrees

Companies like Tesla, Google, Facebook, Apple, Airbnb, Oracle, Netflix, and others, are no longer requiring a four-year degree for many of their job positions.[44] There's a shift towards an emphasis on skills and experience over college degrees as these companies seek out top talent that will actually bring value to their organizations, not a piece of paper that says you sat through Marxist indoctrination camp.[45]

"College Isn't Just About Increasing Your
Employment Prospects. It's the Whole Experience"

Yea, college can be fun, but so can being a successful adult who doesn't struggle financially for the next three+ decades because of poor financial choices, like giving up four years of your time postponing entering the workforce and taking on $50,000 or $100,000+ of loans to do so.

If your children have or develop good social skills, charisma, and a little sense of adventure, they can make friends with people in their local community, such as in a work environment, church, or a local sports meetup like CrossFit, running, etc.

What Some of Today's Most Successful Entrepreneurs Think of College:

- **Mike Rowe** (Discovery Channel's series Dirty Jobs): "If we're lending money that ostensibly we don't have to kids who really have no hope of paying it back in order to train

---

44 Catey Hill, "You don't need a 4-year college degree for these high-paying jobs at Google, Apple, Netflix" *Market Watch* (Apr 17, 2019), marketwatch.com/story/you-dont-need-a-4-year-college-degree-for-these-high-paying-jobs-at-google-apple-netflix-2019-04-08

45 *Ibid*

them for jobs that clearly don't exist, I might suggest that we've gone around the bend [crazy] a little bit."

- **Kevin O' Leary** (Businessman, investor, co-host on Shark Tank, 2020 net worth $400 million): "We ask kids that are 16 to 18 year old to make hundred thousand dollar debt decisions when they go off to university, and they're not prepared for that, they don't know what they're getting themselves into, they just assume 'ok I'm going to pay four years of education at twenty-five thousand a pop, and when I come out the other side somehow I'll be able to pay it back,' that's not how life works anymore."

- **Elon Musk** (Founder and CEO of SpaceX, Tesla, and founder of X.com in 1999 which later became PayPal, 2020 net worth $42.5 billion): "There's no need even to have a college degree...at all...if somebody graduated from a great university that may be an indication they will be capable of great things, but it's not necessarily the case...if you look at people like...Larry Ellison, Steve Jobs, these guys didn't graduate from college, but if you had a chance to hire them, of course that would be a good idea."

- **Seth Godin** (Author and former dot com business executive): "The problem with most colleges is they are high school but with more binge drinking..."

- **Mark Cuban** (Entrepreneur, founder of Broadcast.com, owner of NBA Dallas Mavericks, co-host on Shark Tank, 2020 net worth $4.3 billion): "It's like the newspaper industry, more printing presses, more big buildings, makes us look grander...there's a point of diminishing returns in terms of what it's worth for a college education and how much debt you're willing to saddle yourself with."

- **Mark Zuckerberg** (Founder and CEO of Facebook, 2020 net worth $86.7 billion): "Let's face it: There is something wrong with our system when I can leave [Harvard] and make billions of dollars in ten years, while millions of students can't afford to pay off their loans, let alone start a business."[46]

"But I Went to College and It Made Me the Person I Am Today!"
When did you graduate? Was it before the year 2005? In addition to reviewing the statistics and performing in-field surveys of college graduates, it's also helpful to look at this paradigm shift through the lens of the exponential growth theory, which is used to explain a variety of concepts in a multitude of disciplines like mathematics, economics, physics, etc. This theory helps conceptualize why things that were true for very long periods of time can suddenly transition into no longer being true.

Exponential growth is essentially a pattern of data that correlates greater increases in the quantity or growth or rate of change of something (represented on the Y axis), with the passing of time (represented on the X axis), creating the curve of an exponential function.

For example, if a population of rabbits doubles every year starting with 2 by end of year (EOY) 1, the population would be 4 by EOY 2, 16 by EOY 3, 256 by EOY 4, 512 by EOY 5, and so on. In our example, this population of rabbits is growing exponentially to the power of 2 each year.

46 Catherine Clifford, "Mark Zuckerberg: Success comes from 'the freedom to fail,' so billionaires like me should pay you to do that", *CNBC* (May 26, 2017), cnbc.com/2017/05/25/mark-zuckerberg-on-success-billionaires-should-pay-you-fail.html

Often times, the rate of change will actually start out in a linear fashion, and eventually reach an inflection point, at which time the rate of change switches from being linear to exponential, rising up and creating what chartists would call a hockey stick pattern. In the below chart, the area in which a circle has been drawn encapsulates the inflection point at which what was once a linear rate of growth made that transition to exponential growth.

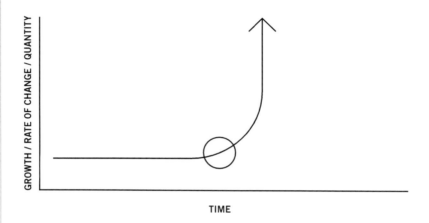

TIME

In the context of why a college degree could have been important for so long in terms of increasing the income potential for college graduates over non-college graduates, there's a key connection to the incredible amount of technological disruption in information storage and transmission.

Prior to the internet revolution, information was essentially guarded and hoarded by the ivy clad walls of academia and government agencies. However, once the internet gained widespread usage in the 1990s and information started pouring back and forth, this may have been the inflection point at which information transmission and evolution went exponential. Today you can hop onto YouTube university or BitChute and learn an incredible amount of information on almost any field imaginable.

Many companies have become fed up with the slow rate of growth of college curriculums to meet the modern labor market's demand for computer science and data analytics skills (as one example), so much so that groups like Microsoft, Linux and other employers have teamed up with Harvard and MIT to develop an online education system over traditional brick and mortar academia to meet their labor needs.

The polling company Gallup found that only 11% of business leaders would agree that higher education is effectively preparing students for work. The Manpower Group reported 40% of employers polled were experiencing difficulty in finding workers with the skills they require. McKinsey found in one of their surveys that 48% of business leaders globally are having a difficult time finding employees who specialize in computer analytics.[47]

Moreover, we've seen *exponential* disruption in many areas of the modern economy due to technological innovation, with entire industries being radically changed or displaced. The affect this has on the labor markets is huge. White-collar jobs like accounting, marketing, law, investment banking, insurance underwriting, stock brokerage, and many others, are becoming increasingly impacted by the use of narrow artificial intelligence (A.I.) by corporations to reduce their operating expenses and increase efficiency.

For example, the majority of lower and middle-class consumers of tax services today can simply log on to online tax prep websites which utilize narrow A.I. algorithms, without the need of an actual human accountant or tax preparer as was done throughout modern history.

Most marketing is now done by software algorithms ("algos"), and the highest paid "marketers" aren't graduates with marketing degrees, they're advanced software and web programmers who

47 Jon Marcus, "Impatient with Colleges, Employers Design Their Own Courses" *Wired* (Dec 18, 2017), wired.com/story/impatient-with-colleges-employers-design-their-own-courses/

have figured out how to design narrow A.I. to sell products based on machine learning of consumer behaviors. Or if we look at the stock exchange, it's run mostly by algos, with the traders on the floor really being software engineers monitoring the systems.

Legal research that used to take an attorney hours, days or weeks is being replaced in the U.S. and Canada by systems like Blue J Legal, where the basic facts and legal question is input, and in moments the A.I. software has searched through and analyzed millions of cases in its database and produces a tailored explanation sensitive to the facts. Currently, narrow A.I. recognition software can analyze MRI and CT scans faster and more accurately than the world's top radiologists, a job that for humans will become close to extinct. Soon, A.I. will diagnose cancer and a robot will perform the surgery, with a very small amount of remaining human oversight.

Notwithstanding all of this exponential evolution of the economy and consumer behaviors, academia as a whole is still churning out graduates with 20th century degrees into a 21st-century labor market.

"But a College Degree is an Insurance Policy My Child Will Have Some Level of Income"

If that were true, there wouldn't be 3.6 million college graduates in the U.S. living in poverty[48] and Americans between the ages of 25 to 34 with college degrees and student debt wouldn't have a median net worth of *negative* $1,900.[49]

---

48 Jillian Berman, "There are 3.6 million college graduates living in poverty", *Market Watch* (Sept. 23, 2018), marketwatch.com/story/there-are-36-million-college-graduates-living-in-poverty-2018-09-12

49 Jillian Berman, "College graduates with student debt have depressing net worth," *Market-Watch* (April 19, 2018), nypost.com/2018/04/19/college-graduates-with-student-debt-have-depressing-net-worth/

Degrees from Top 10 School's Still Have Scarcity

A degree from one of the top 10 universities like Yale, Harvard, MIT, Wharton, the University of Oxford, and so forth, still carry a degree of clout, particularly with alumni, and given the difficulty of admission and completion of the programs, it at least demonstrates that the graduate was, at one point in time, a highly intelligent, studious hard worker.

Top 10 university diplomas do still have scarcity and stand out against diplomas from the other more than 4,000 degree granting post-secondary institutions in the U.S. (and more than 3,300 in Europe), making it easier to at least get an audience with potential employers or business partners. If these top 10 universities dramatically increased enrollment, for any reason at all no matter what the justification, then you can count on their future employment value to drop. Of course, at the end of the day the only *real* success insurance is your child's ability to self-teach, their heart and their work ethic, even with a diploma from one of these elite institutions.

If your child has the ability to self-teach, a strong heart and work ethic, and after performing a cost-benefit analysis, they still think the cost is worth it for the career path they have in mind, then they should do everything they can to get into a top 10 university like the ones mentioned AND major in a field that actually has strong current and future market demand.

Opportunity Cost of a College Degree

The decision to attend a university is a major one, and should be viewed from the lens of opportunity cost. As you'll recall, this is a powerful mindset tool to use before making any major purchasing or investing decisions, and the definition of opportunity cost is *"the loss of potential gain from other alternatives when one alternative is chosen."*

What are the opportunity costs of getting a four-year college degree?

1.) **Time** – This is so incredibly valuable, especially when you're younger and have huge reserves of energy. By sacrificing four years to college, your child is foregoing alternate uses of their time, such as going to trade school or starting their own business. Bryan Caplan, a professor of economics at George Mason University, was interviewed by John Stossel on a special he did specifically on college, in which Caplan raised the following questions: "how many thousands of hours did you spend in classes studying subjects you never thought about again?...How many years should people be made to study stuff when the odds they'll ever utilize it are 1/100, or 1/1000?"[50]

2.) **Tuition Expense** – Unless your child is on a full-ride scholarship, either they will have to pay for their college degree, housing and books, in which case they'll likely have to take out student loans and give themselves a multi-decade debt sentence, or their parents will have to pay. Even if their parents are okay footing the bill for college tuition, imagine what alternative ways that tuition money could have been used to help their child in life. Perhaps it could be invested in a rental property, a small business, or go towards purchasing their first home or condo, or helping their parents retire comfortably.

3.) **Income from Working** – By dedicating four years to college, your child is losing potential income from joining

50 John Stossel, "The College Scam", *YouTube* (May 29, 2018), youtu.be/m4gLDXfXgbs

the workforce earlier. While college Jimmy is graduating and likely $40,000 to $100,000 in debt, workforce Alex has already been working and if he's read this book, has likely built up some savings with which to invest or purchase a home. If Alex makes $40,000 per year after tax, and at this stage is only able to save 35% of his gross income (but is working to get that percentage up to the 50% rule), workforce Alex would have saved up $56,000. If he had invested his 35% savings on a monthly basis, at a compound rate of return of 6%, as college Jimmy is graduating with a mountain of student debt and no real work experience or skills, workforce Alex would have approximately $63,000 in savings and four years of work and investing experience.

Note the above opportunity costs are only exacerbated if the college degree pursued necessitates a graduate degree.

Whether the decision to attend college is upon you, your children or your grandchildren, it would behoove you to spend some time with the young adult to reflect on the points discussed and perform a cost-benefit analysis together, to ensure the time, foregone opportunities and money that would be given to the university administrators and professors couldn't be used more wisely.

If the conclusion of the analysis is that the aforementioned opportunity costs are outweighed by the perceived benefits of the particular college education being considered, that's great! The decision was made with intelligent analysis as opposed to the average approach taken by the masses which is to enroll in college as if their brains are on autopilot (because my mom/teachers/guidance counselor/tv told me so).

Be Willing to Say NO!

A recurring theme in this book is often an emphasis on what NOT to do, just as much as what to do, in order to become a *Rational Saver*, which we earlier defined as: one who has or aspires to have zero consumer debt, a sizeable savings that gets bigger every month by employing the 50% Rule of Savings, and is consistently invested to accelerate the growth of one's net worth.

Steve Jobs put it best when he said:

"People think focus means saying yes to the thing you've got to focus on. But that's not what it means at all. It means saying no to the hundred other good ideas that there are. You have to pick carefully. I'm actually as proud of the things we haven't done as the things I have done. Innovation is saying no to 1,000 things."[51]

Jobs was a master at having laser like focus on his goals, and saying no to all the things that may sound good but would have diminished his attention or caused him to deviate from his primary goals. This book isn't about becoming a billionaire entrepreneur, but that piece of wisdom can help everyone, even the person just starting out in life.

If you are at the point of deciding on whether to attend college, looking at it with laser like focus and really analyzing if there are better options out there that will more quickly help you achieve your goals, and if so, to have the ability Jobs had to be ruthless and SAY NO to college, and say yes to that path that will increase your odds of achieving your goals.

Just because getting student loans or spending your parent's money and going to college is the easy option, doesn't mean it's the best option; and it arguably is easier than weighing your alternatives and venturing into the unknown or the path less traveled, because as you can see from the data, 70% of all high

---

51 "Quotable Quote", *Good Reads*, goodreads.com/quotes/629613-people-think-focus-means-saying-yes-to-the-thing-you-ve

school graduates in the U.S. will immediately attend college in lockstep in the coming school year.[52]

Assuming college will prepare your child for life and give them the ability to secure meaningful employment post-graduation is the easy path for a parent who doesn't want to face reality – which is that ship set sail many decades ago (with the exception of a few in-demand majors like some of the STEM fields at a top 10 school whose diploma still has **scarcity**; or the doctor or dentist path.)

Do NOT Go to College to Figure Out What You Want to Do

Mark Zuckerberg does have some good advice regarding attending college: *"explore what you want to do before committing, and keep yourself flexible."*[53] Do NOT commit to spending four years in college and being tens or hundreds of thousands of dollars in debt to "find yourself" or figure out what you like or want to do. The costs are too great today to go to university for that purpose.

If you're considering a certain field, try to intern, apprentice or learn the basic knowledge and skills you'd need in that field for free. Indeed, you can even rent in a college town and shadow a few classes without having to actually enroll or pay any tuition. If you're interested in dentistry, befriend some dentists, buy them a cup of coffee or lunch to pick their brains on their thoughts on the career, tell them you'd really appreciate their honest opinions of the good and the bad, and get their thoughts.

See if you can shadow them at work, do everything you can to get a feel for the profession first, so you're not in the position of

---

52 U.S. Bureau of Labor Statistics, "69.7 percent of 2016 high school graduates enrolled in college in October 2016", (May 22, 2017), bls.gov/opub/ted/2017/69-point-7-percent-of-2016-high-school-graduates-enrolled-in-college-in-october-2016.htm

53 forbes.com/sites/tomiogeron/2012/10/20/mark-zuckerberg-dont-just-start-a-company-do-something-fundamental/#4648069c1f51

spending multiple years at college before you realize that career path isn't for you and have to switch majors, spend more money, or even worse, find this out after you've graduated college and start working in a field.

ALTERNATIVES TO COLLEGE

Apprentice and gain skills and experience under a successful business or tradesperson in a field you find interesting. This experience will help you climb the ladder in your field if you choose to move onto a new company. Or, you may add so much value to their business that they insist on bringing you aboard, perhaps even partnering with you one day.

Trade school and certifications (electrician, HVAC, plumber, welder, computer technology, stone masonry, home inspector, and other well-paid trades in demand with high probability of employment). These are not only opportunities for the young adult to generate income long before their college peers, but also give themselves a paid education, which they can take later on after getting the required certifications and use to start their own business if they so choose.

Start your own business. Let's assume workforce Alex starts a landscaping business around the time college Jimmy takes out student loans and enters a four-year college. Alex purchases some basic landscaping equipment for $1,000 and books on selling. Alex then goes door to door in markets with his target clientele, offering to mow lawns for free the 1st time to demonstrate the quality of his service. By the time college Jimmy graduates from college with $75,000+ in student loans, no real world experience, and still has to obtain meaningful employment, workforce Alex has spent four years facing and overcoming the challenges of building a business, has a book of clients, and now has three independent contractors doing landscaping jobs for him. Alex has recurring annual income to invest. Perhaps in another four years, workforce Alex may have enough money to buy his home outright with no mortgage, has no credit card debt or student loans, a cash flowing business with people under him, and can afford to start a family, with continued upward economic mobility as his business grows. Where is college Jimmy likely to be?

Go pro early. This term refers to working for a company first that will in turn pay for your college education. This path is becoming increasingly popular. First, the young adult won't end up a debt slave to their student loans, and their family won't have to waste a large chunk of their savings paying for a diploma. Second, the employers now offering this track are usually doing it with specific academic institutions they've teamed up with to provide an education curriculum designed by the employer, essentially providing something more resembling trade school. This means more of the information taught will actually be applicable on a day to day basis during the course of the young adult's career. Employers such as Price Waterhouse Coopers (PwC) are already providing this type of career track whereby students after high school enter apprenticeship programs and PwC supports the student obtaining the requisite credentials and college degree simultaneously.[54]

---

54 Brandon Busteed, "This Will Be The Biggest Disruption In Education" *Forbes* (Apr 30, 2019), forbes.com/sites/brandonbusteed/2019/04/30/this-will-be-the-biggest-disruption-in-higher-education/#610f77ea608a

Have a Story on Why You Chose an Alternate Path

Whichever route you choose, if any of the professional positions you seek are often applied to by job candidates with college degrees, simply have an intelligent story prepared explaining your choice not to go to college, including that you performed a cost-benefit analysis, and why your experience and skills will enable you to add tremendous value to that company, above what a college degree could have enabled you to bring to the table.[55] BOOM! You just stood out from 99% of the other applicants.

55 Catey Hill, "You don't need a 4-year college degree for these high-paying jobs at Google, Apple, Netflix" *Market Watch* (Apr 17, 2019), marketwatch.com/story/you-dont-need-a-4-year-college-degree-for-these-high-paying-jobs-at-google-apple-netflix-2019-04-08

CHAPTER 11

THE 20% RULE OF HOUSING

The single biggest financial mistake most people make, especially as they get into their 30s and 40s when they're looking to settle down, start a family and have their little slice of the middle class dream, is to buy or rent WAY more house than they really can afford. Being financially free requires having enough income to save and invest (in things other than your home). Remember, a home is not an investment. It doesn't pay you every month; you pay it every month.

The standard measure of housing affordability preached by the mainstream media and personal finance blogs is to spend no more than 30% of your gross (pre-tax) household income on housing. Therefore, we're not going to follow the traditional 30% guidance, instead we'll use 20% because most people are up to their eyeballs in debt with very little savings, so the mainstream approach isn't working. Thus, we'll spend no more than 20% of our pre-tax annual household income on housing.

If you're a renter, housing includes rent and utilities. If you're an owner, housing includes mortgage payments, maintenance, utilities, property taxes, and insurance.[56]

---

56 Lauren Lyons Cole, "Forget coffee and avocado toast – most people blow nearly 40% of their money in the same place" *Business Insider* (Apr 26, 2019), businessinsider.com/ personal-finance/how-to-save-more-money-2017-8#:~:text=Housing%20accounts%20for%20 about%2037,is%2030%25%20of%20pretax%20income

Note there are free "cost of homeownership calculators" online which, based on the mortgage amount, term, interest rate, and other variables you can tweak given your specific situation (for example, you can put the heating cost at $0 if you live in a hot climate) will give you an approximate monthly total housing expense figure you can then use to see if over the course of a year that residence you're looking at complies with the 20% Rule of Housing.

20% IS TOO LITTLE FOR HOUSING!

Well, let's crunch some numbers. A hypothetical single filer named Lauren with an income of $80,000 is filing for 2020. Let's assume she read chapter 13 and moved to a state with no state income taxes, so she only owes federal income taxes. To calculate her estimated income taxes for 2020, our single filer takes the $12,400 standard deduction, reducing her taxable income from $80,000 to $67,600, placing her in the 22% tax bracket. She then would take $4,617.50 + 22% of $27,475 (the amount over $40,125) and end up owing $10,662 in federal income tax. If we deduct $10,662 in federal income tax from her $80,000 income, she's left with roughly $69,338 of after-tax income.

When we employ the 20% Rule of Housing and take 20% of her pre-tax income of $80,000, we get $16,000 per year or $1,333 per month she can spend on housing total. In September of 2020, the market interest rate on a 30-year fixed home mortgage was 3.92%. If we assume Lauren buys a starter home for a purchase price of $200,000, with a 20% down payment to avoid PMI, this means her monthly mortgage payments will be $757. We'll also make the following additional assumptions for this hypothetical case study:

- Her property tax rate is 1.1% (the 2020 nationwide average), or roughly $183 per month will go towards her property taxes;

- Lauren avoided an HOA property so she does not have HOA fees;

- Her monthly utilities are $250 total, with electricity at $104, water at $46, internet $75, trash $25, and no oil, natural gas or snow removal costs as she lives in a warm climate;

- Her homeowner's insurance is $65 per month; and

- She puts $78 per month into reserves for repairs and maintenance.

Her total housing expenses including mortgage payments equate to $1,333 per month.

If her living expenses are higher than that, well, maybe Lauren will have to buy a $175,000 or $150,000 property instead of a $200,000 home. Or, maybe she buys a duplex and rents the bottom story out, or lives with a roommate. The point is, if Lauren values building long term wealth and financial freedom over the additional comfort of having an extra 500 SF or living in a flashier part of town, she can adapt and make the 20% Rule of Housing work.

If we take the $16,000 per year ($1,333 per month) housing expense limit Lauren has under the 20% Rule of Housing and divide it by her after-tax take-home income of $69,338, she ends up spending closer to 1/4th of her after-tax income on housing.

This leaves roughly 3/4ths of her after-tax income to cover other living expenses, hopefully leaving her enough of the pie left over to honor the 50% Rule of Savings. Note Lauren will likely have to work up to being able to save 50% of her gross income by (a) increasing her income and (b) decreasing her living expenditures.

An added bonus of the 20% Rule of Housing is you'll prevent your household from inadvertently incurring all the additional higher expenses (beyond the higher mortgage payments) that come with buying too much house, including more expensive:

- Property taxes;

- HOA fees (if applicable);

- Home owners insurance;

- Utilities;

- Recurring landscaping costs (monetary or time costs if you do the landscaping yourself, time you could have spent earning more currency).

"My Household Income Isn't Enough to Buy a House Under the 20% Rule!"

Then, renting may be a better option in the interim. Or, perhaps live with a roommate or family until you increase your income enough to do something different. Is it going to suck? Maybe, maybe not. Could be a lot of fun if you have friends or family you get along with. If it sucks, that's good too! It will help motivate you to increase the amount of value you bring to the market, thereby increasing your income and ability to save and invest.

WHAT THE MAINSTREAM 30% HOUSING ALLOWANCE LOOKS LIKE

The average American consumer unit (this includes families, single persons living alone or sharing a household with others but who are financially independent, or two or more persons living together who share major expenses) in 2018 spent the below percentages of their PRE-TAX annual income on the following[57]:

- Food: 10.1%

- Healthcare: 6.3%

- Entertainment: 4.1%

- Gas and motor oil: 2.7%

- Apparel and services: 2.4%

- Education: 2.0%

- Personal care products and services: 1.0%

If we add these up, we get 28.6% of the American consumer unit's pre-tax income going towards the above average living expenses. Note that there are additional living expenses not accounted for in the BLS data like car insurance, car maintenance, other miscellaneous taxes (payroll tax, sales tax, etc.).

If we take 28.6% of Lauren's $80,000 pre-tax annual income, that's $22,880. After Lauren pays her federal income taxes, she will have $69,338 of after-tax income left over. If we then subtract the $22,880 of average living expenses for the

---

57   "CONSUMER EXPENDITURES—2018" *U.S. Bureau of Labor Statistics* (Sep 10, 2019), bls.gov/news.release/cesan.nr0.htm

previously listed items from that figure, we're left with $46,458 Lauren has to pay for housing AND put into savings and investing.

If we then used the mainstream 30% housing allowance, we would take 30% of $80,000 and get $24,000 as our annual housing allowance, or $2,000 a month ($24,000 per year). If we subtract $24,000 from $46,458 (what was left over after federal income taxes and average living expenses), we're left with $22,458. If we assume the remaining $22,458 is saved and invested, we get a measly savings rate of 28% ($22,458/$80,000). This is a FAR cry from the 50% Rule of Savings.

On the other hand, if Lauren obeys the 20% Rule of Housing, she'll be spending $16,000 per year on housing instead of $24,000 and have an additional $8,000 per year to save and invest, leaving her $30,458 (after paying her Federal income tax, average living expenses and annual housing expenses). In this case, instead of a savings rate of 28%, Lauren's savings rate jumps to 38% ($30,458/$80,000), which is a 36% increase in savings over the savings she would have using the mainstream 30% housing allowance.

By now, it should be obvious that when you crunch the numbers, it's incredibly difficult to have any meaningful income left over at the end of each month to put towards savings and investments when you use lamestream 30% housing allowance. Do yourself a favor, give your savings a chance to grow by using the 20% Rule of Housing instead.

"BUT I ALREADY BOUGHT TOO MUCH HOUSE...HELP!"

If you've already purchased a home with annual housing costs that exceed the 20% Rule of Housing, and you're serious about growing your savings and investing, you may want to consider downsizing. Or, if you have a spare bedroom, you could consider renting the additional room out via a traditional monthly lease, or using an online vacation rental website like Airbnb. If you have a spare parking spot or storage space, consider renting those out as well, the internet is a wonderful thing.

If you're renting too much house, that's easy, simply don't renew your lease and move to a cheaper rental unit!

DISCIPLINE CREATES FREEDOM

By being disciplined enough to cap your annual housing expenses to no more than 20% of your pre-tax household income, you will EXPLODE your wealth compared to your peers, especially when combined with the rest of the hacks this book provides for saving money.

"THOU SHALT NOT SPEND MORE THAN 20% OF THY PRE-TAX HOUSEHOLD ANNUAL INCOME ON HOUSING!"

CHAPTER 12

YOUR HOME ≠ INVESTMENT

Undeniably the largest expense for most people is their home. Because of this, it's crucial we set the record straight regarding some misconceptions about homes that have been VERY profitable for banks over the past 100+ years.

The **#1 misconception about your home is that "it's an investment."** This is totally false. The right investments at the right time have the potential to make you wealthy. No one has ever gotten wealthy because they bought a home. An investment is defined as an asset or good acquired with the intent of generating income or appreciation.[58] Thus, by definition it's not an investment because you purchase your home with the intent to live in it rather than sell it for profit, and it's not paying you cash flow (unless you're renting part of it out, like with a duplex).

HOME APPRECIATION

You may have heard people say, "real estate over the long run goes up so your home is a good investment." They'll pull up median housing price charts and see the long-term rise in nominal prices

---

58 James Chen, "Investment" *Investopedia* (Feb 27, 2020), investopedia.com/terms/i/investment.asp

and say "look how much housing goes up over the long run." This is misleading and fails to take into account the difference between nominal growth and real growth.

One's wealth doesn't increase just because their assets appreciate in nominal terms, their wealth increases if the assets go up in real terms, meaning the currency the owner receives upon selling the asset net of taxes and all other disposition costs, will buy them more goods and services than they could have purchased with the total currency they spent acquiring (total initial investment) AND holding the asset (maintenance and repairs, property taxes, insurance, etc.).

For example, a home in the year 1890 that was purchased with $10,000 would be worth close to the same as a home in 2010 worth $350,000, that is, the amount of goods and services the home buyer in 1890 could have purchased with that $10,000 is relatively similar to the amount of goods and services a home buyer in 2010 could purchase with $350,000 (obviously not taking into account technological advancements with things like electronics, but general living expenses like food, housing, clothing, etc.), thanks to inflation (not a natural phenomenon, but a deliberate policy to siphon off the productivity and labor of the masses to the benefit of the central banking cabal).

On the following page is a graph which shows that nationally in the U.S., over the long run the real growth (i.e., accounting for inflation) of U.S. housing is less than 1% a year. When you compare this with the real growth of the major stock market indexes or gold, you'll realize why calling your home an "investment" is false.

REAL GROWTH IN US HOUSING PRICES

1890-2015

This chart takes into account changes in housing size, quality and adjusts for inflation. Note the long-term return is less than 1% per annum.

Price Index (1890=100)

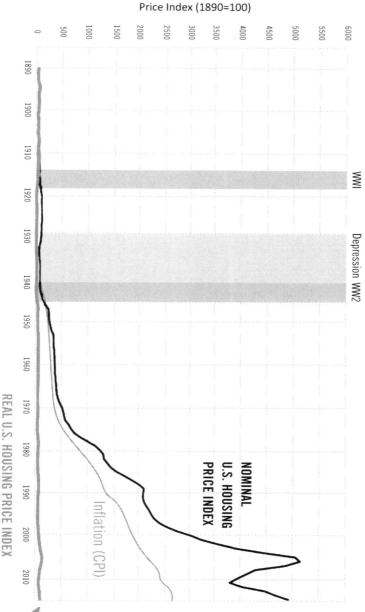

WWI

Great Depression WW2

NOMINAL U.S. HOUSING PRICE INDEX

Inflation (CPI)

REAL U.S. HOUSING PRICE INDEX
(Average change in urban home prices adjusted for inflation)

Source: Robert J. Shiller's Irrational Exuberance, http://www.econ.yale.edu/~shiller/data/Fig3-1.xls; US Census Table 14a: Quarterly Seasonally Adjusted Homeownership Rates for: 1980-2015, http://www.census.gov/housing/hvs/data/histtabs.html; Lawrence H. Officer and Samuel H. Williamson, "The Annual Consumer Price Index for the United States, 1774-2015," MeasuringWorth, 2016, http://www.measuringworth.com/uscpi/

229

That said, when we really do the math, you'll see this under 1% real growth figure doesn't tell the whole story behind profit and loss when you purchase a home as it doesn't account for major ancillary housing costs such as recurring annual non-mortgage homeowner expenses and the closing costs to purchase and the cost of sale should one actually try to sell and take profits if their home appreciates.

"You Should Buy Your Home so You can Build Home Equity"
Consider the following hypothetical: you're very good at market timing and buy a home at the bottom of the market for $300,000. You live in the home for 13 years (median U.S. duration of homeownership). For 13 years straight your home appreciates by 5.11% per year (non-compounding) from the original $300,000 purchase price; in other words, during each one of those 13 years your home appreciates by a rate of 4% (compounding), which means it will be worth $499,522 by the time you decide to sell and take profits at the peak of the market at the end of year 13, your home having increased from its original purchase price by 66.5% or an extra $199,522. Awesome, buying a home was a great investment! Right?

Well, let's crunch the numbers.

When you purchased you put 20% down ($60,000) to avoid triggering private mortgage insurance (PMI) payments. When you buy a home there's closing costs, generally anywhere from 2% to 5% of the purchase price.[59] We'll assume you are crafty and kept it at 2% or $6,000. The interest rate secured in this hypothetical was 3.0% for a 30-year fixed self-amortizing mortgage.

For non-mortgage expenses, *GOBankingRates.com* estimates that the average maintenance costs for U.S. homes is $1,204

---

59 Aly J. Yale, "More Than a Mortgage: The Cost of Owning a Home" *The Balance* (Jun 07, 2020), thebalance.com/more-than-a-mortgage-the-cost-of-owning-a-home-453819

per month, this figure includes the average monthly expenses for things like utility bills, property taxes, snow removal and lawn care, home insurance, repairs and general maintenance, HOA fees and PMI. Note $250 of the $1,204 per month is from average HOA fees, and $158 per month from average PMI.[60] Since you put 20% down, we'll subtract the $158 of PMI, and we'll assume you found a residence without HOA fees and subtract the $250. That puts our estimated average monthly cost at $796, or $9,552 annually, which is a reasonable figure for housing in this price range, and we'll assume the inflation of those expenses is 2%, the Fed's target inflation rate (in Chapter 15, we discuss why the real rate of inflation is likely much higher, but for arguments sake we'll use 2%).

For the mortgage interest tax write-off, we'll assume your annual income is $120,000 per year for the entire 13 years of ownership and you're a single filer in the 24% tax bracket and the income tax section of the tax code stays the same. We'll take each year's interest portion of your mortgage payments and multiply that by 24%, then subtract that amount from your annual cash outlay (money leaving your pocket) to account for the positive financial impact the tax write-off has on your "investment."

At the end of year 13 you sell your home for $499,522, you pay off the remaining mortgage balance of $161,540 and a 6% cost of sale (real estate broker fees AND seller closing costs like transfer taxes, title insurance fees, attorney fees and any credits to buyer for any repairs), which leaves you with $308,011, and you don't have to pay any capital gains due to being within the $250,000 single filer exclusion.

In order to see how well this hypothetical "investment" performed, we'll perform our analysis using both the Internal Rate

60 Michael Keenan, "Here's Why It Costs $1,204 a Month to Maintain the Average Home" *GOBankingRates.com* (Apr 21, 2017), gobankingrates.com/investing/real-estate/heres-costs-1126-month-maintain-average-american-home/

231

of Return (IRR) and the Return on Investment (ROI) metrics. The IRR is the more helpful of the two in this scenario because it enables you to better judge an investment with a longer time horizon.

So, how'd we do on our phenomenal "home investment" that appreciated by 66.5% in just 13 years?

Holding Period (Years): 13			
EOY	**Cash Flows**		**Sale Proceeds**
0	-$66,000		
1	-$19,982		
2	-$20,210		
3	-$20,443		
4	-$20,680		
5	-$20,923		
6	-$21,171		
7	-$21,424		
8	-$21,683		
9	-$21,948		
10	-$22,218		
11	-$22,494		
12	-$22,777		
13	-$23,065	+	$308,011
Internal Rate of Return: -1.60%			

Note the cash outlay (denoted in parenthesis) for the EOY 0 period is $66,000, because the down payment was $60,000 and the closing costs were $6,000. Notice years 1-13 on the Cash Flows (outflows in this case) column slightly increase each year, that's because the mortgage interest tax write-off goes down as you pay less interest on the loan each year as a natural function of amortization, and because of inflation of non-mortgage expenses. The calculus for each cash flow outlay from EOYs 1-13 is the annual debt service – mortgage interest tax write-off savings + annual non-mortgage expenses (adjusted for expense inflation). The $308,011 sale proceeds at EOY 13 are what's left when the home was sold for $499,522 after paying off the mortgage balance and the 6% cost of sale.

So, our "investment" yielded -1.60% in nominal terms, since we only accounted for inflation of the annual non-mortgage expenses, but still need to account for the loss of purchasing power of our dollars we put into the "investment," which causes the yield to drop to -3.60% in real terms. This is without PMI and HOA fees, and with a home that appreciated 66.5% from its purchase price... Over the 13-year period our homebuyer put $345,018 into the home and got $308,011 out of it, resulting in an investment loss of ($37,007). From an ROI perspective, the return is -10.72%. That doesn't sound like a very good investment.

Remember, in this hypothetical we bought the home at the bottom of the market and enjoyed 13 years of continuous 4% compounding appreciation. That's pretty optimistic. Most people's homes don't experience that kind of appreciation, and many actually depreciate in nominal terms from when they purchased it. The set back to those people's wealth is massive.

Who Wins Here?
There's one party that doesn't lose in this game and makes out like the mischievous Cheshire cat.

That would be the bank. If the loan's interest rate is 3.0% for 30 years, the bank is going to make 3.0% on their money every year for thirty years, or possibly higher if they foreclose on the homeowner, auction the house and create a new mortgage for the next buyer.

So, while the homeowner takes all the risk, pays all the property taxes, insurance, repairs and maintenance costs, and puts in their time and effort keeping the collateral in good condition, the bank sits back and just gets 3.0% per year because they loaned fiat currency into existence by typing a few keystrokes into their computer network (they created the currency out of thin air on the spot when they gave you the loan), further debasing our currency via fractional reserve lending. Sounds fair to me.

COMPARE "BUILDING HOME EQUITY" TO INVESTING

Let's compare the negative rate of return from our "building equity in your home" example to what those same cash outlays at the same time intervals could do if instead they were invested in the S&P 500 Index, which has historically averaged returns of 10% (un-adjusted for inflation) or 7% (adjusted for inflation), so we'll use a rate of 6% to adjust for inflation and be conservative (in chapter 15 we'll discuss why in the investing landscape of the 2020s general equities market returns may be lower than years past, and what better opportunities exist).[61]

Under that new scenario, the sale proceeds at EOY 13 if our investor sold all of the S&P shares would be $551,495, assuming each year's cash outlays are invested at the same monthly intervals as the mortgage payments and non-mortgage expenses.

This wouldn't be an honest comparison if we didn't account for capital gains tax. To keep things simple, capital gains = selling price – purchase price. The capital gains are taxed by the capital gains tax rate which can fall within a range depending on the individual's finances. To get a ballpark figure, we'll just

---

61 J.B. Maverick, "What Is the Average Annual Return for the S&P 500?" *Investopedia* (Feb 19, 2020), investopedia.com/ask/answers/042415/what-average-annual-return-sp-500.asp

take the entire amount our investor put into the S&P 500 over the 13 year period, $345,018, and subtract that from the total S&P 500 sales proceeds at EOY 13 of $551,495, which leaves $206,447 in capital gains, which if we assume a capital gains tax rate of 20%, would mean capital gains taxes of $41,295, which we'll then subtract from our stock sale proceeds and be left with after-tax sale proceeds of $510,200.

Actual taxation wouldn't be this simple given each individual's finances for tax purposes can vary, but this is sufficient for demonstration purposes.

Holding Period (Years): 13			
EOY	**Cash Flows**		**Sale Proceeds**
0	-$66,000		
1	-$19,982		
2	-$20,210		
3	-$20,443		
4	-$20,680		
5	-$20,923		
6	-$21,171		
7	-$21,424		
8	-$21,683		
9	-$21,948		
10	-$22,218		
11	-$22,494		
12	-$22,777		
13	-$23,065	+	$510,200
Internal Rate of Return: 5.22%			

In this hypothetical, we get an after-tax IRR of 5.22% in real terms, because we accounted for 2% inflation by using a 6% rate of return instead of the historical S&P 500 average of 10% (un-adjusted for inflation). Moreover, our after-tax inflation adjusted ROI is close to 48%, or an equity multiple of 1.48x as we put a total of $345,018 into the stock index and after tax got an estimated $510,200 out, resulting in an investment gain of $165,182. That sounds like a better investment than the -3.60% IRR and ($37,007) investment loss from our "home investment."

Remember, this chapter is talking about a home to live in. Fix and flips or cash flowing investment properties are an entirely different story and a good deal would have a higher probability of experiencing great investment returns simply because smart investors force appreciation through value-add strategies like rehabbing, rebranding, increasing cash flow and lowering operating expenses.

"BUYING A HOME IS THE LESSER OF THE TWO EVILS!"

"Okay, after reviewing the numbers it now makes sense why your home isn't an investment, but you still need to live somewhere, and the previous example of investing in the S&P 500 doesn't take into account the money you lose every year to rent while doing that, at least buying your home lets you keep some of the currency you spent on housing in the form of home equity, whereas with renting your money totally disappears!"

In the home purchase example on page 152, we used an unlikely 4% rate of compound appreciation to demonstrate the point that even under the best circumstances in which you buy a home that experiences a lot of appreciation, it's still usually a terrible investment because it isn't paying you cash flow, it's taking cash out of your pocket every year, a large percentage of which you do not recapture upon sale. What if the home appreciated by a more realistic annual rate of 1% in real terms (adjusted for inflation), close to the long-term growth rate of the Real US Housing Price Index?

If the $300,000 home appreciated in market value by 1% per year (compounding) in real terms, at the end of 13 years the sale value is $341,428. When we apply a 6% cost of sale, we're left with $320,942. Then when we subtract the remaining mortgage balance of $161,540, our homeowner walks away with $159,402 (inflation-adjusted).

What if we rent a comparable $300,000 home and invest the difference between the cash outlays we would have made purchasing the home and the cash outlays we make renting? We'll rent in the center of Tampa, FL. In July, 2020, a starter home in Tampa is in the $300,000 price range and will have around 1,500 square feet or so and 3 bedrooms and 2 baths. Comparable rental properties in that market are around $1,600 per month. We'll account for inflation in rent and assume the landlord raises the rent by 2% every three years (most landlords aren't going to raise rent every year lest they enjoy lots of vacancy).

Finally, for demonstration purposes we'll invest the extra cash saved by renting instead of owning into the S&P 500 at a 6% compound rate of growth in real terms instead of 10% (the un-adjusted average historical rate), so everything is inflation adjusted and we're comparing apples to apples. We'll sell the S&P 500 shares at EOY 13 and pay the capital gains taxes at a 20% capital gains tax rate.

EOY	Extra $ to Invest	EOY Balance if Invested in S&P 500 @ 6%
0	$66,000	
1	$782	$70,765
2	$1,010	$76,051
3	$1,243	$81,902

4	$1,096	$87,943
5	$1,339	$94,607
6	$1,587	$101,918
7	$1,448	$109,532
8	$1,707	$117,863
9	$1,972	$126,966
10	$1,842	$136,491
11	$2,118	$146,873
12	$2,401	$158,163
13	$2,281	$170,006

$170,006 ‹ **Sales Proceeds Before Tax**

$86,826

Cash OUT $170,006
minus
CASH IN $86,826
EQUALS $83,180   ‹ Capital Gains
            x
            20%   ‹ Capital Gains Tax Rate
            $16,636   ‹ Capital Gains Tax Owed

$170,006 -
$16,636
$153,370 ‹ **Proceeds After Taxes**

So, at the end of 13 years, we walk away with $153,370 after tax (adjusted for inflation) from investing the extra money we have from renting over purchasing, while if you recall the homeowner walked away with $159,402.

That's only an extra $6,032, and in fact is less than the renter walks away with when you factor in the homeowner's money value of time (covered in Chapter 5) given the hundreds of hours our homeowner likely will have spent over 13 years landscaping, maintaining, and repairing the home. In addition, the homeowner has far less mobility than the renter, as the homeowner's equity is trapped while the renter is liquid and can move wherever he wants or needs to move, not being restrained by having to time his local housing market.

The point of this exercise wasn't that renting and investing the difference into the stock market is a good strategy. The point was to dispel the myth that purchasing your home is the lesser of two evils and therefore necessarily the better option. If in this same example our renter invested the money in some of the fast track to wealth alternatives we outline in the next chapter, his returns would likely be far greater, and in those instances renting (if it's cheaper than buying) your place of residence to free up additional cash to put into those fast track to wealth alternative investments would be the optimal financial decision.

YOUR HOME IS AN ASSET ON THE BANK'S BALANCE SHEET...

Another frequent platitude you may have heard from people encouraging homeownership is that "your home is an asset." This is partially true, but that's because it's an asset on the bank's balance sheet. You see, as long your home has a mortgage on it, your mortgage will be taking money out of your pocket every month and giving it to the bank.

Thus, your mortgage payments are liabilities, because liabilities take money away from us, hence why mortgage payments are listed on the liabilities side of a net worth statement (NWS). The bank has your mortgage (the note or deed of trust in some states) as listed under the assets section of their balance sheet (the institutional equivalent of an NWS), as it pays them cash flow in the form of your principal and interest payments. Remember, one person's liability is another's asset.

This is an important mindset shift because people frequently justify their decision to buy a home, or to buy a more expensive home than they should, by telling themselves that they're "buying an asset" so it's a wise financial decision…

THEN WHAT IS A HOME?

If your home isn't an investment, and it's not an asset (on your balance sheet) when you've a mortgage on it, what is it? Quite simply, your home is an immovable, very expensive consumer product, used to live in, that's likely your biggest liability.

This is a helpful mindset shift for those *Rational Savers* looking to build wealth as quickly as possible. This doesn't mean you shouldn't buy a home, or that buying a home isn't the optimal financial choice for *you!* There are housing markets around the world where buying a home can be cheaper than renting. The rent vs. purchase decision will be covered in the next chapter. The purpose of this chapter is to destroy an age-old lie that the banks have used to enslave the lower and middle classes for 100+ years.

BEWARE THE MIDDLE-CLASS TRAP

For those of you looking to build a lot of wealth in the shortest time frame, be careful, a home is the most common middle-class trap there is. That is, they trap people in the middle class by taking away their mobility, both in a geographic sense if a better employment or business opportunity arises in a different city, state or country, and in terms of lowering one's tolerance for risk. Anyone who has built wealth knows it requires calculated risk, whether that's starting a business, learning a new vocation, creating a new product or service, becoming a skilled investor, and so forth.

When you have mortgage payments due every month, property taxes, insurance, repairs and maintenance, the longer you stay in the home, the more you have invested in that home financially and emotionally. Because of this, people often end up trapped in jobs and routines with no further upward socio-economic mobility (in any reasonable timeframe) simply because they're afraid of losing the income stream upon which their house is dependent upon, the house they spent so many years pumping economic energy into.

They also hold back from starting a new business venture or making sizeable investments, often because they're living paycheck to paycheck and can't afford to wait until the new business venture or investments start positively cash flowing.

Moreover, for those who buy more home than they can afford, i.e. violate the 20% Rule of Housing and all their spare income after other living expenses goes toward their home, they become the quintessential example of the old adage "house rich, cash poor." These people will have a very difficult time investing and playing the money game to win.

Perform an internet search: "Grant Cardone: Nobody Ever Achieved Financial Freedom from Buying a Home (Part 3)" to watch an excellent interview with Grant on this very topic in which he makes some powerful and insightful points to consider.

BUYING A HOME MAY STILL BE A GOOD DECISION

The point of this chapter isn't to discourage buying a home. For people who aren't on the fast track to building wealth, but are instead looking to build wealth over time while maintaining a balance between work and life, OR for people who know they aren't disciplined enough to invest the extra income, a home may be the better financial decision there as well and we'll show why.

The point of this chapter is to stop people from buying a house (or buying more house than they can really afford) when that purchase decision was based on false premises like "your home is an investment" or blanket statements that in fact aren't true for everyone such as "it's a good financial decision to buy a home so you can build up equity." That may be the case for some people, particularly those who aren't willing to learn how to become disciplined enough to save and invest their income.

Disclaimer Regarding Stock Indexing

In the examples so far, we've looked at your opportunity cost of buying a home using investing in the S&P 500 as an alternative. This is simply for demonstration purposes, and as you'll see in the next chapter, the returns from the fast track to wealth alternatives covered in the next chapter could dwarf the returns of things like stock market indexes.

CHAPTER 13

RENT VS. PURCHASE

The "do I rent or buy my residence" decision is much easier to make when we use the Cost-Benefit Analysis tool from chapter 3, which shouldn't take more than 30 minutes. In order to do that, you will need to brainstorm ALL of the costs and benefits of renting vs. purchasing, which of course will have varying degrees of importance and probability of being true for each person(s) depending on their unique circumstances.

Note when performing your analysis, one of the biggest factors to consider is MOBILITY. Depending on who you are and your career goals, mobility may have a higher or lower level of importance in your analysis. Just be aware that a home can seriously hinder one's mobility, particularly if the absorption time (real estate parlance for how quickly you can find a buyer) is slow when you need to sell; or your home's market value has significantly depreciated.

For example, suppose your $300,000 home depreciates by 20% in nominal terms from the price you purchased it for. If you have to sell, you'd better be ready to take a $60,000 loss from what you purchased it for, PLUS closing costs (6%) or $14,400, plus the loss in purchasing power of the currency you do get back out of it.

For the person intent on climbing the corporate ladder in a multi-national company, depending on their work situation, they may be required to move to another city or state for the desired promotion or expanded scope of responsibility. For the entrepreneur who is trying to bring a new product or service to the marketplace, or gain notoriety and market exposure, they may have to live in different areas for different periods of time in order to connect with the right people who can help make those goals a reality.

That said, BEFORE performing a Cost-Benefit Analysis, there's a question to ask yourself, the answer to which is paramount to discovering whether renting or purchasing is the better financial decision for YOU! In the last chapter, we demonstrated that your home is not an investment, and arguably should not even be viewed as an asset if you have a mortgage on it. We also hinted that a home may still be the better financial decision over renting, depending on who the *Rational Saver* is.

The question you should ask yourself is this: "am I on the fast track to wealth? Or am I on the slow track to wealth?" which, by the way, is still far better than the track most people are on, which is a track to financial mediocrity. I don't believe there's a medium track, or if there is, trying to distinguish it from the slow track and the fast track is a futile endeavor.

SLOW TRACK TO WEALTH

Basically, the slow track to wealth means your primary source of income is from a job that will always require you to *trade your time and labor for currency,* for example, you work for the government, or you work in academia, or a corporate position but with a clear ceiling on your income, or you're an entrepreneur but your business depends on you being there and performing, either day to day management like if you owned a coffee shop but it can't run on its own and you only own one (as opposed to owning a dozen and having management setup so it can run autonomously without you for long periods of time), or any other job where you create a product or perform a service but without you that product or service doesn't make it to the marketplace, like a skilled craftsman or a digital "content creator."

We're defining these jobs as "slow tracks to wealth" because even if you're extremely talented and in demand, if you stop laboring the cash flow stops coming in. Having to trade your time and labor for currency for your entire life will not get you wealthy as fast as building a system or systems which eventually yield you currency while you sleep, i.e. the fast track to wealth.

The slow track to wealth does enable you to have more of a balance between work and life which most people innately desire, as building these systems can be incredibly arduous and time consuming. Also note the slow track to wealth could eventually speed up if you chose the right company and team to work with and make the right moves.

There is nothing wrong with the slow track to wealth, and if you employ the hacks and strategies discussed in this book, you will still build wealth and financial freedom far beyond what most people will achieve and in a much faster time frame. But you MUST diligently save and invest (wisely), or these slow tracks to wealth will become slow tracks to financial mediocrity.

FAST TRACK TO WEALTH

If you're in the minority of people truly committed to becoming wealthy as fast as possible, are willing to risk everything to get there and make substantial sacrifices AND the avenue you're pursuing is something that has the structural ability to scale (either you eventually can have it run semi-autonomously with minimal weekly oversight, or you can sell the business for an attractive earnings multiple), like: running your own landscaping, plumbing, waste removal, HVAC, or trucking distribution business and growing it to where you have employees managing employees and it can successfully operate autonomous of your day to day oversight; building a portfolio of cash flowing real estate; building a successful e-commerce business; creating a product that can get into the hands of tens of thousands, hundreds of thousands or millions of consumers; leveraging capital into millions through skilled trading and investing; and things of that nature, you're on a *potential* fast track to wealth.

Note the fast track to wealth is far more difficult and riskier than the slow track to wealth, as you may spend years on something and completely fail and have nothing to show for it but hard lessons, broken relationships, loss of your savings and loss of your time. In fact, most successful entrepreneurs have failed at multiple endeavors before they succeeded. This is why successful entrepreneurs have an almost cult like status in our society, because people instinctively know deep down how incredibly difficult it is to step into the arena of entrepreneurship and come out of it victorious.

This is why most people join an already working business system rather than create their own, or they make a job by being in business for themselves, but their business model is such that without them there laboring every day, the business ceases to function, such as the shop owner who only has one shop and has to be there to oversee the day to day operations; or the chiropractor who does not have chiropractors below him operating the business, but rather, he is the business.

For those intent on pursuing the fast track to wealth, when it comes to the decision to rent or purchase your residence, you should be asking "which option will help enable me to get wealthy the fastest!?" The answer is: whichever option has the smallest TOTAL annual cash outlay.

This is of course counter intuitive when the option turns out to be renting and you consider how rent disappears forever yet the principal portion of your mortgage payments goes into your home's equity. That's understandable, hold tight and it will make more sense as we dive into it further.

WHICH OPTION HAS THE SMALLEST TOTAL ANNUAL CASH OUTLAY?

Before you can figure out which option has the smallest **total** annual cash outlay (in some markets buying a home can actually have a smaller annual cash outlay than renting), you'll need to do a few things so that you're comparing apples to apples instead of apples to oranges:

(1) Take the down payment you anticipate making to purchase a home and divide that down payment amount by 13.3 years (the median duration of homeownership in the U.S. as of 2018)[62], unless you know how many

---

62 Chris Moon and Madison Miller, "How Long Do Homeowners Stay in Their homes?" *Value Penguin* (June 4, 2018), valuepenguin.com/how-long-homeowners-stay-in-their-homes

years you will live in the house then use that number instead of 13.3, which will give you what we'll call the down payment quotient;

(2) Estimate all the additional non-mortgage expenses that come with home ownership versus renting, using data that's specific to the home you're considering purchasing, such as: property taxes, repairs and maintenance, home insurance, HOA fees if any, utilities, lawn care and snow removal in cold climate. Annualize and add up all of these estimated costs to give what we'll call the annual non-mortgage expenses;

(3) Calculate what your annual mortgage payments would be, making sure you use the same down payment amount you used in step 1;

(4) Perform the following calculation: [down payment quotient] + [annual non-mortgage expenses] + [**annual** mortgage payments] = TOTAL annual home expense.

(5) For the rental unit you're considering, take the monthly rent payment, add any additional monthly fees you'd have to make separate from your monthly rent payment (utilities, parking and other expenses may be separate depending on the lease), and multiply that sum by 12 to get your TOTAL annual rent cost.

If the TOTAL annual rent cost is less than the TOTAL annual home expense, renting is the option with the smaller total annual cash outlay and thus is the better option if you're trying to build wealth the fastest.

For example, let's assume your choices come down to renting

for an estimated $18,000 per year, or buying a home for an estimated TOTAL annual home expense of $27,450 per year. We'll also assume both of these options do not violate the 20% Rule of Housing. In this case, renting would help you get wealthy faster because you would have an additional $9,450 per year to invest. Remember, buying a home (even though you're building equity) is not the same as investing.

That's an additional $9,450 per year (your opportunity cost if you had purchased the home) that could be invested into the following fast tracks to wealth:

(a) **Yourself** by acquiring or enhancing your marketable skills via private training and courses or industry and trade certifications. What would the return be from investing an additional $9,450 in yourself by getting top notch training to increase your sales skills? Do you think you'd sell more products or services, or sell yourself into a higher paying job? What about if you're in tech and that extra $9,450 can help you attain a higher-level industry certification that makes you eligible for a position paying $30,000 more per year?

- WARNING: regarding private training, if it's anything non-technical like sales, business, real estate, marketing, etc., steer clear of "seminars" as these are notorious for being incredibly overpriced, even ones I know are taught by qualified experts with incredibly useful knowledge, you can get that same knowledge for 1/100th the seminar price by buying their books, taking a reasonably priced online course and watching videos of them for free on YouTube.

(b) **Building and growing your business**. What if you recently started a stone masonry business and you're a one man show, what kind of ROI do you think you could get using that additional $9,450 per year towards contracting a part time stone mason to do some of the manual labor you would normally do, so you can instead spend more time increasing your market share (building a bigger book of business), so you can afford to hire and train more laborers, attract more clients, and create a snowball of success which explodes your revenues?

(c) **Cash flowing investments** such as rental real estate, if you have expertise or are willing to gain expertise in this asset class and continually learn as much as possible, or if you're investing alongside an expert you fully trust who has skin in the deal and isn't just taking your money to the tables. Depending on how fast you can build up your savings, you may have to save up for a few years, and possibly take on a partner.

But would postponing buying a home be worth it? Well, would having 4, 8 or 12+ multi-family rental units bringing in cash flow into your net worth while you sleep make your life better? Let's say going this route you eventually acquire two small 4-unit apartment buildings, which collectively give you a net operating income (NOI) of $40,000 to $60,000 per year. Would that kind of passive income have been worth waiting an extra 5 to 7 years to buy a home?

(d) **Unique appreciation opportunities**. These are opportunities to invest in an asset you believe will experience significant upside (appreciation) beyond normal market returns, either on its own or through your efforts improving the asset (also known as value-add), in an asset class you're knowledgeable about, or alongside an expert whom you trust.

For example, I grew up building computers for fun. When I discovered cryptocurrency in late 2013, I was priced out of mining Bitcoin (BTC) at the time given I was in law school and on a budget, as the blockchain mining difficulty for BTC required application-specific integrated circuit (ASIC) bitcoin miners, and the good ones were expensive, like $5,000 to $20,000 per unit expensive.

Luckily, I discovered Litecoin (LTC), which was still profitable to mine using gaming graphical processing units (GPU's). I saw LTC's future appreciation occurring when the crypto markets eventually viewed it as the cheaper alternative to BTC, akin to how silver is viewed alongside gold.

After I was convinced of my investment thesis, I built half a dozen LTC mining rigs using motherboards, gaming GPUs, power supply units (PSUs), and went to local gas stations to ask for the plastic milk crates they throw away to use as computer cases to lower my initial investment cost. I had to keep my A/C on max as these things generated immense heat.

I also had to accept the very loud buzzing of CPU, PSU, GPU and space fans running day and night. After a year and a half of full-time mining, I had accumulated a modest sized digital wallet full of LTC. Unfortunately, I ceased mining operations as I was finishing law school and the price of Litecoin was not going up like I had anticipated. Fortunately, I held onto some of my LTC and completely forgot about them until sometime in 2017 my friend called and told me they had gone up in price, A LOT.

I then got re-engaged into the crypto space and bought into Ethereum's (ETH) investment thesis (who's value proposition centered around smart contracts) and traded my Litecoins for Ethereum when it was somewhere around $200 per ETH. By the time the cryptocurrencies had reached their peak at the height of the crypto craze near the end of 2017, I started getting calls from friends who had never been in the crypto space before; I started seeing it all over the news; I started seeing relatives in their fifties, sixties, and seventies get excited about cryptocurrency and want to invest. It was a classic speculative bubble like the Dutch Tulip Mania.

This set off alarm bells within my subconscious that told me perhaps it would be a good time to take profits and transition into another investment vehicle. This spurred me to fortuitously liquidate my ETH at around $1,200 (close to its peak). The pre-tax returns from the Litecoin to Ethereum trade alone were around 6x (600%) in about 6 months time.

If I had owned a home in law school like some of my peers instead of rented, I would not have had the extra cash necessary to invest in LTC mining and partake in that unique appreciation opportunity. And while that specific opportunity has passed, there will always be unique appreciation opportunities either in certain types of equities, real estate, gold and silver, commodities, bonds, currencies, cryptocurrencies, and so forth. It's just a matter of timing. Timing is everything.

The truth is, the returns from the extra money saved per year by choosing the option with the smaller total annual cash outlay may be incalculable if it enables you to hop onto any of the above-mentioned fast tracks to wealth and explode your income or net worth.

"IS RENTING OVER PURCHASING MY HOME A SMART MOVE BECAUSE I'LL HAVE EXTRA MONEY TO INVEST INTO THE S&P 500 OR THE NASDAQ?"

Probably not. If the after-tax real yield on the investments or appreciation opportunities you're looking at are simply market-level returns, such as 6% or 7% inflation-adjusted historical average returns of the S&P 500, your net worth may be worse off by renting and investing the difference (with those kinds of returns) than had you of just purchased your home. This is because a 6% or 7% return, depending on your mortgage payments and annual non-mortgage homeowner expenses, may not be enough to offset the currency you lose to renting, and your net worth may be better off owning.

This isn't to say allocating a portion of your investment portfolio towards major stock market indexes isn't a valid strategy, just that investing ALL your additional savings into the stock market indexes isn't likely to get you wealthier faster than if you just purchase your home and avoid paying rent.

THE THIRD OPTION: CO-LIVING WITH FAMILY OR FRIENDS

For those desiring to build wealth quickly, another choice that may or may not exist for you is to live with immediate or extended family members that you get along with for a period of time. You may have family members who would be glad to have you in their home, albeit you may want to help out with things here and there, nobody likes a freeloader!

Many very wealthy people have done this during the earlier

stages of their journey in order to save up as much money as they could to accelerate their investing either into themselves, their business, or acquiring passive income yielding investments, all of which enabled them to escape the rat race. The money saved otherwise would have been wasted on rent or house payments, both of which are not fast track avenues to wealth.

If your family demands rent, perhaps you can offer to trade your labor in the place of rent. For example, if the family member(s) you think you could get along living with have a small business, and they could legitimately use your help, particularly if you have skills that would benefit their business.

If living with family is out of the question, perhaps you and your friends could rent a place together, lowering the cost of living dramatically from living on your own.

"I'D RATHER TAKE THE SLOW TRACK TO WEALTH AND HAVE A HEALTHIER WORK/LIFE BALANCE"

That's completely understandable! Most people will not have a healthy work-life balance if they take the fast track to wealth and want to be successful at it. You will work many times harder than most people with a regular job and salary, sacrificing an incredible amount of your life away with no guarantee of success.

Notwithstanding this decision, you may still want to review some of the previously mentioned fast track to wealth alternatives, particularly the investing in yourself by acquiring or enhancing your marketable skills, such as investing in some quality sales training (check out Grant Cardone's book *Sell or Be Sold*) and courses pertinent to your profession to heighten the level of service you can provide to the market, as well as any industry or trade certifications that could help you move up in your respective profession. Being patient when it comes to buying a home and using that extra cash to invest in yourself could pay off in spades over the long run.

THE HOME CAN BE A FORCED SAVINGS ACCOUNT

For most people, even if it's a terrible investment (having a very low or negative real rate of return), a home does act as a kind of forced savings account. For people who are not disciplined enough to save a large chunk of their income and successfully invest on a regular basis, a home may be a good choice.

Owning one's home outright without a mortgage would be the best choice, but for those that can only obtain a home via a mortgage, it may be a necessary evil. At least the principal portions of their mortgage payments go into "equity," while with renting, the rent money is gone and then what they have left over they blow.

And what do savings accounts have in common? Very low returns. Just be sure to have realistic expectations. As previously demonstrated in our example in chapter 12 of a home appreciating by 66.5%, when the actual ancillary homeownership expenses and inflation are taken into consideration, your home will likely give you a very low or even negative real rate of return should you sell.

On the flipside, a 0% or even -5% rate of return is better than -100%, which is the rate of return you'll get if you rent and blow your leftover income on discretionary consumer expenditures like eating out all the time, alcohol, expensive trips and vacations, new vehicles, unnecessarily expensive electronics, and so forth.

HOMEBUYING TIPS

Tip #1: Abide by the 20% Rule of Housing. This will keep you from buying more house than you should. I know it's difficult when your friends buy an oversized home that has them living paycheck to paycheck, and you want to live that lifestyle too. Or when you watch HGTV and see regular people with regular incomes buying $700,000 homes. Just remind yourself that for most of these people it's simply feeding an illusion of wealth, most of them are house rich and cash poor debt slaves to the banks.

Tip #2: Avoid private mortgage insurance (PMI) like the plague. This has zero benefit to you and is a completely unnecessary additional monthly non-mortgage expense, money that could otherwise have gone to pay down the principal faster or to invest; PMI only benefits the banks as it's additional insurance for them if you default. If you can't afford a large enough down payment to purchase a home without triggering PMI, you're buying WAY too much house. For readers in the UK this is the mortgage indemnity guarantee.

Tip #3: Avoid adjustable rate mortgages (ARMs), also called "variable interest rate" mortgages. With these, the interest rate is "floating" and changes depending on the fed funds rate, which changes on the whims of our central banksters, rather than the devices of the free market. Over the long term, this can be dangerous, particularly if the prime rate increases from what it was when you secured the loan to purchase your house, meaning your cost of debt goes up, and in turn, your mortgage payments go up. This unnecessarily adds risk when you can just get a fixed-rate mortgage.

Tip #4: STAY AWAY from homeowners associations (HOAs). If you're a real estate investor looking to rent property out, HOAs can be a good thing if they pass certain qualifications, but that's beyond the scope of this book. Yes, an HOA can help ensure property owners around you don't do dumb things that lower the property values in your neighborhood, but if you purchase in the right neighborhood with the right quality neighbors in the first place, this isn't necessary. For your personal home, an HOA adds monthly fees which over the years will unnecessarily drain your net worth, and when you consider the opportunity cost of those wasted dollars, you'll find the costs vastly outweigh the benefits.

For example, let's assume your HOA fee is $300 per month (some can be as high as $700 per month), and you live in that home for 20 years. We'll assume inflation is 0% for demonstration purposes because if inflation goes up almost every HOA's fees will go up to match inflation. Over 20 years at an opportunity cost of 6% compounding annual interest, $300 per month of HOA fees ends up costing you $136,694, that's $136,694 you're guaranteed to lose (as long as you can get a 6% return), while on the other hand having an HOA does NOT guarantee your neighborhood's property values won't go down.

Tip #5: Avoid buying your home in states with large unfunded pension liabilities. These are states that have massive pension obligations coming due because of the upcoming tidal wave of retiring baby boomers, and their pension obligations are unfunded, meaning the states do not have the funds to service them (notwithstanding their current tax revenues), because of fiscal mismanagement by career politicians uneducated in real-world economics and finance.

The states with the largest total pension shortfalls (i.e., the states whose politicians made the most promises they couldn't honor) include: California (the largest), New Jersey (2nd largest), and Illinois (3rd largest).[63] This issue is also called the "pension crisis" and even Warren Buffet is telling people to stay away from the states that have it the worst.[64]

Why would buying a home in one of these financially insolvent states be a potential problem for you as an individual homeowner? Who do you think the politicians are going to turn to in order to get the funds to cover these obligations? This brand of politicians, who had no qualms about making promises to their voters they couldn't keep, will become increasingly predatory towards any productive citizens (not on the welfare system) that haven't yet fled their state.

Property taxes in these already highly taxed states are going to skyrocket in the coming years, so be prepared to pay ever-higher property taxes year after year. In addition to stealing your hard-earned currency every year, it will also put downward pressure on your home's market value.

In addition to raising property taxes, they're going to raise taxes on businesses. What happens when these states, which already have extreme regulatory environments with huge legal and compliance costs, continue to raise taxes on their already over-taxed and over-regulated businesses?

Those businesses shut down or leave the state and *take their jobs with them*. This is already playing out as companies flee California and New York for states like Texas and Florida. In

---

63 Evan Comen, "Is your money safe? These states are getting hit hardest by the pension crisis" *USA Today* (Oct 15, 2019), usatoday.com/story/money/2019/10/15/every-states-pension-crisis-ranked/40302439/

64 Anil Niraula, "Warren Buffett: Avoid States With Large Unfunded Pension Liabilities" *Reason Foundation* (May 7, 2019), reason.org/commentary/warren-buffett-avoid-states-with-large-unfunded-pension-liabilities/

2016 alone some 1,800 companies fled California, with Texas being their #1 destination.[65]

Commercial real estate investors and developers are keenly aware of the importance of basic-job providers, that is, companies that create jobs (called basic-jobs) that bring in cashflow from outside the local economy. These jobs are more important than non-basic jobs, because basic jobs allow non-basic jobs to exist in the first place, as they have a multiplier effect called the economic base multiplier (EBM), creating X number of non-basic jobs per basic job. Thus, if a company creates 50 basic jobs in a market, and the EBM in that local economy is 5 (the EBM can vary from market to market); that means that in addition to those 50 basic-jobs, that company has also created roughly 200 non-basic jobs (jobs like police, firefighters, EMTs, teachers, doctors, nurses, dentists, restaurant and retail workers, and so forth).

Without basic jobs, there is no money to pay police, firefighters, EMTs, teachers, doctors, dentists, and so on. Unless you expect those people to work for free and not be able to pay for their own housing or feed their own families.

Why would a loss in basic jobs affect the market value of your home? Because people migrate to where there is employment opportunity, so when there's diminished job opportunities in your area, demand for housing is also diminished and with it the buyer pool for your home. This inevitably destroys a significant portion of your home's equity, which will really have an impact on your net worth when you sell or refinance.

An extreme example of this is the city of Detroit, whose primary basic-job providers were the auto manufacturing industry. When they left, they took not just their basic jobs with them, but

65 Bill Hethcock, "1,800 companies left California in a year – with most bound for Texas" *The Business Journals* (Dec 13, 2018), bizjournals.com/bizjournals/news/2018/12/13/1-800-companies-left-california-in-a-year-with.html

the cash inflows and demand that sustained hundreds of thousands of non-basic jobs. Property values plummeted, eventually to the point that in many neighborhoods' owners couldn't give their homes away and just abandoned them.

Tip #6: Consider moving to fiscally responsible states.
The states you may want to consider buying a home in, if your work and life situation permits, are states that we'll call fiscally responsible states, such as:

- Texas*
- Florida*
- Nevada*
- Alaska*
- Wyoming*
- Tennessee (no state tax on wages or salaries)
- New Hampshire (no state tax on wages or salaries)
- Kentucky
- Arizona
- Utah
- South Carolina
- Idaho
- Arkansas

* denotes states without income tax as of 2020. This is a VERY attractive attribute, as state income taxes absolutely eat away at your potential savings. The home values in fiscally responsible states are likely to fair substantially better than the rest of the U.S.

Tip #7: Live outside the city if possible.

Generally speaking, most cities are more expensive to live in than the suburbs or rural areas, particularly in terms of housing costs, taxes, groceries, and other day-to-day consumer purchases. Of course, you have to factor in time and cost traveling into the city if your work requires that.

Tip #8: Take property taxes into account.

Even if a state does not have state income tax, there are localities that may have high property taxes, and that is an important factor to consider when comparing homes and areas to live in. Be sure to look at the property tax trend; is it continually being increased year after year? If so, perhaps you might want to consider a home in an area with a more property rights friendly appraiser and local government.

If you're comparing two homes, assuming they're close to even in all other respects, but one is an extra $1,500 per year in property taxes, over 20 years that's an extra $30,000 expense you're incurring. Perhaps you should buy the home with lower property taxes so that $30,000 can go to something more useful than government bureaucrats...

Tip #9: Look into whether your state and county have a homestead exemption.

These are laws that provide certain financial and legal protections to homeowners on their principal residence. Most states and counties that have a homestead exemption require you to submit an application. Generally speaking, the benefits of getting a homestead exemption are:

- Lower property taxes via a reduced assessed value of your property, either by a fixed amount or based on a specified percentage. For example, if your property tax rate is 1.1%, and your property prior to filing for the homestead exemption was assessed at $300,000, you were paying $3,300 per year, or $33,000 over 10 years (assuming the assessed value is constant for demonstration purposes). If your state's exemption is $50,000, this lets you reduce $50,000 from the assessed value and in our hypothetical situation, the assessed value is reduced from $300,000 to $250,000, with your annual property tax now reduced from $3,300 to $2,750 per year, or $27,500 over 10 years (leaving you with an extra $5,500 in your pocket over the 10 year period), or a 16.7% annual savings. Check your county as well which may have additional homestead benefits.

- Asset protection from a forced sale of your home by specified unsecured creditors in the event of bankruptcy or default.

Speak with your local attorney and county tax assessor regarding your specific state and county's homestead exemption require-ments, benefits, and application process.

CHAPTER 14

TWO PRIMARY GOALS OF INVESTING

Save or Slave was written for people who want better lives for themselves and their loved ones. By employing the mindsets, tools, and hacks contained in this book, the reader should be able to EXPLODE their savings to such levels that, when invested (wisely) on a regular basis, over time will create life-changing financial freedom.

With that said, having just $1,000 to your name and investing that isn't going to make a big difference in your life. Yes, the habit is important and all that jazz, but let's face it, unless you invested your $1,000 in Bitcoin when it was one dollar, $1,000 simply isn't enough to meaningfully create life-changing results and financial freedom.

So before reading this chapter and embarking on the investing side of this journey, MAKE SURE you have used the information in the previous chapters to become a proficient *Rational Saver*, otherwise, investing would be putting the cart before the horse (doing things backwards to your detriment). This means that, among other things:

- you're diligently employing the savings hacks and mindsets covered in *Save or Slave*, and you have created a net worth statement which you update weekly;

- you've performed a diagnostic budget (that you review weekly) and are using the hacks in chapter 5 to dramatically lower your operating expense ratio and boost your savings rate;

- you're free of bad debts (consumer debts like credit cards, auto and student loans, etc.), because investing when you've outstanding credit card debt at 22% interest is counterproductive;

- you have an emergency fund to cover at least 6 months of living expenses; and

- you're actively working on a viable plan to increase your income and the amount of value you can provide to the marketplace or your employer.

If you've done the above, now it's time to start putting our money to work (instead of just working for money). First, we need to define our goals in investing and always keep these in mind so we stay on track.

The *Rational Saver's* two primary goals of investing are:

Goal #1: **To NOT LOSE WEALTH**. This means (a) protect yourself from the hidden enemy we're going to discuss shortly, and (b) invest wisely. Otherwise, you can lose your hard-earned money and do more harm than good.

Goal #2: **To create passive income systems**, also called cashflow, so your wealth starts increasing even when you're sleeping, i.e., so your active income (where you trade your time and labor for currency) is not your only income source.

Goal #1 always supersedes **Goal #2**. Never sacrifice **Goal #1** by making foolish investment decisions trying to attain **Goal #2**.

CHAPTER 15

THE HIDDEN TAX OF INFLATION

This chapter will explore the topic of inflation further, as it pertains to your efforts in building wealth for yourself and your loved ones.

WEALTH, MONEY, AND CURRENCY

The definition of wealth is *"an abundance of valuable possessions or money."* Of course, what constitutes valuable possessions is subjective, but in the context of finance, it's likely to mean private property that is objectively valuable. They have a high degree of market liquidity (i.e., are relatively easy to sell), things such as: real estate, stocks, bonds, commodities, and so forth.

Note after the words "valuable possessions" the word "money" is used. So far, we've used the words "money" and "currency" interchangeably to make this book more reader-friendly. However, at this juncture, it's important we distinguish currency from money. Currency and money have many similar attributes; however, they differ in two significant ways:

First, we're forced to use currency (dollars if you're in the U.S., Euros if you're in Europe, etc.), for our day-to-day purchases of goods and services because providers of goods and services need currency in order to service their debts and pay taxes, thanks to the legal tender and tax laws passed at the behest of private central bankers that lobbied congress (not out of the kindness of their hearts).

Second, money is a store of value, whereas currency is NOT a store of value, as evidenced by the U.S. Dollar having lost 97% of its value since the establishment of the Federal Reserve in 1913.[66] Value can also be thought of as synonymous with purchasing power, that is, how much goods and services you can purchase. In other words, money is a store of purchasing power, whereas currency is not a store of purchasing power.

DOLLAR DEVALUATION DENIAL SYNDROME

I can already hear the Keynesians with their $100,000+ economics degrees not worth the paper they're printed on exclaiming "but you can't compare dollars in 1913 to dollars now, because they didn't have iPhones back then, so that would be comparing apples to oranges..." If we're still using logic, acceptance of this argument would necessarily entail that we should ignore inflation because every year new technological gadgets come out...

In 1912, a man's tailored suit cost around $20. In 2020, a medium quality man's tailored suit is around $800. Is a tailored suit today 40 times better than a tailored suit in 1912 because we have smart phones?! How about food? The average price of a loaf of bread in 1913 was 5.6 cents. In 2020 it was $2.07. Is 2020 bread 37 times better than bread in 1913 because we have the internet? Organic eggs were 37.3 cents per dozen in 1913.[67] In

66 Tom Lewis, "The Failure of Fiat Currencies" *The Gold Telegraph* (Feb 28, 2018), http://goldtelegraph.com/failure-fiat-currencies/

67 Tim McMahon, "Food Price Inflation Since 1913" *InflationData.com* (Mar 21, 2013), inflationdata.com/articles/2013/03/21/food-price-inflation-1913/

2020, the average price for a dozen organic eggs ranged from $4 to $7. If we use the lower end figure of $4, does that mean that a dozen organic eggs in 2020 are 11 times better than a dozen organic eggs in 1913 because you have a smart TV?

Another argument I come across as to why we should ignore the dollar's long-term loss in purchasing is because people could always use their dollars to buy U.S. treasuries...

Forgetting the immoral aspect of this argument, that every day people and your grandma should know their dollars are hot potatoes and going to be devalued if they don't quickly exchange them for treasuries (as if there's a disclaimer on dollars saying "you'd better get rid of this quick it's purchasing power is going to drop"), this argument is moot because when we take into account actual inflation versus the skewed government reported CPI, real yields on treasuries have been negative since February of 2008, and as of this writing in 2020 they're still negative.

We will discuss actual inflation versus the government's reported CPI shortly.

WHAT DOES IT MEAN TO GROW YOUR WEALTH?

When we go back to the definition of wealth, part of which is the amount of money you have, this consequently means **growing your wealth entails *increasing your purchasing power*.** As an example, if you have $100,000 invested into an asset, and in one year it appreciates 30% net of taxes and disposition costs (at the end of the day you keep $130,000 from the sale), but due to inflation spiking that $130,000 can now only buy $90,000 worth of goods and services, well you didn't grow your wealth, you LOST WEALTH (and violated Goal #1), because your purchasing power was diminished; your net **nominal rate of return** was 30%, but your net **real rate of return** (the rate that's more important) was -10%.

FIAT CURRENCY –
A USEFUL TOOL FOR STEALTH CONFISCATION

Because all currencies are fiat (as of 2020), i.e., backed by the issuer's word instead of something tangible like a commodity, governments can simply print/type it into existence through open market operation shell games with their friendly central bankers whenever they need to pay for stuff, inflating the monetary supply which increases the prices of assets, goods, and services in the sectors of the economy that receive the fiat currency injections.

To date, there is no historical precedence of a fiat currency successfully holding its value.[68] They have all persistently and substantially lost most of their value over time, and many have gone to virtually zero. This is by design.

Fiat currencies were conjured up by unscrupulous central bankers, also called the "international banking cartel," "money masters," the "globalist cabal," or the "lords of finance," as a trick to steal the economic energy (time and labor) from the masses undetected, turning that accumulated economic energy into geopolitical power...

This explains why in the U.S. in 1955 you could buy a starter home for around $31,000 that in 2020 would cost $300,000.[69] This wouldn't be *as* devastating if wages matched the rate of inflation, but they don't. Wage and income growth for the middle

---

68 "The Rise and Fall of Fiat Currencies" *Dinar Dirham* (Oct 12, 2018), dinardirham.com/the-rise-and-fall-of-fiat-currencies/

69 UsInflationCalculator.com

and lower classes are NOWHERE NEAR in keeping with the rate of inflation.

As proof, in 1985 the median U.S. household income was $23,620,[70] and the median cost for a home was $82,800.[71] That means it took approximately 3.5 years of median income labor to gross the amount of dollars needed to purchase the median home. In 2019, the median U.S. household income was $68,703,[72] and the median cost for a home was $313,000, requiring 4.55 years of median income labor to purchase the same home. That's a 30% increase in the cost of housing relative to wages in just 34 years.

The Manhattan Institute issued a report on whether the American family has been prospering or languishing over time. In the report they created a "Cost-of-Thriving Index" (COTI) which tracks the cost of a basket of products and services a family of four are likely to want to purchase. They then compared the median weekly income over time to the increase in costs of goods and services in that basket. They found that in 1985 it took 30 weeks of the median weekly wage to afford a 3-bedroom house at the 40th percentile (local market pricing), a semester of public college, a family health-insurance policy, and the operation of an automobile.[73] By 2018, it took 53

70 "Money Income of Households, Families, and Persons in the United States: 1985", *United States Census Bureau* (Aug 1987), census.gov/library/publications/1987/demo/p60-156.html

71 "Median Sales Prices of Houses Sold for the United States", *Federal Reserve Bank of St. Louis Economic Research* (accessed 9/18/2020), fred.stlouisfed.org/series/MSPUS

72 "Income, Poverty and Health Insurance Coverage in the United States: 2019", *United States Census Bureau* (Sep 15, 2020), census.gov/newsroom/press-releases/2020/income-poverty.html

73 Oren Cass, "The Cost-of-Thriving Index: Reevaluating the Prosperity of the American Family" *Manhattan Institute* (Feb 20, 2020), manhattan-institute.org/reevaluating-prosperity-of-american-family

weeks of labor to afford those same goods and services. This means that a full-time job at the median weekly wage would no longer be sufficient to even afford that same standard of living because there are only 52 weeks in a year.[74]

Accordingly, if median wages matched inflation, the number of weeks of laboring at the median wage needed for the same standard of living should still be 30 weeks, rather than having increased to 53 weeks (a 76% increase). Clearly, median wage growth has been dismal, while the cost of living has skyrocketed.

There are many consequences of this long-term currency devaluation asides from the cost of living going up for each successive generation (housing, education, food, energy, vehicles, healthcare, and so forth). One of these consequences is the uneven distribution of the monetary supply inflation (the Cantillon Effect) which further exacerbates the disparity of wealth in society, and creates misdirected blame towards "capitalism" when the root cause of the problem, central banking, is in fact textbook communism (see Karl Marx's calls for "centralization of credit" in his *Manifesto of the Communist Party*).[75]

Capitalists abhor manipulation or interference with the free markets by government and central banks, as well as government-sanctioned monopolies for special interest groups and criminal cabals.

This has resulted in citizens uneducated in economics and history (even ones with degrees from top-ranked universities) crying out for more socialism as the answer, akin to passengers on the Titanic yelling at the captain to go faster towards the

---

74 *Ibid*

75 Thorsten Polleit, "Why Marx Loved Central Banks" *Mises Institute* (02/08/2018), mises.org/wire/why-marx-loved-central-banks

iceberg, rather than to change course and head to the safe harbor of capitalism.

How does this personally affect us with regards to our Goal #1 of not losing wealth? Let's go back to our 1955 example and suppose it took your grandparents 10 years of hard work to save that $31,000, the cost of a respectable starter home in 1955. Suppose they took that $31,000 and instead of buying a home, put it in the family safe, and told their kids to hold onto it for emergencies and to tell their kids to do the same. By 2020, that $31,000 your grandparents saved would have lost 90% of its purchasing power, and 9 of the 10 years of time and labor your grandparents traded for that $31,000 would be erased.

This is why billionaire hedge fund manager Ray Dalio famously said, "cash is trash." As a *Rational Saver*, know that **an ever-present enemy we have to fight is the hidden tax of inflation.** Many people are not aware of this hidden tax, or are only vaguely aware but not enough for it to alter their savings strategy, hence why so many people from 2008 to this writing in 2020 have had their savings sitting in bank certificates of deposit (CDs), savings accounts and U.S. treasuries, all with negative yields in real terms, meaning they've all been guaranteed to lose the holder's purchasing power, i.e., their wealth.

So if you have a 10-year U.S. Treasury that's yielding 0.60% in nominal terms, and we suppose the actual non-skewed average rate of inflation for the duration of the note's term is 5%, this means every year that 10-year Treasury note's real yield is -4.4%, that's a 4.4% loss of purchasing power per year.

"But...xyz government agency said inflation is/was only ___%!" See below.

ACTUAL INFLATION VS. GOVERNMENT SKEWED CPI

So far, when inflation has come up, for demonstration purposes we've used the Fed's stated target inflation rate of 2%. However, the Bureau of Labor Statistics (BLS) reported headline inflation, i.e. the Consumer Price Index (CPI), as well as the Core Inflation rate, have both been MASSIVELY manipulated since the early 1980s to under-report the real rate of inflation felt by the median American consumer unit (the majority of people).

This was done through a multitude of statistics tricks, such as taking the old CPI, which originally measured a pre-defined consistently weighted basket of goods and services the median consumer unit realistically purchased with regularity, and overwhelm that original basket with some 80,000+ items, most of which the everyday consumer does not buy on a regular basis.[76] Anyone with an elementary understanding of statistics would catch the fatal flaw here – by adding tens of thousands of goods and services not consumed on a regular basis, you're drowning out meaningful data on increases in costs of goods and services that ARE consumed on a regular basis, portraying the real rate of inflation felt by the median consumer unit as lower than it really is.

Another gimmick is to exclude essential items from the Core CPI, such as food, energy, and income and social security taxes. I guess the government doesn't think increases in the cost of food, energy, and taxes effect our lives enough to include it in the Core CPI…

In the early 1980s, they also transitioned from the traditional way of measuring the cost of housing, which was based on the price to buy a new home, to home owner's equivalent

---

76 "Problems with the Consumer Price Index", *Chapwood Index* (accessed 9/19/2020), chapwoodindex.com/problems-with-the-consumer-price-index/

rent (OER) which is what a homeowner would have to pay themselves in rent in order to have housing equivalent to their cost of ownership...this is just another convoluted trick to under-report inflation, and it worked, subtracting over a full percentage point from the headline CPI when the transition was made in 1982.[77]

One of the most egregious tricks was transitioning from the Cost of Goods Index (COGI) originally used to track inflation, to a Cost of Living Index (COLI). With the COGI, they simply tracked the prices of common everyday consumer goods and services. But with the current COLI, they make adjustments to the prices of those goods and services for quality, which is entirely subjective.

So, if the cost of a new car has increased from $15,000 to $19,500, the old COGI method would simply say the new car item has increased by 30%, while the dishonest current COLI method would put the cost increase far below 30% because of improvements in the underlying good or service... "well, this newer car has a better ABS system, seat warmers for if your buttocks are cold, and an LCD navigation screen!"

Which method more honestly reflects the cost increase of a new car? The one that tracks the actual cost increase, or the one that downplays the increase in price due to subjective quality enhancements? People don't buy cars to have their butts warmed or to have the upgraded ABS system, they buy cars for transportation. That added LCD screen inside the car didn't offset the extra $4,500 on the new car's sticker price.

They also began making substitution adjustments. Traditionally, the government would track fixed goods, for example, a steak was a steak and chicken was chicken. But then they began substituting items, for example, if steak became more expensive, they'd figure people will buy less steak and buy more chicken

---

77 "False Stats Cannot Hide The Collapse: John Williams", *Liberty and Finance* YouTube Channel (Jun 22, 2020), youtube.com/watch?v=GW5O1creMO4

due to the increase in the price of steak, in other words sub-stitute chicken for steak, and they would give chicken a greater weighting, skewing the fact that the cost of steak increased.

They've done this with all sorts of goods and services. The CPI is supposed to let people know the cost for maintaining a constant standard of living, not a diminishing standard of living...

Who benefited from the government manipulation and gim-micks to hide the real rate of consumer price inflation? The gov-ernment. By reducing headline inflation, they reduced the cost of living adjustments that government would have to make on social security benefits and government pensions (to include military and VA pensions), as a means for reducing their budget deficits...

This is why you may have spoken to retirees on social security or government pensions who have indicated it's become increas-ingly difficult to get by on that pension or social security. That's because the CPI is massively under reported, so it's a hidden device for robbing social security and retirement pensions right from under the retirees' noses.

The family dynasties that control and profit from the cen-tral banking system also benefited from these changes in the measurement of inflation, as it helps them hide from the gen-eral trusting (naïve) public the continued theft of our economic energy (causing ever-increasing wealth disparity and decimation of the middle class) through fractional reserve lending and issu-ing fiat currency over sound money (see Article 1, Section 10 of the U.S. Constitution).

The result of all this CPI dishonesty as it pertains to us indi-vidual *Rational Savers*? Well, let's suppose in January of 2017, before this book came out, your run of the mill financial advisor told you to have a 60/40 portfolio allocation of stocks to bonds (the mainstream financial advice), and at that time your total liquid net worth is $250,000, so after talking to this financial

THE HIDDEN TAX OF INFLATION

"advisor" you put $100,000 into 5-year U.S. Treasury Series EE notes, which on January 23 of 2017 had a nominal yield of 1.95%. We'll presume you lived in Philadelphia.

According to the Chapwood Index, which gathers inflation data and drills down by market, the actual consumer price inflation rate for the years 2017, 2018 and 2019 in Philadelphia would have averaged out to 10.86% (not 1% or 2% like the BLS reported).

For demonstration purposes, assuming the 10.86% average actual consumer inflation rate for Philadelphia continued on through 2022, this means that when your $100,000 Treasury Note with a nominal yield of 1.95% matures, the maturity value would only be able to purchase $65,775 worth of goods and services in 2017 (when you made the initial investment). In other words, you lost 34% of your purchasing power in only 5 years and violated **Goal #1: TO NOT LOSE WEALTH.**

Let's assume you're a "somewhere in the middle" person and the Chapwood Index says your particular market's average inflation rate is 9%. You might think "well, 9% inflation that's just way too high, but after doing more research into the statistical tricks and gimmicks listed, 2% probably is way under-reporting, so I think it's probably somewhere in the middle." Okay, so 2% is the lower bound and 9% the upper bound, the middle would be 5.5% inflation PER YEAR.

At 5.5% inflation per year, if you invested $100,000 of your savings into a 10-year note with a **nominal yield** of 1.95%, in 10 years the maturity value of your note is $121,303, but in terms of buying power after 10 years of 5.5% inflation, would be the equivalent to $71,015 in today's dollars (when you made the initial investment), meaning your "investment" would have lost 29% of its initial purchasing power. That is a serious problem for those trying to preserve, or God forbid, grow their wealth!

The Keynesian economists who criticize those that question

the **BLS's** reported inflation bring up MIT's Billion Prices Project which arrives at an inflation rate similar to the **BLS's** reported rate. Hey, they're using data aggregation from hundreds of online retailers, sounds high tech, and it's MIT + macro economists (Keynesians), so they must be right, case closed...

Of course, there's no way they're using a similar flawed methodology as the government... such as measuring too many goods and services that the median consumer unit does not actually purchase on a regular basis, or adding subjective quality adjustments or substitutions to pricing just as the **BLS** does... or dozens of other statistical tricks to arrive at a similar rate of inflation..."But in 2018 the Billion Prices Project won the Economics in Central Banking Award, so central bankers approve of their findings![78]" Let that sink in for a bit...

For those that do not believe the government would lie to you and under-report the real rate of inflation through statistics games, head on over to George Gammon, creator of the Rebel Capitalist Show, who put out an excellent video on this topic titled "Consumer Price Index: Biggest Scam In US History Revealed."

THE ANTIDOTE TO INFLATION

For those who don't believe the government's bogus inflation stats, the antidote to this problem I use is to have a higher allocation of savings in money as opposed to fiat currency. So, what is money? J.P. Morgan, an agent of the Rothschilds (the creators of the central banking scam) who financed Rockefeller's

---

78 Central Banking, "Economics in central banking: Alberto Cavallo and Roberto Rigobon – Billion Prices Project/PriceStats" *CentralBanking.com* (Jan 24, 2018), centralbanking. com/awards/3346716/economics-in-central-banking-alberto-cavallo-and-roberto-rigobon-billion-prices-projectpricestats

Standard Oil empire, answered this question shortly before his death in 1912 while testifying before U.S. Congress: *"gold is money; everything else is credit."*

If we go back to our 1955 example, and suppose instead of putting that $31,000 in the family safe, our hypothetical grandparents purchased physical gold with it, which in January of 1955 was around $35.31 per ounce, they would have been able to acquire roughly 878 one-ounce American Gold Eagles (AGEs). In September of 2020, the spot price of gold was around $1,950 per ounce, and the premiums on 1-ounce AGEs were around $100, so that 878 ounces of gold would be worth roughly $1,712,000 plus $87,800 (878 x $100 premium), for a total of $1,800,000.

Pop quiz: Of the three uses for the $31,000 in our hypothetical 1955 example, which one would have done the best job preserving the grandparent's wealth?

(a) Leaving $31,000 in cash in the family safe so the grandkids in 2020 can use it to buy a new luxury SUV or cover one year of college tuition at a mid-tier school;

(b) Buy a $31,000 house that in 2020 might be worth $300,000;

(c) Buy 878 ounces of gold for $31,000 that in 2020 would be worth $1.8 MILLION DOLLARS!

Yes, C is the correct answer. Gold preserved and GREW the family's wealth far beyond just being able to buy a starter home; with $1.8 million dollars in 2020, you could buy six $300,000 starter homes, or even better, a quality 16-unit cash flowing apartment building with all cash and zero debt, or perhaps three 16-unit apartment buildings (in 2020 dollars) if using leverage (i.e., a mortgage).

Gold and Silver's Track Record as International Money

The history of gold and silver as money goes as far back as the Sumerians in 2700 B.C., whose civilization was located in the southernmost region of ancient Mesopotamia (modern-day Iraq and Kuwait) between the Tigris and Euphrates rivers.[79] The Sumerian's neighbors to the west, ancient Egypt, by that time was also using gold for the exchange of goods and services. That's over 4,700 years ago.

The Old Testament, Quran, and Hadiths all speak of the king of Israel, King Solomon, and numerous references to his wealth in gold and silver, and the legendary lost "Ophir" gold mine that provided King Solomon's Temple and the Kingdom of Israel with their immense riches.

The Achaemenid Empire, an ancient Iranian civilization founded by Cyrus the Great, began issuing gold and silver coins in 520 B.C., with the most notable being the imperial Persian Daric gold coin and the Siglos silver coin. Silver coins were used as money in ancient Greece during Alexander the Great's reign and remained so throughout the Mediterranean for over four centuries after his death. In the east, gold and silver coins were used in India as money starting in the 6th century B.C., and in China during the Han Dynasty between 202 B.C. and 220 A.D.

The Romans considered gold a metal of their pagan gods, having descended from the sun. It was commonly used in jewelry and ornaments to signify one's social status, wealth and prosperity. Gold and silver coins (the Aureus and Denarius) were the predominant form of Roman money, from 753 B.C. and the regal period, to 509 B.C. with the founding of the Republic, to the establishment of the Roman Empire in 27 B.C., and the

---

79 Nathan Lewis, "Gold Has Always Been The Best Money" *Forbes* (Aug 12, 2020), forbes.com/sites/nathanlewis/2020/08/12/gold-has-always-been-the-best-money/

formation of the Byzantine Empire in the East in 330 A.D. which used gold and silver up into medieval times.

The Arab caliphates that arose from the Islamic prophet Mohammed, starting with the 3rd Caliph Uthman of the Rashidun Caliphate, used gold coins in trade like their Byzantine neighbors. The gold Dinar was the most notable minted coin of the Arab empire, and this was used throughout their massive controlled territory, which at the height of the caliphate spanned from Baghdad to Barcelona.

During the dark ages, outside of Byzantium, gold was too scarce to be used as money in every day trade in medieval Europe; rather, most gold was hoarded by kings for bribes, reserves for military conflict, and gifts to advance royal political objectives. It was also used by the church for its most coveted objects such as altars and crowns.

The local economy in the countryside, comprised primarily of peasant farmers, was predominantly a barter economy. However, merchants, high officials in the church and nobility did use gold and silver coins for storing wealth and more significant transactions.

People have embarked on voyages across the globe and conquered new lands in search of gold and silver. Beginning around the 8th century A.D., the Vikings engaged in numerous raiding campaigns along the coastal regions of Western and Northern Europe, Ireland and Great Britain, looting some 400 tons of silver from the Anglo-Saxon kingdom alone.[80]

The rise of Italian city-states such as the Republic of Florence, with their advancements in culture, economics, art, and politics, were largely responsible for uplifting the rest of Europe out of the dark ages during what is now called the Renaissance

80 Jade Davenport, "Gold, silver in Medieval Europe" *Mining Weekly* (Aug 24, 2012), miningweekly.com/article/gold-and-silver-in-medieval-europe-2012-08-17

period. In 1252, Florence began minting gold coins, known as Florins, for use in regular transactions. In 1280, the Republic of Venice, after witnessing the powerful positive economic effects in Florence, copied their neighbor and began minting their own gold coins called Ducats.

Swiss economist Ferdinand Lips theorized that "gold money was the economic and financial basis of the Renaissance. Culture flourishes under conditions of wealth and not poverty."[81]

America's discovery in the 15th century was largely attributable to this thirst for gold, as Christopher Columbus's idea to connect Europe to Asia by sailing west was said to have been partially motivated by his desire to discover gold and silver in the new world.

Moreover, the sanctioning of his voyage by the Spanish monarchs, Ferdinand of Aragon and Isabella of Castile, was likely motivated by their desire for riches as well (in addition to spreading Catholicism), both in terms of expropriation of gold and silver directly from foreign lands, as well as from the creation of profitable trading routes that would indirectly result in more gold and silver accumulating in the royal treasury.[82]

The discovery of America spurred what many historians consider to be the first great gold rush of western civilization, with armies of Conquistadors risking death on perilous journeys across the Atlantic Ocean just to plunder gold from the New World. So much was seized that it increased 16th century Europe's gold supply by an estimated 500%.[83]

81 Ferdinand Lips (2001), *Gold Wars: The Battle Against Sound Money as Seen From a Swiss Perspective*. New York NY: Foundation for the Advancement of Monetary Education.

82 History.com Editors, "Christopher Columbus" *History.com* (Nov 9, 2009), history.com/topics/exploration/christopher-columbus

83 Nick Lioudis, "What is the Gold Standard?" *Investopedia* (Feb 3, 2019), investopedia.com/ask/answers/09/gold-standard.asp#

Gold and silver played a crucial role in the domestic economies and international trade and diplomacy of the Dutch and British Empires. Some historians believe the American revolution was largely caused by a loss of gold and silver in the colonies from acts of British parliament that siphoned gold and silver out of the colonies and into England's treasury by requiring all colonial debts to England be paid in gold and silver, while simultaneously preventing the export of gold and silver into the colonies, acts which were a part of England's broader economic policy of mercantilism.

This forced the colonies to resort to using their own local paper fiat currencies for trade with each other and British merchants, until King George III signed the Currency Act of 1764, outlawing most colonial currencies to the benefit of British merchants. The result was even higher inflation and exacerbated economic troubles, along with increased animosity between the colonies and tyrannical England.

In geopolitics, this is what's called a currency war, and throughout modern history, most shooting wars have been preceded by currency wars. In 1785, the fiat Continental dollar went into hyperinflation and became worthless, influencing the drafters of the U.S. Constitution during the Philadelphia Convention of 1787 to think gold and silver's use as money important enough to ensure it followed the preamble by placing it in Article I, Section 10, stating, *inter alia "No state shall...coin Money; emit Bills of Credit; make any Thing but gold and silver Coin a Tender in Payment of Debts."*

To the American people's detriment and the international central banking cartel's benefit, in 1884, a corrupted U.S. Supreme Court ruled in *Juilliard v. Greenman* that somehow the founder's intent was to leave an exception for congress to use fiat currency prone to inflation and possible collapse. This is despite the fact they just experienced a fiat currency collapse in 1785, and specifically wrote a prohibition on emitting anything but gold and silver as legal tender, and founders like James Madison made specific comments as to the legislative intent behind the provision, stating *"the pretext for paper currency, and particularly for making the bills a tender either for public or private debts, was cut off."*

In 1792, the states through Congress established a bimetallic GOLD AND SILVER standard for the U.S. currency... In 1821, England was the first nation to officially adopt a paper gold standard (a system whereby paper money is backed by and freely convertible into a fixed amount of gold).

In 1871, Germany followed England's example and there came about an international gold standard among many western nations. This ended in 1914 at the onset of World War One, as central bankers and the nations they controlled ditched the gold standard for fiat currency, that way they could finance the incredibly costly war for longer periods of time than a true gold standard would have permitted (it would have required peace terms far sooner, rather than fiat currency which can continue to be printed and allow armed conflicts to go on almost indefinitely).

In 1931, Britain officially abandoned their gold standard and in 1933 the tyrant FDR unconstitutionally outlawed private gold ownership by U.S. citizens under executive order # 6102. The National Socialists (Nazis) helped fund their war machine from the theft of Austrian gold during their invasion of Austria in 1938, stealing some 90 tons of gold.[84] Likewise, the communist Soviet Union was regularly sending its gold to the U.K.

---

84 George M. Taber, "The Epic Gold Heists that Financed the War for Hitler" *Knowledge@ Wharton* (Feb 11, 2016), knowledge.wharton.upenn.edu/article/the-epic-gold-heist-that-financed-the-war-for-hitler/

for war materials and military equipment to fight the Nazis on the eastern front.[85]

Prior to the U.S entering World War Two, the U.S. was the largest supplier of war materials to the allied countries, often in exchange for gold, resulting in the U.S. owning most of the world's gold reserves by the end of the war. This hindered any sort of return to a gold standard by the allied nations that had depleted their gold reserves buying U.S. war materials, along with defeated Axis powers whose gold reserves were confiscated by the U.S.[86]

In 1944, 44 Allied nations entered into an agreement known as the Bretton Woods Agreement whereby the world's currencies couldn't be linked to gold, rather, they were linked to the U.S. dollar (Federal Reserve notes), which was linked to gold, and the central banks would maintain fixed exchange rates between their currencies and the dollar, and in turn, the U.S. promised to redeem U.S. dollars for gold on demand (for the signatories, not U.S. citizens who were still prohibited from owning gold).

In 1971, Nixon unilaterally closed the gold window for foreign holders of dollars (dishonorably breaking the Bretton Woods treaty), preventing them from being able to convert their U.S. dollar holdings into gold per the terms of the agreement, finalizing the de-linkage of gold to the dollar.

While sound money was slowly being moved out of the hands of everyday people, the governments, big banks, and wealthy elites hoarded gold for themselves, using those as reserves to establish creditworthiness, shore up trade imbalances, and as a means of preserving dynastic wealth and protecting against

---

85 Charlie Parker, "HMS Edinburgh: diver ends silence on Soviet gold" *The Times* (Mar 16, 2020), thetimes.co.uk/article/hms-edinburgh-diver-ends-silence-on-soviet-gold-fsbns0g9q

86 David E. Sanger, "Nazi Gold Was Recast And Issued In the U.S." *The New York Times* (Nov 2, 1997), nytimes.com/1997/11/02/world/nazi-gold-was-recast-and-issued-in-the-us.html

unsound monetary policy (central bank debasement of currencies and theft of purchasing power from holders of those currencies, i.e., the everyday citizen).

Throughout history, gold has been viewed as a nation's real
reserves (along with commodities like oil), not how many IOUs
they print. Gold gives its holders autarky (economic indepen-
dence) for three primary reasons: (1) it's internationally recognized as money; (2) it has a high degree of liquidity; and (3) it
has zero counter-party risk.

Regarding #3, this is evidenced when a nation at war seeks
to acquire crucial supplies for its survival like armaments, food,
vehicles, oil, steel, and so forth, but potential trading partners
refuse to accept that nation's paper currency for risk of it being
worthless should that nation be defeated. However, that same
nation in crisis can get access to all of those supplies as long as
it comes to the trading table with gold, because regardless of the
outcome of the military conflict, the gold's value is unaffected
and as such has zero counter-party risk.

Suffice it to say, gold and silver have a VERY long track
record (almost 5,000 years) of being an international store of
value or money, a track record that is unparalleled. Nothing else
on Earth has preserved its value and acted as money anywhere
near as long as gold and silver.

WHY ARE GOLD AND SILVER PRECIOUS AND NOT SOMETHING ELSE?

When the topic of gold comes up, there are always those who will
say something along the lines of "gold only has value because
people say it does, it just as easily could be beads or feathers
or seashells, that's why I don't believe it is a good thing to own,

because humans may at some time randomly value some other arbitrary thing."

First, this argument doesn't hold much water when one looks at history in conjunction with the branch of mathematics concerning numerical descriptions of how likely an event is to occur or how likely it is that a proposition is true, also known as probability theory.

When we consider the probability of civilizations all over Earth for almost 5,000 years choosing gold as the predominant means of storing economic energy, out of all the other possible elements and objects available, the theory that gold was arbitrarily or randomly chosen becomes somewhat preposterous.

Do those positing this argument really believe one day people around the world will wake up and start coveting feathers and beads? Why do the world's top 10 most powerful nation states maintain the top 10 largest gold reserves, and not reserves of feathers and beads?[87] No Chairman Bernanke, it's not just because of "long-term tradition." The answer is: chemistry.

There are 118 elements on the periodic table of elements that humans have had to choose from for storing economic energy. There are 38 elements that have negative reactions to the environment, such as lithium, which if exposed to air will create an extremely powerful fire capable of burning through concrete. 11 of the elements are gasses, and for obvious reasons gas doesn't make a good form of money, you can't put gas in your pocket, you'd have to carry around a jar and every time you opened it up, you'd go broke...

Two elements are liquids: mercury and bromine. Mercury is highly toxic in a variety of forms, and as such it's not good for humans to be handling and hauling it around. Inhalation

---

87 "Top 10 Countries with Largest Gold Reserves" *U.S. Global Reserves* (Aug 25, 2020), http://usfunds.com/investor-library/frank-talk/top-10-countries-with-largest-gold-reserves/

of mercury vapors can be extremely harmful or even fatal to humans. Bromine is corrosive to human tissue in its liquid state, and bromine vapors are also highly toxic upon inhalation.

Fifteen elements are actinides and 14 elements are lanthanides. Both the actinides and lanthanides series of elements are highly radioactive and lethal...you might think twice about that cup of coffee if it entailed getting a nice dose of radiation in order to purchase it, yea?

The thing which is to be a store of wealth has to be rare, because human beings value things which are scarce. Why do Lamborghinis turn heads when people drive them? Because of their scarcity. If every person in the U.S. drove a Lamborghini, they wouldn't turn heads or command anywhere near the price they do.

This requirement of scarcity removes all the common elements like copper, nickel, iron, magnesium, silicon, tin, lead, and so forth. But it also can't be so rare that almost no one could obtain it or recognize what it is, like Osmium (the rarest element in the Earth's crust). Iridium, although not a part of the actinoid or lanthanoid series, is a rare transition metal that is classified by the IAEA as a category-2 radioactive substance that can permanently injure anyone who handles it for minutes to hours, and can kill people within close proximity within hours to days.

After we remove elements that:

- are too common to have scarcity;
- are too rare to be accumulated in sufficient quantities for trade;
- will escape because they're gasses;
- are toxic to handle or can create poisonous vapors;
- are radioactive; and

- will spontaneously combust or have other negative reactions to the environment...

We're left with the five remaining elements out of the 118 on the periodic table: palladium, rhodium, silver, platinum, and gold.

Of the 5 remaining elements, gold is the only one that does not tarnish, corrode, rust, or change colors over the years. Gold gives off a bright yellow reminiscent of the sun and rays of light, creating a beautiful aura that signifies life and success, and looks great not only in jewelry, but architecture, artifacts, religious objects, paintings and so forth.

Gold is unique in its color when compared to palladium, rhodium, and platinum, which all look similar in color to each other and to silver to the everyday person, who could easily confuse them for each other, making them an inferior choice for the primary store of economic energy when compared to gold.

Moreover, mining and processing platinum, rhodium and palladium are far more difficult than mining and processing silver, making silver the logical choice as the store of economic energy for smaller transactions than those that would warrant gold.

As should be obvious by now, chemistry and history show us gold and silver inherently have the ideal qualities of a store of economic energy (i.e. money):

- General recognition by all civilizations as being valuable (as proven by history);

- Portability (can be easily carried and traded);

- Durability (the ability to withstand pressure, wear or damage including from the elements, which gold does perfectly as it never rusts);

- Homogeneity (1 ounce of gold or silver no matter the source will have the same chemical composition everywhere);

- Divisibility (can be formed in different denominations such as one ounce, half ounce, quarter ounce, and so forth);

- Malleability (able to be minted into coins, bars and jewelry); and

- Stability of value (1 ounce of gold will always be 1 ounce of gold).

This is in contrast to seashells, sand, feathers, beads, and other trivial things that Keynesians and the profiteers off of the current fiat currency system will say could just as easily have been used as money but for people arbitrarily choosing gold and silver...the chemistry proves this argument false.

Keynesians and their friends also hate when intrinsic value in the context of money is brought up. Digital currency is created with a few keystrokes, and paper currency is created with a printing press, paper and some ink. These are not hard to do and require very little energy and labor.

Gold and silver, on the other hand, require substantial human labor, energy, risk and time to produce. Before any gold and silver can even be extracted from the Earth's crust, there is significant exploration (prospecting) in order to find ore sites capable of yielding enough gold or silver for the project to be financially feasible and make a profit.

There's the development process of the mine which can take as long as five years. This involves planning and construction of the mine and associated infrastructure, including obtaining the requisite permits and licenses.

Then there's the actual operation of the gold or silver mine, where the ore is extracted and processed. This involves trans-forming rock and ore into a metallic alloy of substantial purity. The older methods of obtaining gold and silver, such as panning, sluicing and dredging, are no longer economically viable on any large scale, as humans have for the most part already exhausted the easily mined gold and silver in the Earth's crust.

Hard rock mining is now the predominant method required, as deposits are increasingly only being found deeper in the Earth, which requires access shafts and vertical pits called stokes to be drilled, explosives then get placed along the length of the stokes and are detonated, with the resultant blast sending chunks of rock to the bottom of the mining shafts, which are then lifted up and out of the mine, put into trucks, hauled off to a mill where the giant boulders are crunched with advanced industrial machinery into a fine dust.

Then, water is mixed with the dust to form a substance called slurry. The slurry then undergoes a chemical process called leaching that extracts gold out of the rock, with the most common method of leaching being to mix the slurry with cyanide and oxygen (gold cyanidation). All the gold is sifted and filtered out of that and smelted, with the little bits of gold thrown into a furnace at approximately 2,100 degrees Fahrenheit.

The gold is then sent to a refinery. A chemical mixture called flux (usually borax and sodium carbonate) is mixed with gold before melting it in order to remove impurities (remaining non-gold elements) before the gold is then melted and poured into solid bars. Samples of the gold are taken to labs for tests, or assays that measure the gold content. The gold if used for bullion is sent off to public and private mints.

All this needs to be done efficiently, safely and responsibly. Note it can take decades before a gold or silver mine is even ready to produce material that can be refined.

Suffice it to say, gold and silver requires an incredible amount of labor, time, energy (oil, gasoline, and electricity), equipment, chemicals, and financial investment and risk to produce, especially today where all the easy gold and silver (gold and silver methods of extraction that our ancestors used) have already been exhausted. All of that is condensed and stored into gold and silver bullion, hence why **gold and silver have intrinsic value.** When one holds a gold coin, they are holding a tremendous amount of stored economic energy. Contrast that to a fiat currency note which is simply paper and ink, or 0's and 1's in a computer network...

"NOBODY I KNOW HAS GOLD, THAT'S OLD TIMEY STUFF"

This is what the central banking elites want the uninformed masses to think (while they and their rich friends hoard gold for themselves). They prefer we forget about the yellow metal and instead plow into already extremely overvalued stock and bond markets, as well as hold fiat currency, all forms of credit that enable them to quietly siphon away our economic energy, as well as control, track, and tax us. It's a lot easier to tax your stocks than your private physical gold holdings.

If gold was some old-timey relic of the past that no longer has importance in a modern technological society, then how do we explain the following:

- Globally, central banks (the bankers' banks) have been net purchasers of gold since 2010, and in 2018 went on the largest gold buying spree in almost 50 years, acquiring some 656.2 tons of gold. [88] In 2019, central banks collectively bought a record 650.3 tons of gold, the 2nd highest level of annual purchases in 50 years, just below their 2018 gold buying spree.[89]

- Russia has been buying gold every month since March of 2015 in keeping with Putin's "fiscal fortress" policy of high gold reserves and low debt obligations. In 2018, the Central Bank of Russia bought a record 274.3 metric tons of gold,[90] while simultaneously selling off nearly all of their U.S. Treasury holdings and implementing a more than 50% reduction in their U.S. dollar forex reserves.[91]

- Since 2008, China has imported 12,000 tons of gold on a net basis, and the Peoples Bank of China (PBOC) has prohibited exportation of gold from the Chinese domestic market, which in layman's terms means China is gold hoarding and prefers it come into the country and not leave.[92]

- The Reserve Bank of India bought 40.45 metric tons of gold in the fiscal year of 2019-2020, putting its reported gold holdings at an estimated 653 tonnes or $40.8

---

88 "The New Tier 1 Asset?" *Pinnacle Digest* (Mar 23, 2019), pinnacledigest.com/mining-stocks/central-bank-purchases-gold/

89 "Central Banks Buy More Gold" *Schiff Gold* (Mar 16, 2020), schiffgold.com/key-gold-news/central-banks-buy-more-gold/

90 Bne IntelliNews "Russia's Gold Reserves Hit Five-Year High" *The Moscow Times* (Apr 9, 2019), themoscowtimes.com/2019/04/09/russias-gold-reserves-hit-five-year-high-a65147

91 Schiff Gold, Mar 16, 2020.

92 Jan Nieuwenhuijs, "China's Gold Hoarding: Will It Cause The Price of Gold to Rise?" *Seeking Alpha* (Jan 16, 2020), seekingalpha.com/article/4317244-chinas-gold-hoarding-will-cause-price-of-gold-to-rise

billion USD, around the market capitalization of General Motors (as of Sep 2020).[93]

- In late 2018, the Hungarian National Bank announced a 10-fold increase in their monetary gold holdings. They had 3.10 tons in September of 2018, and by mid-October of 2018 they purchased 28.4 tons of gold, increasing their stockpile from 3.10 tons to 31.5 tons or by 1,000%.[94] In 2019, Poland announced that over 2018-2019, the National Bank of Poland in Warsaw bought 125.7 metric tons of gold, bringing their reserves to 228.6 tonnes, which is more than double their original holdings.[95]

- Countries around the world have been diligently repatriating their gold stored abroad. This indicates increased perceived value of those gold stockpiles, enough to pay for them to come home. In 2013, Germany began a five-year operation that resulted in 374 metric tons of German gold repatriated from vaults in Paris and 300 metric tons from vaults in New York, back into Bundesbank vaults in Frankfurt.[96]

- In 2014, the Netherlands repatriated 122.5 tons of gold from the New York Federal Reserve Bank over a period

93 George Mathew, "RBI gold reserves up 40.4 tonnes in 2019-20, more than half of total holdings held overseas" *The Indian Express* (May 11, 2020), indianexpress.com/article/business/banking-and-finance/rbi-gold-reserves-up-40-4-tonnes-in-2019-20-more-than-half-of-total-holdings-held-overseas-6403555/#

94 Ronan Manly, "Poland joins Hungary with Huge Gold Purchase and Repatriation" *Bullion Star* (Jul 7, 2019), bullionstar.com/blogs/ronan-manly/poland-joins-hungary-with-huge-gold-purchase-and-repatriation/

95 *Ibid.*

96 Preeti Varathan, "Germany has pulled all of its gold out of Paris"

of a few weeks, back to their vaults in Amsterdam.[97] In the same year, Austria repatriated an estimated 15 tons of their gold reserves from vaults in London.[98] Poland and Hungary have also jumped aboard the repatriation train, with the latter in 2019 taking back almost half of its gold that was stored in the Bank of England, and the former bringing all of its gold back to its vaults in Budapest.[99] In April of 2019, Romania's parliament passed a bill to repatriate their gold from the U.K. as well, and it appears Slovakia and Serbia will be joining this new trend soon.[100]

- **Jeffrey Gundlach**, billionaire bond investor and founder of the firm DoubleLine Capital LP, known as the "King of Bonds," on June 9, 2020, affirmed he's bearish on the dollar and over the long term he's bullish on gold.[101] Gundlach stated in May 2019 "I love gold. I have owned gold since it was trading at $300 [2002]."[102]

---

97 Olav Dirkmaat, "Why the Netherlands Repatriated 4 Billions of Gold" *Gold Republic* (Nov 24, 2014), goldrepublic.com/news/why-the-dutch-central-bank-secretly-repatriated-4-billions-of-gold

98 "Austria says it has repatriated 15 tonnes of gold from London" *Reuters* (Dec 11, 2015), reuters.com/article/austria-gold/austria-says-it-has-repatriated-15-tonnes-of-gold-from-london-idUSL8N1401VQ20151211#

99 Manly, 2019.

100 Drew Woodhouse, "Countries went on a gold-buying spree before coronavirus took hold – here's why" *The Conversation* (May 21, 2020), theconversation.com/countries-went-on-a-gold-buying-spree-before-coronavirus-took-hold-heres-why-138173

101 Tyler Durden, "Gundlach Warns Stock Market Likely To Fall From 'Lofty Perch' Despite 'Superman' Powell, Says Buy Gold" *Zero Hedge* (Jun 9, 2020), zerohedge.com/markets/superman-jeffrey-gundlach-live-webcast

102 John Rothans, "Do Billionaires Buy Gold?" *US Money Reserve* (Sep 11, 2019), usmoneyreserve.com/blog/billionaires-buy-gold/

- **Warren Buffet**, billionaire equities activist investor directed Berkshire Hathaway in the 2nd quarter of 2020 to purchase $564 million of stock in Barrick Gold, a large cap gold mining company.[103]

- **Sam Zell**, billionaire real estate investor stated "for the first time in my life, I bought gold because it is a good hedge."[104] Gold has always been an excellent **hedge** (investment position to offset potential losses incurred by another investment) against currency depreciation, geopolitical crises, and deflation of other assets classes.

- **Jim Rogers**, billionaire commodities investor, in an interview with Kitco News on August 19, 2020, said he's owned gold for decades, and believes it's going to go "much, much higher" before the global fiat currency printing spree is over.

- **Ray Dalio**, billionaire and founder of the world's largest hedge fund, Bridgewater Associates, invested $400 million dollars into gold ETFs in the 2nd quarter of 2020, indicating extreme bullishness for gold itself.[105] Dalio believes gold is great both as a **store of wealth** and a means of **portfolio diversification**.[106]

103 Michael McCrae, "Warren Buffet buys gold" *Kitco News* (Aug 14, 2020), kitco.com/news/2020-08-14/Warren-Buffett-buys-gold.html

104 Luzi-Ann Javier, "Billionaire Sam Zell Buys Gold for First Time in Bet on Tight Supply" *Bloomberg* (Jan 17, 2019), bloomberg.com/news/articles/2019-01-17/billionaire-zell-buys-gold-for-first-time-in-bet-on-tight-supply

105 Saloni Sardana, "Billionaire Ray Dalio's Bridgewater fund poured almost half a billion dollars into gold in Q2" *Markets Business Insider* (Aug 13, 2020), markets.businessinsider.com/commodities/news/gold-price-ray-dalio-invested-400-million-precious-metal-q2-2020-8-1029501695#

106 Rothans, 2019.

- **Naguib Sawiris**, an Egyptian billionaire telecom mogul, invested half of his net worth in gold in 2018.[107]

- **Paul Tudor Jones**, billionaire hedge fund manager, stated in a Bloomberg interview in summer of 2019 that gold "has everything going for it in a world where rates in the U.S. are conceivably going to zero."[108]

- **Jacob Rothschild** in 2016 increased RIT Capital Partners plc gold holdings to protect against "the greatest experiment in monetary policy in the history of the world" and the "unintended consequences of very low interest rates, with some 30% of global government debt at negative yields, combined with quantitative easing on a massive scale... In times like these, preservation of capital in **real terms** continues to be as important an objective as any in the management of your company's assets."[109] This is ironic considering the family connection to the central banking system responsible for this great "experiment in monetary policy" ...

- In the 2nd quarter of 2020, **Blackrock**, the world's largest asset manager with $7.4 Trillion of assets under management, made the 2nd largest purchase of units in SLV (a large cap silver ETF that tracks the price performance of underlying holdings in the London silver price fix), acquiring 6.5 million units.

---

107 *Ibid.*

108 *Ibid.*

109 Jacob Rothschild, "Half-Yearly Financial Report" *RIT Capital Partners plc* (30, June 2016), ritcap.com/reports

- One of the top three largest commercial banks in the world, **JP Morgan Chase,** has an estimated 25 million ounces of gold and around 1 billion ounces of silver stockpiled in its vaults, making it the largest silver holder in the United States.[110]

- In the 3rd quarter of 2020, the **Ohio Police and Fire Pension Fund** announced it will be allocating 5% of its assets to gold.[111] There is a reasonable probability other pension funds may follow Ohio's lead in the future.

Given the world's largest and most powerful nation states, central banks, hedge funds and billionaire investors are buying and repatriating gold and silver, i.e., the smart money and institutional money, this is indicative that perhaps gold and silver will continue it's almost 5,000-year trend as a store of value.

"GOLD IS THE MONEY OF KINGS; SILVER IS THE MONEY OF GENTLEMEN; BARTER IS THE MONEY OF PEASANTS; BUT DEBT IS THE MONEY OF SLAVES."
—NORM FRANZ

---

110 Anthony Anderson, "JP Morgan Now Bullish On Silver With 1 Billion Ounces and Gold with 25 Million Ounces" *GSI Exchange* (Apr 11, 2020), gsiexchange.com/with-jpmorgan-back-in-the-mix-the-hammer-is-now-about-to-fall/

111 Jeff Clark, "Pension Funds Join the Gold Party-Things Are About to Get Interesting" *GoldSilver.com* (Sep 4, 2020), goldsilver.com/blog/pension-funds-join-the-gold-partythings-are-about-to-get-interesting/

"What about Cash Flow?"

By now, some readers are probably wondering *"what about cash flow?"* Well, before we get into cash flow and ways to create it (investing Goal #2), we need to remember our baseline is Goal #1 – to NOT LOSE WEALTH. Therefore, we need to prevent the hidden tax of inflation from stealing our purchasing power away from us while we accumulate enough savings to acquire the *right* cash flowing investments.

For example, let's suppose it's the year 2016 and hypothetical Bob fixed his personal finances and operating expense ratio so that he's able to start saving $35,000 per year to invest. Bob's chosen real estate as his avenue for acquiring cash flow. He's read numerous books about apartment investing and is confident that when he's built up enough savings, he will be able to successfully play the apartment game.

Bob lives in Tampa and has strategically decided to acquire apartments where he lives, that way he's close enough to self-manage, eliminating management fees that could be 10% or more of the investment's gross income, and he can make sure it's not mismanaged.

Let's assume for a four-unit multifamily property in Bob's market, the most lenders will give Bob a mortgage at is a 65% LTV ratio, so he'll need to come up with a 35% down payment. If the market price per unit for the apartment class Bob wants to own is $100,000 per unit in 2016, for a 4-unit building he'll need roughly $140,000 for the down payment. This will take him 4 years to save up at $35,000 savings per year.

From 2010 to 2020, the average annual real estate appreciation rate for Tampa was around 5.44%.[112] If we assume the apartments Bob is considering purchasing reflect that average

112 Marco Santarelli, "Tampa Real Estate Market 2020 Overview" *Norada Real Estate* (May 30, 2020), noradarealestate.com/blog/tampa-fl-real-estate-market/

appreciation rate of 5.44%, in the 1st quarter of 2020, after Bob has finally saved $140,000, that will no longer be enough to cover the 35% down payment, as the apartment buildings he was looking at appreciated roughly 5.44% per year.

The $400,000 four-unit apartment building appreciated to $494,400, which means he's roughly $33,000 short and will need to add another year (and then some) of working and saving in order to invest. That's another year of missed opportunities because competitors continue to take the good deals, and another year of missed cashflow.

What if instead of keeping his savings in U.S. dollars, which from 2016-2019 depreciated 5.44% per year relative to Tampa housing, Bob had instead put his monthly savings into gold? From 2016-2019, the average annual rate of appreciation for gold comes out to 9.72%.

This means that Bob will have enough savings to buy that 4-unit apartment building in a shorter timeframe than anticipated, before the end of four years, because the average annual appreciation rate of the apartment building was 5.44%, while his gold's average annual appreciation rate was 9.72%, a positive differential of 4.28%.

"What About Storing Savings in Stock Market Indexes and ETFs?"

An investing methodology that has been beat to death into the minds of the average investor by the mainstream media and financial advisor industry is to just "buy the market" by investing in the S&P 500, Down Jones Industrial Average, and NASDAQ indexes, or in broad ETFs and mutual funds. All of these strategies have proven over the very long term to be solid strategies, particularly for the baby boomer generation.

If your only other options are to (a) lose your savings to inflation through holding only cash, negative real yielding bonds, savings accounts and CD's; or (b) try to pick individual stocks, then "buying the market" probably is the superior strategy. Losing your wealth to inflation is a guaranteed avenue for failure, and trying to pick individual stocks is an incredibly risky strategy and something professionals spend decades trying to get good at.

However, there are a host of major macro-economic structural changes underway that may dramatically diminish the efficacy of the "buy the market" strategy for growing and preserving one's wealth in the investing landscape of the 2020s and 2030s. This structural shift already began at the turn of the century, as evidenced by gold's outperformance of the major stock indexes, making gold the top performing broad market asset class since the year 2000 (excluding Bitcoin and cryptocurrencies).

As you can see from the graph below, which compares the historical percentage returns for the Dow Jones Industrial Average (DIJA) against gold from September 2000 to September 2020, gold's historical returns for this timeframe are 605%, while the DJIA's are only 160% (including dividends).[113]

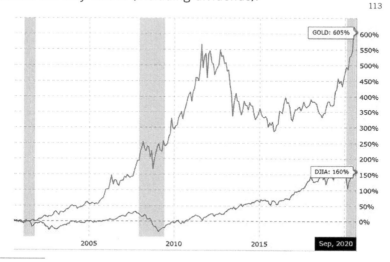

113 Gold vs. Stock Market, *MacroTrends.Net* (accessed 9/20/2020), macrotrends.net/2608/gold-price-vs-stock-market-100-year-chart

The S&P 500 performance during this time frame is even lower, at closer to 129%. This is a major shift from the 20th-century status quo of stock market indexes dramatically outperforming gold.

If one had invested $10,000 into the DJIA, which was $10,650.92 in September of 2000, by September of 2020, that investment would be worth roughly $25,967. In contrast, if that same investor instead bought $10,000 worth of physical gold in September of 2000, which was around $276.60 per ounce, by September of 2020, that gold investment would be worth roughly $69,718.

Why the change from stocks outperforming gold in the 20th century to gold outperforming stocks in the first twenty years of the 21st century? I believe this is a consequence of major structural changes underway that will alter economies and markets in general. Many highly respected macro-investors and economists are warning that the old 20th-century passive investing strategies of indexing, mutual funds, and ETFs, will become less effective in the coming investment landscape of the 2020s and 2030s, with greater risk and lower returns.

What are these structural changes? Niels Jensen in his book *The End of Indexing: Six structural mega-trends that will threaten passive investment*, identifies six, three of which are particularly compelling and come up with regularity in presentations and comments by some big-name macro investors and hedge fund managers:

- The end of the debt super-cycle;

- The coming wave of retiring baby boomers;

- The decline of spending by the middle classes;

The end of the debt super-cycle goes back to interest rates and the cost of debt. A quick summary for those not already familiar, the most important rate in the world is the federal funds rate, which is the interest rate at which banks and credit unions lend reserve balances to each other overnight, and is set by decree by the Federal Open Market Committee (FOMC).

The fed funds rate has an enormous impact not only on the U.S. economy but on the world's economies due to the U.S. Dollar being the world's reserve currency (for now). When the fed funds rate is lowered, banks lower interest rates to consumers for things like auto and home loans, which encourages more borrowing and spending, bidding up prices because consumers can afford to pay more as the cost of debt is cheaper.

As we can see from the graph below, in December of 1980 the fed funds rate was 20% and has been declining ever since, with brief periods where it's raised but then subsequently dropped further.

Federal Funds Rate

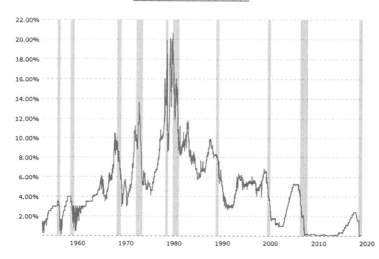

The fed funds rate also affects short-term interest rates on trea-suries. Without veering outside of the scope of this book into macro-economic land, long term rates (like the 10 Year U.S. Treasury Note) tend to follow short-term rates, as shown by the graph below tracking the interest rate on the 10-year U.S. Treasury note.

10 Year U.S. Treasury Note

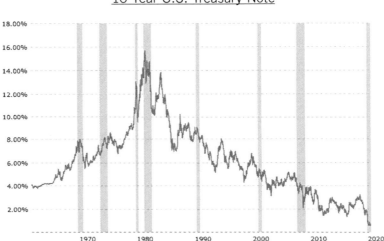

This four-decade artificial lowering of interest rates has resulted in MASSIVE levels of individual, corporate, and government debt, with huge multi-decade inflows of capital into the stock markets chasing returns to beat inflation and achieve growth not obtainable in the bond markets (particularly after the GFC of 2008-2009 when real yields went negative).

This is a global trend, as central banks around the world have instituted this "monetary policy" trajectory towards the Zero Lower Bound - where short-term nominal interest rates are at or near zero, causing a liquidity trap and limiting central banks' ability to further "stimulate economic growth."

The central banks of the world and our Federal Reserve in the U.S. have been "stimulating economic growth" since 1980, and put this policy in hyperdrive after 2008, which has MASSIVELY inflated asset prices, especially bonds, stocks, and commercial real estate, and simultaneously lowered yields on those assets for new investors and new capital, as there is an inverse relationship between prices and yields. This situation is NOT capitalism and certainly not indicative of a free market economy.

The consensus amongst many leading macro investors and hedge fund managers is that we're indeed coming to the end of this debt super cycle now that we're at the Zero Lower Bound and the central banks are out of metaphorical ammunition to inflate these bubbles any longer.[114] [115] [116] This is one reason there is likely to be lower returns and higher risk of capital loss in the decades to come from the old "buy the market" strategy of passively investing into the stock market.

The second major structural change underway is what some call the "baby boomer retirement crisis." This has to do with the waves of retiring baby boomers, who possess a disproportionate majority of the world's wealth relative to the younger generations and will likely move away from the trend of "buying the dips" (buying stocks after major corrections) in the equities markets, towards a trend of de-risking (moving capital out of equities and into lower-risk assets and U.S. dollars) so they can ensure

---

114 Ben Moshinsky, "RAY DALIO: The 75-year debt supercycle is coming to an end" *Business Insider* (Jan 27, 2016), businessinsider.com/ray-dalio-ft-opinion-long-term-debt-2016-1

115 Jennifer Ablan, "Bull market 'supercycle' for stocks, bonds ending: Bill Gross" *Reuters* (May 4, 2015), reuters.com/article/us-investing-gross-outlook/bull-market-supercycle-for-stocks-bonds-ending-bill-gross-idUSKBN0NP12G20150504

116 Jennifer Ablan, "U.S. growth would have contracted without trillions in government, consumer debt: Gundlach" *Reuters* (May 14, 2019), reuters.com/article/us-funds-doubleline-gundlach/u-s-growth-would-have-contracted-without-trillions-in-government-consumer-debt-gundlach-idUSKCN1SK2KW

they're able to afford retirement and healthcare.[117] This again doesn't bode well for the broad equities indexes in the 2020s and 2030s, as inflows of currency is what results in appreciation, not massive outflows.

The third major structural change is the decline in spending by the middle classes (and the decline in the middle class itself). This was a trend already well underway by the 2000s and 2010s,[118] but made many times worse by the government forced shutdowns of 2020. As of September 2020, personal consumption makes up roughly 67% (reportedly) of America's Gross Domestic Product (GDP), a metric used to judge the size and health of an economy.[119]

In a nutshell, we have an economy driven by consumption, rather than manufacturing where goods are made and sold abroad. This makes us incredibly economically fragile to declines in domestic spending (consumption), as the majority of our nation's businesses are dependent on selling goods and services to American consumers for their revenue streams, and with major declines in consumption, those revenue streams get cut, and as a natural consequence, jobs are slashed as are the inflows of capital into the equities markets from 401(k) contributions and independent investment by employees via indexing, ETFs and mutual funds.

On the other hand, if we had a stronger percentage of our GDP come from manufacturing, we would weather drops in

---

117 Raoul Pal, "The Coming Retirement Crisis Explained and Explored (w/ Raoul Pal)" *Real Vision Finance* (Oct 28, 2018), youtube.com/watch?v=5OFaZcCOIRU&t=14s

118 Jessie X. Fan & Hua Zan, "The Decline of the American Middle Class: Evidence from the Consumer Expenditure Surveys 1988-2015" *Journal of Family and Economic Issues* (Nov 14, 2019), link.springer.com/article/10.1007%2Fs10834-019-09651-1

119 "Shares of gross domestic product: Personal consumption expenditures" *Federal Reserve Bank of St. Louis* (accessed 9/21/2020), fred.stlouisfed.org/series/DPCERE1Q156NBEA

domestic spending far better because a larger percentage of our jobs would be related to selling goods and services to foreign importers around the globe.

This is why there's been such a resurgence in interest for bringing manufacturing jobs back into the U.S., manufacturing that was exported to China and elsewhere by politicians who could care less about future generations of Americans that had to live in the hollowed out economy they created where the most common jobs are rideshare drivers, e-commerce delivery, and retail/restaurant workers (all jobs centered around consumption).

There are many other structural changes and systemic risks that are outside the scope of this book, but which do not appear to bode well for the equities markets of the 2020s and 2030s, such as further technological disruption and displacement of job sectors due to automation and artificial intelligence, and the looming unfunded pension liability crisis discussed earlier, which may result in bankrupt states imposing "wealth taxes" on equities, causing massive outflows of capital to other assets by residents of those states.

JOHN EXTER'S PYRAMID

John Exter was an American economist (1910-2006), member of the Board of Governors of the Federal Reserve, and advisor to former Fed Chairman Paul Volcker. He's best known for creating a visual representation organizing asset classes in terms of risk and size in the form of an inverted pyramid, with the safest (and smallest) asset classes at the bottom, and riskier (and larger) asset classes towards the top.

Some macro economists believe that in times of economic crisis where markets engage in massive de-leveraging and/or de-risking, liquidity will flow from the riskier asset classes at the higher levels of the inverted pyramid, down to the less risky assets in the lower levels, as creditors move down the pyramid out of the most illiquid and risky debts into safer assets, with the safest being gold (and silver). The higher debtors sit on the pyramid, the less liquid they will be in these times of "credit contraction" which will also likely result in deflation of prices of the assets higher up the pyramid.

Remember, you can have asset price deflation while simultaneously experiencing consumer price inflation, meaning stocks, real estate, and bonds can drop in price (deflation), while the cost of groceries and everyday consumer goods can increase (inflation).

Below is a modern adaptation of Exter's pyramid, reflecting the approximate size of global asset classes as of 2019. If you look up older adaptations, you'll notice a MASSIVE difference in quantities, with the 2019 adaptation having increased exponentially in size, thanks to the never-ending financialization of everything (mortgage backed securities, collateralized debt obligations, credit default swaps) and huge levels of money printing (typing) or "monetary easing" our central banks have done to inflate asset prices to record levels.

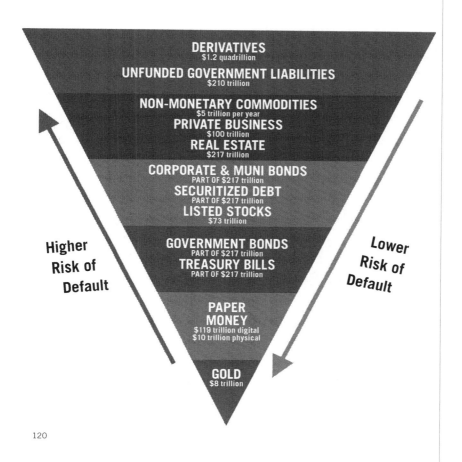

I believe it's plausible that certain segments of real estate, such as farm and agricultural land or well-positioned multi-family, may actually be further down the pyramid than the blanket real estate asset class is shown to be, but overall, this visual representation is helpful in understanding the current state of things. Also, somewhere near the bottom perhaps is very rare, famous, and collectible fine artwork, such as works by Rembrandt, Picasso, and Dali.

120 James Anderson, "Financial Crisis Protection John Exter Pyramid" SD Bullion (Oct 30, 2019), sdbullion.com/blog/financial-crisis-protection

WHAT DOES ALL THIS MEAN?

While nothing contained herein should be construed as financial advice, from an academic perspective, this means that in the investment landscape of the 2020s and 2030s, gold is probably a better alternative for protecting wealth from currency debasement than traditional passive investing into stock market indexes, ETFs and mutual funds, given the likelihood of financial markets de-leveraging and de-risking from the four-decade asset hyper bubbles that have been created by central bank monetary policy.

It also means that gold is also likely a better alternative for protecting wealth than bonds, at least until (or if) real yields go up significantly from where they are presently (which is negative).

In a Bloomberg interview on July 29, 2020, Scott Minerd, Guggenheim Partners co-founder and chief investment officer, said, "one of the major functions of money is to be a store of value, when you get to the point that real returns [i.e., yields] are negative on cash or bonds, you've gotten to the point where what's the downside of owning gold? I think that precious metals as a store of value are to be expected at this point, I think despite the run-up we've got a lot more room to the upside...in times of uncertainty and where the printing press is running full course, precious metals are the place to be."[121]

For those that still believe in central banker's ability to keep the stock markets going higher forever, having some allocation to gold and silver may be good hedges or insurance in the event your thesis is wrong.

---

121 "Minerd Says Precious Metals Are the Place to Be" *Bloomberg Markets and Finance* YouTube Channel (Jul 29, 2020)

PORTFOLIO ALLOCATION TO GOLD AND SILVER

The first consideration is portfolio allocation, that is, if you do decide to buy gold and silver, what percentage of your net worth should be allocated to it? Over the past few decades, a 4% up to 10% gold allocation was the standard for many investors and money managers.

Given we're approaching the end of the debt super-cycle, since 2016 I've had a much higher allocation to gold and silver. We are somewhat in uncharted economic territory in global modern history, so you will need to decide for yourself what allocation you think will confidently safeguard your savings.

Remember, having an emergency fund with 6 months of living expenses in dollars should come before investing (unless inflation goes parabolic like in Argentina or Venezuela), as well as some cash reserves for any business or real estate investments you have. Additionally, extinguishing your bad debts (consumer debt), especially credit card debt, should come before investing, as you're guaranteed to owe the onerous interest rate that accompanies credit cards.

BENEFITS OF PHYSICAL GOLD AND SILVER

The first question for those new to the precious metals space is how to buy it, whether to buy physical or gold and silver ETFs. First, if you don't have anywhere safe to store it, such as in a safe in your home, and you intend on just leaving it in a drawer or something, ETFs might be safer since having gold and silver laying around your home unsecured is a recipe for theft.

That said, by buying into gold and silver ETFs as opposed to physical, you're relinquishing some of the major advantages that come with owning physical precious metals.

First, physical gold and silver are wealth insurance against cyberwarfare and EMP attacks, and while the risk at first may seem remote, consider the advancements in modern asymmetrical warfare and A.I., along with our increased dependence on digital information storage and transmission (most people's "wealth" other than their home is now stored digitally). The odds increase every year of some sort of major cyber-attack on our financial system, to include brokerage accounts where you would purchase gold and silver ETFs.

The recent formation of the U.S. Space Force in 2019 has to do with cyber-warfare and Signals Intelligence defense via satellites around Earth's orbit. Part of the appeal to nation-states of cyberwarfare is the concept of plausible deniability – that is, nation (or rogue non-state actor) A could attack nation B and make it look like the attack came from nation C, causing nation B harm in the initial cyber-attack as well as further harm from engaging in military conflict with nation C. This plausible deniability doctrine, much like how the doctrine of mutually assured destruction spurred the nuclear arms race in the cold war, is now spurring a present-day digital arms race, exponentially increasing the odds of such an attack. Have fun trying to get reimbursed for your gold and silver ETF holdings you supposedly had prior to the attack...

Second, physical gold and silver in your own possession allows you to avoid management fees that you'd otherwise pay owning gold and silver ETFs, presently anywhere from 0.25% to 0.40% per year. So, if you have $50,000 in a gold ETF with a 0.40% annual management fee, that's $200 per year.

Third, physical gold and silver are independent of the financial system and there's no counter-party risk. You're not dependent on the managers of that ETF and your brokerage honoring their obligations. Moreover, no matter how off the rails the politicians or central banks get, if you have a hundred ounces of gold, you have a hundred ounces of gold.

Fourth, physical gold and silver are truly decentralized and anonymous. Depending on what country and jurisdiction one lives in, one could theoretically exchange it with local farmers, fisherman and vegetable growers for food, private sellers of goods and services essential to one's survival like vehicles, fuel, tools, building materials, and so forth...I've even heard of people trading gold and silver to contractors to build their home. This is truly an anonymous form of money. One can have the worst credit history in the world (or worst "social score" if you're in Communist China), but if one has gold and silver, there are plenty of private individuals to trade with.

This will become increasingly important as the globalist international banking cartel pushes us towards central banker controlled crypto-currencies, giving them the ability to force negative interest rates onto the holders of currency or force time limits with which to spend their currency (in previous times these policies would not work as savers could simply withdraw their cash and "put it under the mattress").

Whether through negative interest rates or time limits with which to spend the central banker currency, both would have the equivalent effect of being harsh penalties on savers. This form of top-down economic control (similar to that of China) is being attempted as I write this book (see the "Banking for All Act" S.3571 introduced in the U.S. Senate on March 23, 2020).

Are there people who won't accept gold and silver? Of course, but there are plenty that will. Moreover, one can always exchange it for one's national currency with local coin shops and gold dealers. In the age of never-ending intrusion into our privacy, it's nice to have some means to privately transact without tyrannical "for your safety" big brother watching over your every move like something out of a dystopian science fiction novel.

In order to take full advantage of the privacy benefits of physical gold and silver, it helps to purchase it in person, from bullion dealers who respect the right to privacy, John or Jane Doe... If one buys it online, there will be a digital record of having purchased it on the front end, but one can still maintain privacy on the back end if one trades it for goods and services with individuals privately.

Fifth, physical gold and silver add a psychological layer between you and foolish spending decisions. If you recall in chapter 7, we discussed studies indicating consumers spend 100% more when using credit cards than when using cash, as cash causes the consumer to feel the loss of their currency when they spend it. This same psychological barrier is there with physical gold and silver.

Stacking gold and silver is great for people who have a hard time not spending their savings, people who will build up some savings, but then sabotage them by giving in to temptation to make discretionary consumer purchases, rather than investing and holding.

I've never even considered selling my physical gold and silver to fund discretionary consumer purchases. I view stacking as building my wealth and emergency reserves, to be used in times of crisis as a last resort, or if gold becomes overvalued (discussed shortly). Stacking gold and silver is a great way to build savings and financial discipline.

HOW TO BUY PHYSICAL GOLD AND SILVER

If you're going to buy physical gold and silver in person from a local coin and bullion dealer, you'll want to buy a Sigma Metalytics Precious Metal Verifier (PMV) Original – Basic Set that can detect if the gold and silver is genuine by measuring the expected electrical characteristics based on the selected metal type. Direct from the manufacturer, as of 2020, these are around $719.

That sounds like an expensive purchase, but that's your insurance for making sure you don't get taken by counterfeit gold or silver coins. It's also useful if you ever do want to trade your gold or silver privately for goods and services, as any seller's or vendor's concerns can be quelled with a quick 10-second test with the PMV unit.

Precious metals fraud is rare, but nevertheless, why take the risk? The machine is very fast and easy to use, your 80-year-old grandma could use it. Also, a cheap $18 digital scale is handy for weighing the coins as well. The machine tests for purity, but by weighing it you also test to ensure it hasn't been shaved or clipped. 1-ounce American Gold Eagles (AGEs) weigh approximately 33.9 grams, half ounce AGEs weigh roughly half that, although your scale may show a little more if the coin is in a protective plastic capsule or cardboard backing. Whatever gold or silver coins you're buying, you can look up their weight in grams online.

If you're not concerned with acquiring physical gold and silver in person, or do not want to buy a PMV, then you can purchase online confidently as long as you use a reputable dealer like:

- GoldSilver.com
- ProvidentMetals.com
- JMBullion.com

- Apmex.com

- SDBullion.com

There are others, but the ones mentioned above are highly trusted with regards to their integrity and security procedures as far as counterfeits or underweight bullion is concerned.

When you buy gold or silver, know what the spot price is the day you're purchasing it. The spot prices are easy to find on any of the above-mentioned websites. You'll also want to know what the premium is for that coin, as bullion dealers need to make a profit to stay in business, and it's unlikely you'll be able to buy gold or silver coins at spot price.

All you have to do is go to one of the above-mentioned sites, and if you're buying a 1-ounce gold coin, look at the cost to purchase that specific coin which will include the spot price and the premium. So, if your coin dealer is asking $2,200 for a one-ounce gold American Eagle, but you can buy one on GoldSilver.com for $2,000, show the dealer what the cost is on one of those online merchants so he can match it. Most dealers will be able to match the online merchants.

Which Gold and Silver Coins/Rounds/Bars are Good?

In the precious metals (PM) world, there are bars, coins, and rounds. Coins are minted by governments, while rounds are minted by private treasuries. Bars can be minted by governments or private mints.

For gold, bars are not a good idea unless you're a billionaire or a central bank. Gold rounds are also not at all desirable. The most liquid and optimal gold to buy are in 1 ounce and ½ ounce denominations in **coin** form, minted by the government of the country in which you live in.

- If you're in the U.S., the American Gold Eagle or the American Gold Buffalo;

- Canada - the Gold Maple Leaf;

- England - the Gold Britannia;

- South Africa - the Gold Krugerrand;

- And Austria – the Gold Vienna Philharmonic.

That's said, any of the above-listed gold coins are highly liquid and easy to buy and sell. Note the face value of each coin has no relationship to its actual worth. The 1-ounce American Gold Eagle face value is $50, but I could sell one today close to $2,000 (as of this writing).

Regarding silver, 10-ounce bars are common in the U.S. and Canada, and kilobars are also fairly common, particularly in Asia, however, the most liquid form is 1-ounce silver coins. I also own silver rounds because the premiums are lower (you get more ounces of silver for your money) and as long as it's from a reputable private mint like APMEX, Johnson Matthey, Sunshine Minting, U.S. Assay, A-Mark, SilverTowne, etc., you're good to go. I use a 50/50 ratio of silver coins to rounds.

It's good to have silver coins as well, even if premiums are higher because they do have increased liquidity and you can profit from an increase in premiums from what you originally paid for the coins if there's a supply crunch.

Be Your Own Bank

Entrusting your gold in a safety deposit box with a bank, or in a vault with a private vault company, both have a risk everyone should be aware of. Should another socialist tyrant like FDR[122] come along and decree by executive order to unconstitutionally (a violation of the 4th amendment if you're in the U.S.) confiscate people's gold "for _____(fill in the blank's) safety", your gold is liable to be stolen from those bank safety deposit boxes and private vaults by government order followers "just following orders" (the Nuremberg Defense) like the Gestapo and the NKVD.[123]

Odds are they aren't going to go house to house. Instead, they'll likely turn to the low hanging fruit - the physical gold ETFs are supposed to hold in trust, and banks and private vault companies within their jurisdiction. They'll walk in, flash the newly enacted illegal confiscation "law," and the stewards of your gold and silver will hand over your property without a fight. As the old saying goes "possession is 9/10ths of the law."

One can get a quality heavy-duty firearm safe for around $750-$1,000 (as of 2020), that would be difficult for most thieves to steal, especially if bolted down to the floor from the inside, and that has good fire resistance.

If one does not have a location in which they're comfortable storing their gold, another option to consider is with a reputable private vault company in a jurisdiction like Singapore or Switzerland that has a higher level of respect for private property rights.

Loose Lips Sink Ships
During World War II, there were posters put out by the U.S. Office of War Information with the slogan "loose lips might sink ships." This was to remind U.S. servicemen and other citizens to avoid careless talk that could be intercepted by enemy spies

---

122 David J. Heinrich, "FDR's Heinous Crimes" *Mises Institute* (Oct 21, 2004), mises.org/wire/fdrs-heinous-crimes

123 Mark Passio, "Order Followers" *Natural Law Seminar* (Oct 19, 2013), bitchute.com/video/7UIjvTJIlcOb/

and compromise military operations. This is also a good slogan to keep in mind as it pertains to one's personal savings and precious metals holdings.

DOLLAR-COST AVERAGING (DCA)

Dollar-cost averaging is an investment strategy that divides up the total amount to be invested across periodic purchases of a target asset(s) to reduce the impact volatility has on the overall purchase. In other words, it lowers the probability of overpaying for an asset. With regards to gold and silver, this means investing a predefined percentage of one's monthly dollars left over for savings (after taxes and all living expenses are paid) into gold and silver (that matches their chosen net worth allocation). This is usually less risky than taking one lump sum amount and buying an asset like gold or silver all at once.

For example, let's suppose Rob has $1,200 left over each month to put into savings, zero bad debt and an emergency fund with enough cash to cover 6 months of total living expenses, and now Rob wants to get started investing. For conceptual ease, we'll assume Rob has chosen a 40% allocation to gold, and 60% allocation into cash flowing storage rental units. 40% of $1,200 is $480 a month for gold. As previously mentioned, it's best to stick to gold denominations of ½ ounce or 1-ounce coins.

As of this writing, a 1-ounce American Gold Eagle (AGE) coin is $1,990, and a ½ ounce AGE is $1,036. Assuming the price doesn't increase or decrease significantly while Rob saves up, it will take him roughly 2 to 2.5 months of saving $480 per month (depending on his payment schedule) to afford to buy a ½ ounce AGE.

Alternatively, Rob could choose 1 month to put all his $1,200 of savings towards the ½ ounce AGE, and another month to save up additional cash to put towards buying the storage rental unit when he's accumulated enough.

The caveat here is the real rate of inflation, which Rob can keep tabs on via the chapwoodindex.com. If the real rate of inflation is in the teens or higher, and real yields on Treasury Bills (T-bills) are positive, meaning the real rate of inflation less the T-bill's advertised nominal yield is positive, then Rob could park the savings he is building up for the storage unit into T-Bills (maturity of 1 year or less) if he's more comfortable doing that than gold, or he could have an allocation in both.

If the current trend of negative real interest rates on T-bills continues, Rob may want to consider putting all of his spare savings into gold, to protect it from a loss of purchasing power due to inflation, and when he's accumulated enough to meet both his desired gold percentage allocation and to cover the purchase of the rental storage unit, he can liquidate the gold portion needed for the rental storage unit and keep the remainder of gold to meet his desired gold percentage allocation.

As long as Rob is aware of the estimated degree of loss of purchasing power of his savings due to inflation, and takes actions to prevent this by parking his savings into gold, Rob will reduce the number of months or years of laboring required to have enough currency saved up to invest in that rental storage unit (or whatever cash flowing investment he's considering).

SELLING GOLD AND SILVER

Gold and silver are very easy monetary assets to liquidate. While selling your home can take months, you can liquidate your gold and silver in a day or so depending on how much you have. Just call a few of your local coin/bullion dealers, and/or any of the previously mentioned online precious metals exchange companies, and you can shop for who will give you the best deal, which should be spot price plus some percentage of the premium depending on the coin/round/bar and market supply and demand conditions.

WHEN TO SELL SOME GOLD AND SILVER?

I cannot give financial advice, but I'm personally following American investor Jim Roger's strategy, that is, to trim my gold and silver holdings once it appears we're in bubble territory (over-valued), and transfer the currency from selling the gold and sil-ver into assets that are undervalued (and have future market demand), preferably assets that produce cash flow. I will still keep a core position of gold and silver regardless of price. So hypothetically speaking, if my current position was 40% gold, and it comes time to sell, I'd begin trimming my position in gold from 40% of my net worth to 10%.

When I think gold is in bubble territory, I wouldn't sell all the gold I intend to trim at once, rather, I would sell in tranches of 20%. For example, if I had 100 ounces of gold I wanted to trim (separate from the core position I aim to keep), I'd sell 20 ounces one month, and the next month sell 20% of the remaining 80 ounces (16 ounces), and the month after that 20% of 64 ounces (approximately 13 ounces). This has similar benefits to the dollar cost averaging strategy, but on the sell side.

How can you tell if gold and/or silver is in bubble territory (overvalued)? On the next page is a graph that can give you an idea of how to tell when an asset is entering bubble territory. How long it takes for an asset to go through these phases can range from months to decades.

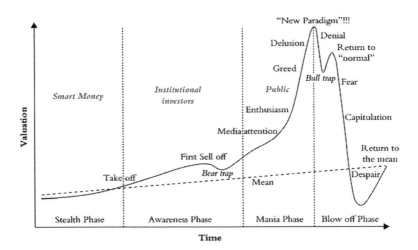

The best way, however, is to follow true market experts in this field like David Morgan at TheMorganReport.com and Mike Maloney at GoldSilver.com and listen to podcasts like Palisade Radio which has interviews with a variety of market experts in this field and a common question that will come up is where they think the gold and silver markets are in terms of valuation.

Combine this with some common sense. I knew to sell my cryptocurrency positions in 2017 shortly after friends who were older and not already in the crypto space or computers at all, started calling me asking about getting into cryptocurrency to make huge profits. Something told me, now's time to take profits, and luckily, I sold near the top when ETH was around $1200 and started moving those gains into what I perceived were undervalued assets, gold and silver.

That said, gold in particular is not like other assets in that it is a form of monetary reserves that duals as an inflation and chaos hedge, and this is why I'll always keep a core position of my net worth in gold (at least 10%), regardless of valuation.

WHAT ABOUT GOLD DURING A DEFLATION?

While gold has always proven to be a great hedge during times of inflation, what about the rare periods of deflation? During one of history's worst deflationary periods, the U.S. Great Depression, the price of gold increased in 1933 from $20.67 per ounce to $35 per ounce in 9 months (a 69% increase in nominal terms).

Because other asset prices were simultaneously depressed (deflated), the actual increase in real terms (purchasing power) of gold was FAR greater than 69% for those who refused to fold to tyranny by voluntarily giving FDR their gold. Yes, the gold price was fixed by the government during this time period. However, droves of U.S. citizens piled into goldmining stocks. While the Dow Jones Industrial Average was down by -73% from the crash in 1929 to January of 1933, the largest gold mining company at the time, Homestake Mining, had seen its stock shares increase by a whopping 474% over that same time period.[124]

During the Global Financial Collapse of 2008-2009, gold dropped at first due to investors needing liquidity to cover margin calls; however, by the end of 2008, gold regained its ground and even appreciated by 5.5% in nominal terms. By the end of 2009, it was up an additional 24% in nominal terms, while markets remained decimated and unemployment high.[125]

While history doesn't always repeat itself, it often rhymes. These two historical deflationary events in U.S. history are indicative of human nature to pile into gold as a safe haven during times of economic chaos.

124 Jeff Clark, "Should Gold Investors Root for Deflation?" *GoldSilver.com* (Apr 15, 2019), goldsilver.com/blog/should-gold-investors-root-for-deflation/

125 *Ibid.*

GOLD PRICE GAUGE

However, even if there is a deflationary collapse so bad gold ends up seeing a price decline and doesn't rapidly recover like in the Great Depression or the Global Financial Collapse of 2008, that doesn't mean your gold has lost purchasing power, or hasn't actually increased your wealth. How is this? Let's suppose gold is $2,000 an ounce, and the median cost of a three-bedroom starter home in your market is $300,000. Using what we'll call your gold price gauge, you figure that median $300,000 home will require you to liquidate (or trade) approximately 150 ounces of gold to purchase (without debt).

Let's say there's a deflationary crash that results in that same median three-bedroom starter home in your market dropping in value by 30% from $300,000 to $210,000, and gold sells off due to liquidity demand and margin calls, dropping from $2,000 per ounce to $1,700. Ouch, you lost $300 per ounce on your gold! In nominal terms...

In real terms, your gold increased in value relative to that median home...whereas your gold price gauge shows it used to cost 150 ounces of gold to buy that median starter home, now that same home can be purchased with 123.5 ounces of gold ($210,000 divided by $1,700), so you get to keep an extra 26.5 ounces of gold and get the house debt-free.

In other words, your gold to median home ratio in your market was 150:1, and even though the gold price dropped in the deflationary crash, because the home dropped further, the ratio dropped to 123.5:1 in golds favor, so your gold INCREASED your purchasing power by roughly 21.5% relative to that median house.

The same gold price gauge can be used to see if your gold has increased in purchasing power relative to anything: land, the Dow

Jones index (Gold to Dow ratio), the NASDAQ index, other commodities, and so forth. This is the true way to measure whether your gold is increasing or decreasing your wealth. By adopting this mindset of looking at investments and big-ticket items not just in nominal terms (like most people), but also in terms of how many ounces of gold does the item cost, you can better time when to purchase/trade your gold for that asset or item.

This ties into the concept of a **wealth transfer opportunity**: that is, selling one asset that has experienced strong appreciation while under your control, before that asset goes into a deflationary drop (i.e., a bust), and then using the proceeds from the sale to buy another asset that is undervalued and will increase in its future value due to heightened future market demand for the asset in its current state or in an improved state (also called forcing appreciation or value add).

CHAPTER 16

CASHFLOW IS KING

Imagine you have a little secret garden behind your home. In that secret garden, there's a small Japanese cherry blossom tree you recently planted, and it's all yours. Twice a week you briefly visit your little tree, watering it and admiring its beauty; its delicate white and pink flower colors, its faint scent of lilac and rose accented with soft almond and creamy vanilla like aroma give you a feeling of calm and tranquility.

You soon discover, however, that this is no ordinary Japanese cherry blossom tree. For some strange reason, once a month when you wake up and go visit your little tree, what were once cherry blossom petals have magically turned into cash, which of course you pick up. How cool would that be!? Would you not want to buy and plant more of these magic cherry blossom trees?

Well, passive income systems (i.e., investments that produce cash flow) are real-life magic cherry blossom trees. Sure, they'll require a lot of effort to find, acquire and plant, but once you do, aside from some weekly monitoring and maintenance, they will give you two very great gifts:

(1) Cash flow without having to trade your labor and time for it like you would with your job, putting time on your side so that the more passive income systems you acquire,

the faster you will become wealthy (so long as you continue to reinvest the cash flow).

(2) Increased resiliency. By having additional income streams completely separate from your primary source of income, you'll be in a far better position to weather storms and hardships that life might throw your way, such as losing your job, economic crashes, industry disruption, or even if your active income is simply lowered for whatever reason.

Notwithstanding the fact that gold and silver are excellent assets for preserving wealth and protecting against currency debasement (investing Goal #1), they do not pay you cash flow, and ultimately the only path to freedom is creating or acquiring passive income systems (investing Goal #2).

While this is not a book about investing, but rather, the lost art of savings, this chapter will outline a few general considerations and pointers that will hopefully be helpful when you begin your journey to acquire passive income systems.

HOPE IS NOT AN INVESTMENT STRATEGY

Jumping into an investment simply because it pays a dividend is how so many new investors lose their savings and quit investing before they really had an opportunity to even begin. Countless personal finance gurus and video bloggers are exacerbating this situation, as most are catering towards people who are new to passive income and portray getting it as something that's easy and quick.

These clickbait videos and articles are everywhere; they're really good at getting clicks, especially videos that have titles like "___(insert number) Passive Income Investments You Can Make Today With $____(usually $500 or $1000)."

One such personal finance guru I'm going to pick on put out a video for people who want to GET STARTED TODAY with passive investing. In the video, her first tip was to invest into a REIT... The first REIT she lists is a major shopping mall REIT, and pays a whopping dividend yield of 5.82%, and if you invest $1000 today, in a year it will give you $58.20 deposited to your account in your sleep!

At the time the video was released (January of 2020), the REIT was trading at around $144 per share. Well, as I write this at the end of September of 2020, that stock is down at around $64.70 per share... meaning that $1,000 investment is now worth $450. This video has over 700,000 views as of this writing. Think about how many people who took her advice are down $650 (or more if they invested more than $1,000), and will probably never get their money back.

She also mentioned a retail department store stock paying a 9.95% dividend! Wow! The stock was trading at $15.18 when she made the video, today at the end of September 2020, it's at $5.70 per share...

This personal finance guru made a newbie investor mistake (and many of her viewers who are also new and trusted her suffered the consequences). She fell for what's called a **dividend trap** in stock market parlance. These are stocks offering dividend yields that are much higher relative to other dividend yields in the market, and are usually too good to be true. They often have unsustainable payout ratios, high debt loads, poor management, a flawed business model, and are a part of a dying industry (which should be the easiest red flag to spot).

These stocks were a part of a dying industry (retail shopping centers and big box fashion department stores), and anyone who took even a half an hour of time to do some research would have found hundreds of articles covering the "retail apocalypse" this industry has been undergoing starting in 2010 going all the way to 2020, with massive disruption of brick and mortars retail, ESPECIALLY shopping malls and retail department stores. This guru released this video in January of 2020 and has absolutely no excuse for not having done research into the industry.

Dividend traps are aimed at attracting capital from newbie investors who are attracted by the relatively high dividend and don't take time to analyze the stock and look for red flags, rather, the investor just "hopes" the investment holds its share price or goes up in the future and keeps spitting off abnormally high dividends in the meantime.

HOPE IS NOT AN INVESTMENT STRATEGY. When you haven't taken time to learn a successful investment strategy for your chosen investment type, sure you'll have a boatload of companies and sellers that will take your money, but when that underlying investment loses 25%, 50% or more of its market value and doesn't recover, the positive impact of that passive income can be destroyed.

Moreover, many dividend trap stocks end up cutting their dividends altogether after they've lost a bunch of value, just as bad real estate investments can lose their cashflow due to vacancy or other problems the newbie investor failed to identify due to poor due diligence.

ACCOUNT FOR REAL INFLATION

This same personal finance guru lady I'm picking on gave as her second tip the idea of investing in a municipal bond fund. Her reason: bonds are safer than stocks. Well, the bond fund she recommended at that time had a yield of 1.73%. If we assume the real rate of inflation is somewhere in between the government's under reported CPI figures and the Chapwood Index or Shadow Stats figures which are closer to 10%, and we settle at 5.5% inflation for the somewhere in the middle crowd, that 1.73% bond fund's real yield would have been -3.77%.

This lady obviously was not aware of what building wealth means, or that she was losing wealth while "invested" in that 1.73% muni bond fund, or about the concept of inflation and the under reporting of CPI that's gone on since the early 1980s.

Fortunately for you, because you are reading this book to educate yourself, you are more aware than most people, so if you're looking at passive income systems, the yields need to be higher than the real rate of inflation.

DIVIDEND STOCKS ARE HIGH RISK LOW RETURN PASSIVE INCOME VEHICLES

As of 2020, the average payback period for U.S. stocks with dividends is around 20-25 years. That means that on average it will take 20 to 25 years of dividend payments to get your principal back, and then you can start making a return on top of the principal you tied up 20 to 25 years ago...[126]

Yes, there is potential for stock price appreciation, however, the average length of time in between major stock market corrections due to the business cycle is between four and ten years. Thus, over that 20-25 year holding period, the odds are that you'll at least have two major reductions to your dividend stock's share price.

126 Robert Kientz, "Re-Imagining Exter's Pyramid In Today's Panicked Market" *Seeking Alpha* (Mar 19, 2020), seekingalpha.com/article/4332917-re-imagining-exters-pyramid-in-to-days-panicked-market

Add real inflation into the mix and your returns are minimized even further. You'll probably find that unless you've identified the very cream of the crop dividend stocks in terms of future performance during your multi-decade holding period, dividend stocks aren't all they're cracked up to be when it comes to cashflow for the passive long-term investor, especially when there are other investment opportunities out there, like real estate.

BECOME AN EXPERT IN YOUR CHOSEN PASSIVE INCOME INVESTMENT FIELD

Before you start investing in passive income systems, you should devote a serious amount of time to studying and learning everything you can from those who are successful in that particular asset type. You have to look at it like giving yourself a master's degree in your chosen investment niche. Otherwise, you'll just be gambling your money, and in the end, the house always wins.

Does this mean you should spend ten years studying investing before actually going out and making investments? Of course not. That's analysis paralysis, and you do learn by doing. You can't learn how to fly a plane without actually ever actually going up and doing it, but you also don't want to make the news because you knew nothing about flying and went up solo hoping to figure it out on the spot...

BARRIERS TO ENTRY

Barrier to entry is a theory in economics that describes the start-up costs or other obstacles that prevent new competitors from easily entering into an area of business or investment class. It's also a helpful concept for filtering through potential passive income investments that could end up being high risk, low return time wasters, diverting your attention from the good stuff.

A few years ago I wanted to test and see what kind of passive income a large commercial real estate crowdfunding site would give, as it was a relatively new investing concept that differed from REITs in that it was not a stock and thus not subject to the whims of the stock market. I went small and only put maybe $30,000 or so in it, to beta test and see.

What was the barrier to entry here? Very low, all you had to do was create an account, transfer money from your bank, and pick from a few options of different real estate portfolios, some oriented more towards appreciation and long-term growth, others like the one I chose oriented towards the most passive income. After a year or so I sold and my after-tax yield with the passive income barely surpassed 3.5%, not even enough to keep up with the real rate of inflation.

Had I used the barrier to entry filter, I would have concluded that this is too easy and good to be true, and it was. The return I got was far less than the advertised projected returns.

Anything you find with words like "easy," "free" or "fast" in relation to making money investing, is probably a scam. The only person making money is the "self-proclaimed expert" selling their method, course, subscription, multi-level marketing system, or just from the ad revenue from clicks.

There is no such thing as "easy," "free" or "fast" passive income investments in the modern investing landscape where interest rates are near the zero bound and yields on all cash flowing assets have been artificially pushed down. Quality passive income investments will not be "easy" to find and acquire at the right price, will not be "free," and will not be "fast," they will require a lot of time learning how to dragnet and underwrite all the bad ones to find the good ones.

By employing this filter from the get go, you can save yourself A LOT of wasted time and money, and orient your focus on passive income investments that have a medium barrier to entry and much greater return potential that will make the investment worth the time, effort and risk.

TIMING IS EVERYTHING

This concept is not stressed nearly enough today in personal finance. Are there always good cash flowing investments at any time of a market cycle? Yes, there are ALWAYS opportunities. But you can dramatically improve your odds of success with good timing, and likewise, dramatically decrease your odds of success with poor timing. We want probability on our side.

Specific to real estate, successful real estate investors consider where a particular investment is in its valuation cycle, which can vary depending on what market it's in. The easiest way to judge where an asset is in its valuation cycle, is to follow trustworthy industry experts who do not have an economic motive to sway you one way or the other as to your opinion.

For example, if you're looking at buying small apartments in Charlotte, NC, you can get professional industry market research reports from IBISWorld specific to Charlotte,[127] which will show you where apartments are on the valuation cycle backed up with all kinds of data including new construction starts, trends in rent, vacancy, absorption times, and so forth. They do a fantastic job as it pertains to commercial real estate.

If it shows multi-family in that market is in the late stages of a bull market and is starting to get overbuilt, rents are beginning

127 IbisWorld.com

to stagnate, and it appears there's too much money chasing too few deals, that's probably the worst time to buy. That's when you want to be patient.

In contrast, the investors who used timing to their advantage and came into the real estate markets in 2010 and 2011 after the housing crash, they made a killing. There were waves of foreclosures and bank auctions, investors could buy properties for 40 cents on the dollar. Lots of foreclosures and properties selling for major discounts from what they were sold for in prior years are obvious clues that the market is in a recession (a buyer's market).

Timing your acquisition of an investment can be the difference between riding a wave of appreciation and cash flow growth (dividend or rent growth) up, or riding the wave down, losing value, cash flow and possibly the asset all together if the investment's revenue stream has been compromised and can no longer service the debt.

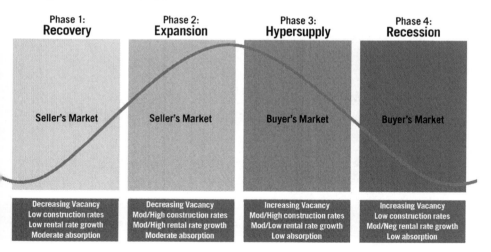

Yes, it's unrealistic to expect to "time the market" exactly and buy at the very bottom and sell at the very top, but one can at least have some idea of what phase they're in with a little research. For real estate, the phases are shown in the illustration above.

Don't Try to Catch a Falling Knife

With investing, you don't want to try to catch a falling knife, you want to wait until it stops, that is, if an investment is falling sharply or quickly, you don't want to rush in right away to "buy the dip" because you're simply gambling in your assumption that you're going to time your purchase when that asset is done dropping.

For example, suppose there's a stock on an investor's watch list that falls by 10% in one day. The investor who jumps in the next day to "buy the dip" is going to get cut if that stock keeps falling, say another 10% and another 10% after that, especially if that stock doesn't ever retrace its losses from where it was purchased at (i.e., what goes down doesn't always come up). That investor's folly was he/she tried to catch a falling knife, rather than waiting for it to stop before taking a position.

I have made this mistake and had to learn this concept the hard way – by losing money. The same principle applies to all investments, whether we're talking cryptocurrencies, commodities, real estate, anything.

BECOME AN EXPERT AT GATHERING INTELLIGENCE AND PERFORMING DUE DILIGENCE

Whatever you choose to invest in, work on becoming an expert in gathering intelligence and performing due diligence on that investment type, to confirm the accuracy of assumptions used in your investment analysis or investment thesis.

As an example, if it's real estate and you're looking at buying a small apartment complex, this means knowing everything there is to know about the complex itself, the neighborhood, and the broader market.

Always consider if the seller's true motive is to abandon a

sinking ship, and you want to find out why it's sinking (if it's due to something you can fix, or something you cannot fix). Perhaps a major employer in that market is shutting down and this means many jobs will be lost and impact renter demand? That's a big development in the market you'll want to know about.

A common theme I saw when I was involved in commercial real estate acquisitions and dispositions of retail shopping centers was sellers abandoning their shopping centers when too many of their tenants gave direct or indirect indications they were not going to renew their leases, and the seller was not able to line up replacement tenants due to falling demand for retail space in those markets.

It was obvious to the listing broker, but of course they (the seller) will always have some other plausible story as to why they want to sell, because if they were to be honest and say "I'm selling because I'm about to have a ton of vacancy and my net operating income is going to plummet, I'm hoping to get out now and let some other sucker get hurt," no one would pay the purchase price those seller's wanted (or needed to pay the balloon payment on their mortgage).

Of course, many sellers of their commercial properties were simply taking profits and moving that money into a new project. The crucial objective for the buyer is to become like a detective and figure out the truth through gathering and analyzing evidence.

Boots on the ground intel gathering is an incredibly helpful tactic. This means going above and beyond just analyzing the P&L Statements, rent roll, general ledger and other financial information given to you by the seller. This means sitting in the parking lot on a Friday night, seeing what kind of renters congregate at the building. Are they mostly grad students and young urban professionals? Are they heavily employed by a particular industry and what is that industry? Do they look like the kind of renters that cause a lot of property damage (increased repairs and maintenance costs)? Is crime going to be an issue?

It means pretending to be a renter and calling up buildings in the immediate neighborhood to get an idea of what the actual rental rates landlords are willing to rent for (rather than the listed rental rate online); finding out how much vacancy there is in that neighborhood and area, and what the actual absorption time is for similar unit types.

There are plenty of excellent resources on performing due diligence specific to the asset type you're interested in acquiring for your passive income systems. This is just to give an idea of what's entailed should you choose real estate. Yes, this is a much higher barrier to entry than dividend stocks, but the yield potential is much greater because of it.

INVESTMENT ANALYSIS METRICS

Below are some powerful financial metrics that will help you in analyzing and comparing investment alternatives, especially when casting a wide dragnet to prospect and find the best passive income opportunities. Note some of these metrics factor in a projected sale event, as many investors take advantage of both cash flow and appreciation, while others prefer to just look at cash flow.

Beware of **"garbage in, garbage out"**: This is a crucial concept that states that if the investment assumptions you used to arrive at the numbers you input into your investment analysis are incorrect, the outputs will be incorrect. This is why being an expert at gathering intelligence and performing due diligence is paramount, so you can acquire accurate investment assumptions.

Return on Investment (ROI): This directly measures the total return of an investment relative to the investment's total cost. Note if your intent is not to take advantage of appreciation and sell the asset, this metric is not very useful, you'll want to skip this and use the cash on cash metric instead. The ROI formula is below:

$$\textbf{ROI} = \frac{\text{Current Value of Investment} - \text{Cost of Investment}}{\text{Cost of Investment}}$$

The current value of investment is the current market value, or if you have enough information to be more precise you can use the total sale proceeds one would receive net of expenses and taxes (what the seller has left over after expenses and taxes are removed).

The cost of investment can be the purchase price, or your total initial investment if using leverage.

The major limitation of the ROI measure when comparing investments is it does not account for time. For example, suppose investor Paul is looking at Investment A which has an ROI of 14%, and Investment B which has an ROI of 10%. From an ROI perspective, Investment A is superior.

However, we always want to factor in time. If Investment A's 14% return occurs over a 2-year period, but Investment B's return occurs over a 1-year period, Investment B's rate of return is actually higher when we look at the **average annual ROI**.

To do that, we take A's 14% return and divide it by how many years it takes to achieve that return, in this case 2, and get an average annual ROI of 7%. We then take B's 10% return, and since it only takes 1 year to achieve that, we divide it by 1 and get an average annual ROI of 10%. Thus, all other things being equal, investment B is in fact the more attractive investment when we factor in time.

Cash on Cash Return: This is the most useful metric to investors looking primarily for long-term cash flow. With these investors, even if the asset appreciates in value, they're likely to continue to own (but may consider a cash out refinance at some point). This metric is commonly used in real estate, but can apply to any cash flowing passive income investments. The cash on cash return formula is below:

$$\textbf{Cash on Cash} = \frac{\text{Annual Pre-Tax Cash Flow}}{\text{Total Cash Invested}}$$

The annual pre-tax cash flow is the overall cash flow the investor would get from the investment net all expenses except for taxes. So, if investment A produces $50,000 per year in gross income (i.e. "top line revenue"), but after all expenses, the investor at the end of the day sees $25,000 in income before taxes, the annual pre-tax cash flow would be $25,000.

For real estate specifically, the annual pre-tax cash flow is calculated with the following formula:

(gross scheduled rent + other income)

–

(amount of scheduled rent lost to vacancy +
operating expenses + annual mortgage payments)

The total cash invested is the total amount of cash the investor has put into the investment, NOT the purchase price. For example, if investor Paul buys a 4-unit apartment building and the purchase price was $400,000, but Paul used a mortgage (also called leverage) and only had to put down 40% or $160,000. Paul also did $35,000 worth of rehab on the units in order to raise the rents. Paul's total cash invested thus far would be $195,000.

So, if the annual pre-tax cash flow is $25,000 and Paul's total cash invested is $195,000, Paul's cash on cash for this property is 12.82%.

Capitalization Rate ("Cap Rate"): This is similar to the ROI metric in that it expresses an expected rate of return, but is specific to cash flowing investment real estate. It is helpful for quickly looking at how a property is priced relative to similar properties in the same market. That said, this by no means should be the only financial measure you perform on a real estate investment, as it doesn't take into account the time value of money (TVM), leverage (i.e., using debt), and increased cash flows due to property improvements (i.e., value-add, such as by renovating and increasing the rents, or decreasing operating expenses).

This is more helpful for seeing if a property is priced above market, at market, or below market, as you can pull sale comps of similar properties in that market and some of the data will have the property's cap rate. The cap rate is calculated with the below formula and expressed as a percentage:

$$\text{Cap Rate} = \frac{\text{Net Operating Income}}{\text{Purchase Price}}$$

The net operating income (NOI) is the property's projected annual revenue less all operating expenses and property taxes. Included in operating expenses are things like insurance, utilities, legal fees, repairs and maintenance, and all other regularly reoccurring costs to run and manage the property. Capital expenditures, such as the cost for a new roof, HVAC system or parking lot, as examples, are not included, as they only occur perhaps once every 10 years or so, and are not considered regularly reoccurring.

As an example, if a small commercial warehouse for sale has

a paying tenant, and the NOI is $50,000, and the purchase price the seller is willing to sell for is $700,000, the cap rate would be 7.14%. If similar properties in that market are selling for cap rates in the 8.5% range, perhaps this seller is asking for higher than what the going market price is for this asset type, or perhaps there are additional factors to support such a price. That's where gathering intel and doing due diligence comes into play.

Payback Period: This measures the amount of time it takes for the investor to recoup the total initial investment, in other words, how long something takes to pay for itself, also called reaching the break-even point.

For example, if investment A has a total initial cost to the investor of $100,000 and the investor receives $25,000 in after-tax net income from the investment per year, in 4 years the investor will have recouped that initial $100,000 investment, and thus the payback period for that investment is 4 years (the break-even point). Profits after the break-even point are all gravy.

Unlike cap rate, which is primarily used in real estate, the payback period is useful with all kinds of investments, as well as for determining the profitability of capital improvements and upgrades.

For example, let's suppose a multi-family investor owns an 8-unit apartment building, and the investor is considering adding washers and dryers to all 8 units and can raise the rents by an extra $30 per month by doing so. Let's suppose by buying in bulk the landlord is able to get 8 sets of washers & dryers for $6,250. By being able to raise the rents by $30 per unit per month, for 8 units, that adds $2,880 per year in net income. Since the tenants are responsible for their own utilities, there are no ancillary costs to the investor that come with the washer and dryers.

To calculate the payback period of those unit upgrades, you'd take the total upgrade cost of $6,250 and divide that by the annual additional net cash flow the upgrades created, in this case, $2,880 per year, and your payback period would be: 2.17 years or roughly 2 years and 2 months. In that scenario, that unit upgrade is a no brainer.

Internal Rate of Return (IRR): Also known as an investment's "yield," this is an excellent financial metric (used throughout this book in many examples) for estimating the rate of growth (or profitability) of a potential investment over time. The IRR takes into consideration the factor of time as well as periodic cash flows.

This is not easy to do by hand, and it's much better to use a free IRR calculator online. The calculator should have a T bar, with initial cash outlay or flow for period 0, and then you should be able to set how many years (periods), and a sale price somewhere for if there's a disposition event.

Be extra careful when it comes to estimated sales proceeds – if you overshoot by how much your investment is actually able to sell for, that could make a huge difference in your IRR, as well as if you forget to account for all disposition expenses and taxes. Remember the garbage in, garbage out concept—the output is only as good as the accuracy of the assumptions you input.

HOPE FOR THE BEST, PREPARE FOR THE WORST

When I had the opportunity to speak with successful commercial real estate investors on a daily basis as a broker, I noticed a recurring theme with all of the successful ones: they always hoped for the best and prepared for the worst. Some called it "starting from the train wreck and working backwards."

By having this yin and yang approach to investing, you first identify what the problems are and what can be done about it, while keeping an eye for great opportunities for upside that others may have overlooked. This way, you see both the wonderful possibilities an investment has, but also have a feasible plan of action for if/when things go bad, so you're not left dumbfounded and caught in the headlights like a deer. If you aren't prepared for disaster, your probabilities of facing and overcoming it drop precipitously.

MARGIN OF ERROR

Building on the above, in your financial analysis of prospective investments, be sure to include a margin of error. One basic example of this in real estate is using a vacancy factor. For example, if you're considering buying a self-storage unit to rent out, and let's say the unit costs $5,000, and you can rent it out for $1,000 per year and based on your research you see the vacancy rate for those units are perhaps 5%, it couldn't hurt to assume a 10% vacancy factor per year.

In that instance, your payback period would be roughly 5 and a half years ($5,000 / $1,000 per year x 0.90). If you luck out and have less vacancy than that, great, but your initial projections left some margin of error, which will affect which investment(s) you ultimately choose, and how much you're willing to pay.

Incorporating a margin of error into your investment analyses will prevent you from pulling the trigger on deals that are too thin, that don't pencil out if Mr. Murphy shows up.

THE GAMBLER'S FALLACY

This cognitive bias is also called the Monte Carlo Fallacy after an infamous game of roulette at the Casino de Monte-Carlo in 1913 in which the ball fell on black 26 times in a row, an extremely rare occurrence. As the ball kept falling on black, gamblers kept betting on red and lost millions of francs in the process, incorrectly reasoning along the way that because of the long streak of black, it had to be followed by a long streak of red.

The gambler's fallacy is something to be cognizant of when you're making investing decisions, to ensure you're not being unduly influenced by it. Essentially, it's where you think because an event occurred many times previously, there's a lower chance of that event happening again in the future.

If you flip a coin and it lands on heads 6 times in a row, does this increase the odds of the 7th toss being tails since it's long overdue? Someone under the influence of the gambler's fallacy would say yes. However, that assumption is false, as the coin does not keep a memory of the previous coin toss. In reality, the odds are still 50%. The past results are not going to change the odds of the 7th coin toss, as each coin toss is an independent probability event.

RECENCY BIAS

This cognitive bias is where one believes what occurred in the recent past will continue to occur in the future based solely on the fact that it occurred recently. This can also be where one believes because something has not occurred in a long time, that it will continue to not occur. It's essentially the opposite of the gambler's fallacy.

Back to our coin flip example. If you flipped a coin 10 times and it landed on tails 10 times in a row, someone under the influence of recency bias would believe the 11th coin flip will also be tails, since the trend for the past 10 flips has been tails. We know in reality the odds are 50% on each flip.

As investors, this cognitive bias translates into not being complacent with regards to trends. An easy example of this is how many U.S. stock market investors cling to the buy the dip strategy, which has worked very well in recent history, considered by many as the holy grail move every time there is a market correction. Eventually, this may end up being a fatal mistake when it no longer works, as experienced by many investors in the Japanese market crash of the early 1990s, after which it took the Nikkei almost 30 years to even come close to recouping its losses just in nominal terms. Those investors learned about recency bias the not-fun way...

GOOD DEBT CAN BE A WEALTH ACCELERATOR

As touched upon in Chapter 7, while debt can enslave you (and is arguably being used to enslave humanity), in the context of this chapter (investing), if used very carefully and strategically, it can turbocharge your net worth's rate of growth. This type of debt is what we'll call good debt.

Most of the wealthiest clients and investors I encountered in commercial real estate brokerage had all employed good debt at some point or another. For debt to be "good," it necessarily must create what's called **positive leverage**, that is, leverage that when introduced increases the investment's return on equity.

With a real estate transaction, positive leverage would exist simply when the cost of debt (the effective interest rate on the money you borrow) is less than the cash-on-cash return the cash flowing investment would have produced prior to introducing debt into the transaction.

For example, suppose you're looking at investing in your first property which happens to be a duplex. We'll assume the contract price is $264,000, and a 0% vacancy rate given there are only two tenants and they just each renewed a full year lease. We'll also assume the annual pre-tax cash flow is $18,500, and you have $264,000 in cash and are able to purchase the property outright. In that scenario, your cash on cash return would be 7%.

But let's suppose you can get a 30 year self-amortizing fixed 4.5% interest mortgage to purchase the property with a 40% down payment, causing your total initial investment to drop from $264,000 to $105,600. Because the cost of debt is 4.5% and the property's cash on cash return is 7%, by using debt, your cash on cash return jumps to 8.4% (140 basis points higher). This may not seem like much, but over time this extra boost to your investment's returns will make a significant difference.

By introducing good debt, you get a higher return on each dollar invested, and in our example, would have an extra $158,400 with which to invest in another property, or to put into your cash and/or gold reserves.

Negative leverage is where the cost of debt is greater than the cash on cash return of the property. For example, if the interest rate on the mortgage is 10%, and the investment property's cash on cash return is 7% without debt, by introducing debt with a higher interest rate than the property's non-leveraged cash on cash return, your cash on cash return drops from 7% without debt to 1.72% with debt...NEGATIVE LEVERAGE IS NO BUENO.

TREAT GOOD DEBT LIKE A HIGHLY RADIOACTIVE SUBSTANCE TO BE HANDLED WITH EXTREME CARE

Even good debt can be quite dangerous if not handled carefully, as you're adding additional risk into the equation. Many real estate investors in the 2008-2009 Global Financial Crisis who had used good debt still ended up going bankrupt and losing their investments, many even losing their homes to foreclosure, because they did not take the necessary precautions ahead of time to deal with unforeseen problems or changes in market conditions.

What are some things an investor can do to lower the risks of adding on good debt?

1. Maintain adequate cash reserves for each investment that has debt on it. Just like you have a personal emergency fund with 6 months' worth of living expenses, it is helpful to have cash reserves set aside for each investment to sustain itself for at least one year without revenue, perhaps more depending on the investment. Then, if disaster strikes, let's say if it's real estate and you lose your tenants, you can still make the mortgage payments while you simultaneously find replacement tenants or perform whatever capital expenditures you need to perform to fix the property.

2. Maintain a conservative debt service coverage ratio (DSCR). Just because you can take out an 80% Loan to Value mortgage, doesn't mean you should. The higher the ratio of debt to value, the lower your debt service coverage ratio will be, which means there is less cushion for any drop in anticipated revenues. Some professional investors will still lever up to the hilt to get the

348

highest rate of return on each dollar invested, but will have very large cash reserves as a cushion to make up for their low DSCR.

3. Avoid recourse loans when possible. In commercial real estate, as an example, there are lenders who will give what's called non-recourse loans, that is, loans whereby if the borrower defaults, the borrower's personal property and home is not on the hook, rather, just the underlying asset the loan was used to purchase. These are always preferable as they lower your risk dramatically. In the 2008 Global Financial Crisis, investors with non-recourse loans on their assets who were in Mr. Murphy's path of destruction simply lost those investments that went under, while investors with recourse loans lost their investments along with their homes, businesses, and savings. One situation sucks, the other is catastrophic. If the investment is a strong high-quality investment, there should be non-recourse loans available.

ADDING CASH FLOWING ASSETS TO YOUR NWS

When adding cash flowing assets to your net worth statement, use the cap rate in order to arrive at a value in the assets column. Let's say you acquire a 4-unit small apartment building with a net operating income of $28,800 per year, and through your ongoing relationships with multi-family brokers in your market you conclude the going cap rate in that market for similar properties is 6.5%, you would divide $28,800 by 0.065 and get a market value of $443,077.

It's also helpful to have a cell at the bottom of your NWS that computes the total annual passive cash flow you will receive from your passive income investments. This will help motivate you to increase it whenever possible and let you keep track of your progress in that endeavor.

REINVEST THE INTEREST
& NEVER SPEND THE PRINCIPAL

As you're accumulating passive cash flowing investments, the golden rule to avoid all your efforts being for naught is to reinvest the interest. This is the fastest way to wealth accumulation.

When you have enough passive cash flow and you think you'd like to spend some of it on discretionary consumer purchases, that's fine, but always remember this maxim: spend only the interest, never the principal.

CONCLUSION

When I began writing this book, I started from the mindset of writing to my future children whom I would one day hand this book to as they approached adulthood.

The information contained herein is what I would want my own children to know regarding personal finance as they venture out into the adult world. With this knowledge, they could protect themselves from being used and abused by modern-day snake oil salesmen trying to sell them the devices of their own enslavement, devices that would ultimately waste their time, money, and energy, holding them back decades from where they could be financially.

The central and commercial bankers, credit card companies, auto dealerships, socialist big government politicians, all these predators and others will try to turn our children into borrowers in one form or another, i.e., place our children into servitude, for the borrower is servant to the lender.[128]

My hope is that the readers of this book will use the knowledge contained herein as a shield to protect themselves, and live life not as servants and debt slaves, but as FREE men and women.

With that said, even if you accomplish this mission, it will all be a total waste if you've become wealthy but neglected your spiritual development and helping your fellow brothers and sisters

---

128 Proverbs 22, Verse 7, King James Bible (KJV)

in these troubling times we're entering, *"For what shall it profit a man, if he shall gain the whole world, and lose his own soul?"*[129]

Some have strongly advised me against putting this in the concluding chapter given this book is about personal finance, and it's sure to stir up lots of negative reviews. I cannot heed their advice, for even if it means this book sells fewer copies, the consequence of the alternative is disobeying God by not preaching the gospel of our Lord Jesus Christ as it is so commanded,[130] only to enjoy the pleasures of sin for a season.[131]

For those that think Christianity and the Bible is silly superstition or a cult (me for the first 30 years of my life), **I dare you** to explain how it is that the Bible, being made up of 66 books between the Old Testament AND the New Testament, HAND written by at least 40 different authors of all different professional backgrounds over a period of 1600 years, in 13 different countries, does not contradict itself ONCE (in the original/old King James Version) historically, scientifically, doctrinally, ethically, morally, theologically, or in any manner whatsoever?

For this to have occurred happenstance without divine intervention would be a statistical anomaly akin to winning the Powerball numerous times in a row, especially when we consider that it was written thousands of years before information could be stored and transmitted digitally and any sort of artificial general intelligence (AGI) algorithms could have been employed for such a colossal undertaking.

For the scientifically inclined, consider that until the 16th and 17th century A.D. with the introduction of the Copernican system (heliocentric model), astronomers believed Earth was stationary

---

129 Mark 8, Verse 36, KJV

130 Acts 5, Verse 42, KJV

131 Hebrews 11, Verse 25, KJV

and at the center of the universe (geocentric model).

Chapter 26 Verse 7 of the Book of Job states a scientific truth that was not known at that time. It says describing God's works: "*He stretcheth out the north over the empty place, and hangeth the earth upon nothing.*"

How would Job have correctly known the Earth hangs upon nothing, i.e. space? This was obviously authored before satellites and rockets were being sent into space, and thousands of years before the Copernican system was even first hypothesized much less put down on paper in the *De revolutionibus orbium coelestium libri VI* ("Six Books Concerning the Revolutions of the Heavenly Orbs") in 1543.

All a person at that time would have known is what they saw when they looked up at the sky (hence why ancient astronomers mistakenly believed the Earth to be on the geocentric system). And since there's not a giant mirror in outer space facing the Earth, anyone who may have possessed an ancient rudimentary telescope would only be able to look up at the celestial bodies, they would not be able to look back and see that Earth is in fact floating in space...

Or in Isaiah chapter 40 verse 22, speaking of God, the Bible says "*It is he that sitteth upon the circle of the earth, and the inhabitants thereof are as grasshoppers; that stretcheth out the heavens as a curtain, and spreadeth them out as a tent to dwell in:*" By stretching out the heavens as a curtain around the circle of the Earth, that is another way of saying sphere or globe. This was written in a time when most people thought the Earth was flat (with the exception of only a select few Greek philosophers).

In Job chapter 38 verse 24, the Bible says "*By what way is the light parted, which scattereth the east wind upon the earth?*" In the meteorological sciences, wind is produced by flowing from high-pressure areas to low-pressure areas due to the uneven heating of the Earth's surface by the sun. Moreover, prevailing winds actually do blow east-west rather than west-east, north-south, or south-north. This is due to the Earth's rotation and the Coriolis effect. These scientific truths were not discovered by humans until recent memory, not over 2000 years ago when the book of Job was written...[132]

When you consider the odds of all these scientific truths being accurately described thousands of years before their scientific discovery, along with the incredible level of consistency throughout all 66 books, for these to all have occurred without divine intervention is <u>statistically impossible</u>. Thus, the <u>original</u> (old) King James Version of the bible (without footnotes) is literally the word of God.

What about evolution? Doesn't that challenge the bible's creation story? Modern scientific discoveries aided by computer technology in the fields of molecular biology and synthetic organic chemistry have all but obliterated Darwin's evolution theory (which is from the 1800s).[133] We're now seeing some of the world's most brilliant and renowned scientists come out against evolution theory, such as computer science professor David Gelernter[134] of Yale University and synthetic organic chemistry and nanoengineering professor James Tour[135] of Rice University, stating unequivocally that Darwin's evolution theory is a mathematical IMPOSSIBILITY and as such is no longer a plausible explanation for the origin of species on our planet.

---

132 Jerry Coffey, "What Causes Wind?" *Universe Today* (Dec 10, 2010), universetoday. com/82329/what-causes-wind/

133 Stephen C. Meyer, *"Darwin's Doubt: The Explosive Origin of Animal Life and the Case for Intelligent Design"* (HarperOne, June 22, 2010).

134 David Gelernter, *"Giving Up Darwin"* (The Claremont Review of Books, Spring 2019).

135 James Tour: The Origin of Life Has Not Been Explained (Science Uprising).

For those interested in **eternal life** (something far greater than any riches one can accumulate on Earth), check out *The Bible Way to Heaven* at RevivalBaptistOrlando.com/sermons

"It's odd that there are people who believe Jesus could not possibly have risen from the dead, yet they believe ALL LIFE arose from the dead..."

RECOMMENDED WEBSITES

Ron Paul Institute for Peace and Prosperity
@ RonPaulInstitute.org

Ron Paul Liberty Report @ RonPaulLibertyReport.com

The **Mises Institute** @ Mises.org

Foundation for Economic Education (FEE) @ Fee.org

Ayn Rand Institute @ AynRand.org

HighImpactTV @ HighImpactTV.com

Stossel TV @ JohnStossel.com

Zero Hedge @ ZeroHedge.com

Dr. Mercola @ Mercola.com

Gerald Celente's Trends Journal @ TrendsResearch.com

Classical Capital @ ClassicalCapital.com

Plutocracy Cartel @ PlutocracyCartel.net

End The Fed @ EndTheFed.org

We Are Change @ WeAreChange.org

RECOMMENDED FILMS

Being Baptist: From the Historical Anabaptists to the Impact of the Independent Fundamental Baptist Church

New World Order Bible Versions a Paul Wittenberger film
The Great Culling: Our Water a Paul Wittenberger film
Mr. Jones (2019)

RECOMMENDED SHORT VIDEOS, CHANNELS AND DOCUMENTARIES

The Money Masters documentary (1996) by Bill Still

All Wars are Bankers' Wars documentary (2013) by Michael Rivero

Hidden Secrets of Money series by Michael Maloney

Princes of the Yen documentary (2014)

G. Edward Griffin – How the Banking Cartel Fooled America Into Creating the Federal Reserve System interview on Silver Bullion TV

Ex-Dutch Banker Ronald Bernard Exposing Illuminati Satanic Child Sacrifice – Testimony for the International Tribunal for Natural Justice (2018)

Consumer Price Index: Biggest Scam in US History Revealed! By George Gammon of the Rebel Capitalist Show

"Voices of Reason: A Nightmare Called Socialism" by Liberty Pen on YouTube channel

092: G. Edward Griffin: Individualism vs Collectivism on the Cashflow Ninja podcast

The Rich Dad Channel by Robert and Kim Kiyosaki

Thrive: What on Earth Will It Take? by Foster Gamble

Collectivism vs Individual Liberty – Ayn Rand

Really Graceful @ bitchute.com/channel/reallygraceful/

John Stossel: Jordan Peterson vs. "Social Justice Warriors" @ ReasonTV

Grant Cardone: Nobody Ever Achieved Financial Freedom from Buying a Home (Part 3) on VLADTV

The **Peter Schiff Show** Podcast

Joe Rogan Experience #1508 - Peter Schiff

Raoul Pal's **Real Vision**

Greg Hunter @ USAWatchdog.com

Jeff Berkowitz's **Dollar Vigilante** @ BitChute.com

Milton Friedman – Your Greed or Their Greed? video of interview with Phil Donahue in 1979

The Biggest Scam in America on Valuetainment by Patrick Bet-David

Liberty and Finance YouTube channel

The **Morgan Report** by David Morgan

"But That Wasn't Real Communism, Socialism, or Marxism!" by Jordan B. Peterson

The Gulag Archipelago and The Wisdom of Aleksandr Solzhenitsyn on Academy of Ideas YouTube channel

Order Followers by Mark Passio

John F. Kennedy's Speech on April 27, 1961 at the Waldorf-Astoria Hotel in NYC to the American Newspaper Publishers Association

RECOMMENDED READING

The Creature from Jekyll Island by G. Edward Griffin

Economics in One Lesson by Henry Hazlitt

End the Fed by Dr. Ron Paul

The Case Against Socialism by Dr. Rand Paul

The Wall Street Trilogy: A History by Antony C. Sutton

America's Secret Establishment: An Introduction to the Order of Skull & Bones by Antony C. Sutton

Rich Dad's Cashflow Quadrant: Guide to Financial Freedom by Robert Kiyosaki

The Case Against Education: Why the Education System Is a Waste of Time and Money by Bryan Caplan

Guide to Investing in Gold & Silver: Protect Your Financial Future by Michael Maloney

You Have the Right to Remain Innocent by James Duane

Permanent Record by Edward Snowden

Aftermath: Seven Secrets of Wealth Preservation in the Coming Chaos by James Rickards

The Fruits of Graft: Great Depressions Then and Now by Wayne Jett

The Gulag Archipelago by Aleksandr Solzhenitsyn

Made in the USA
Middletown, DE
03 January 2023

21129978R00205